# CONTAMINATION, POLLUTION AND THE PLANNING PROCESS

## A PRACTITIONER'S GUIDE

Tom Graham

Published November 2023

ISBN 978-1-9163023-9-6

Text © Tom Graham

Typography © Bath Publishing

Bath Publishing Limited

27 Charmouth Road

Bath

BA1 3LJ

Tel: 01225 577810

email: info@bathpublishing.co.uk

www.bathpublishing.com

Bath Publishing is a company registered in England: 5209173

Registered Office: As above

**TO**

Thomas, my favourite grandson

and

Linda, my favourite wife!

# About the author

Tom Graham is a barrister and former solicitor with over 40 years' experience in town and country planning and highway law. He has advised, and continues to advise, in both the private and public sectors and has taken the lead in a number of major public inquiries.

Tom has been a lecturer in a range of topics for over 20 years.

He has a particular interest in climate change and currently writes and lectures on the topic. He has written books on Highways and Development and the Environment Act 2021 (also published by Bath Publishing Ltd). He is currently writing a book with the provisional title 'Climate Change on Trial – A Forensic Study of Competing Claims'.

# Acknowledgments

I need to proffer some acknowledgements, and there are a number of them. First, of course I must thank my long-suffering wife, Linda, for putting up with my writing yet another book. Then I would like to thank David Chaplin and Helen Lacey at Bath Publishing. Once again, David and Helen have had the confidence to risk the publication of a new book on my behalf and Helen has performed her usual miracles in turning the manuscript into the finished product.

I have, along the way, participated in a number of webinars and seminars in working up the book and learned a lot from my fellow speakers in doing so.

Finally, my usual thanks to Linda Jackson for her help in choosing the cover to this book.

Tom Graham

October 2023

# CONTENTS

# Table Of Cases

# Table Of Statutes

# Table Of Statutory Instruments

# Table Of Circulars, Guidance And Frameworks

# Preface

*"It is not so long ago that a member of the Diplomatic Body in London, who had spent some years of his service in China, told me that there was a Chinese curse which took the form of saying, 'May you live in interesting times'..."*

Sir Austen Chamberlain, addressing the annual meeting of Birmingham Unionist Association – The Yorkshire Post – March 1936

The abiding question for all would be authors is *"Why write a book at all?"* In many cases the answer is obscure. The question is amplified when, as here, there are already some good books on the topic in question and, as here, a lot of technical guidance. The short answer is that there may be merit in a concise bespoke handbook on the town and country planning aspects of land contamination and pollution which has been written by a practitioner with other practitioners in mind. The reality is that there is little published material which fulfils this exact role.

In the Halcyon days before the inception of the National Planning Policy Framework (2012) (NPPF) heralded the death of many well-known circulars and guidance, one could look to national guidance as a source of reliable advice. However, the NPPF is *"concise"* to the point of obscurity and the somewhat simplistic supporting advice published on the National Planning Practice Guidance (NPPG) website is no substitute for the advice which was provided before 2012. Those who suggest that this is a heresy against the new order might look to the detailed advice on mining which was lost with the withdrawal of the series of Minerals Planning Guidance Notes and ask whether the NPPG is a fair replacement. As to planning and land contamination, one could have looked to Planning Policy Statement 23 (PPS 23) and the helpful advice contained in that document. Truth be told, the current position is not helpful to the earnest student of the topic.

For example, and somewhat surprisingly, it is difficult to find realistic and useable guidance on the use of planning conditions in connection with land which is, or might be, affected by contamination. The NPPG states:

*"Model land contamination conditions can be found in Appendix A of circular 11/95."*[1]

The model planning conditions in Circular 11/95 are, therefore, an appropriate starting point, albeit one then comes to a strange affectation; namely, that, in 2012, the then extant version of the NPPF withdrew the useful explanatory narrative in the Circular but retained the model conditions in the annex to the Circular. Thus, in theory, the model conditions remained intact, but the text which explained them was deleted.

---

[1]  Paragraph 010: Reference ID: 33–010–20190722.

The position had been made more complicated by a letter dated 30 May 2008 which was sent by the Deputy Director; Planning – Resources and Environment Policy at the Department of Communities and Local Government to all Chief Planning Officers in England. The letter was said to circulate a new set of model conditions which would supersede Circular 11/95 and which were intended for use by local planning authorities during development on land affected by contamination.

Be that as it may, as noted above, the model conditions in the appendix to Circular 11/95 appear to have been revived by the NPPG, albeit this letter of 2008 does not appear to have been expressly withdrawn. Presumably, it was deemed to be otiose when PPS23 was withdrawn in 2012.

The confusion is compounded by the fact that, for some reason known only to itself, the Planning Inspectorate produced its own suggested conditions in 2016.[2]

It should, therefore, come as no surprise that the use of conditions in connection with applications for the development of land which is said to be affected by contamination came before the courts in 2020.[3]

So, to revert to the initial question, there is a need for commentary on these difficult issues and a book is justified. At least that is my story, and I am sticking to it!

## The scope of this book
Whilst matters such as climate change have been mentioned above, this book is concerned with the development or redevelopment of land which may be affected by contamination or pollution within the UK and, as such, proceeds on the basis of the perceived wisdom on the topic as expressed in legislation, policy and through the courts. This is to say, it must, within reason, react to and interpret those base materials without seeking to judge whether they are right or wrong when subjected to full scientific analysis. The reason for this is quite simple, which is that the bodies which are involved in the determination of planning applications do not normally subject every proposition promulgated by those who enjoy higher positions in the hierarchy to rigorous forensic examination.

## Note on timing
So far as possible, all cross-references, extracts etc are up-to-date at the time of writing (September 2023).

---

[2]   Updated in 2023.

[3]   See Paragraph 14.3.

# Chapter 1

# What Are "*Contaminated Land*" And "*Pollution*"?

**1.1      What is "*contaminated land*"?**

The question of what is "*contaminated land*" is more vexed than might appear to be the case at the outset, not least because it is almost always not defined in planning conditions or planning obligations.

The problem for both lawyer and planner, in this topic area, is that terminology is used in an inconsistent and often contradictory manner with the result that it is sometimes difficult to define what the author of a particular commentary is alluding to. Whether helpful or not, it is apposite to consider a number of definitions in the hope of, at least, throwing some light on this matter.

Commentators often rely on the statutory definition in Section 78A(2) of the Environmental Protection Act 1990. This defines "*contaminated land*" as being:

> "*... any land which appears to the local authority in whose area it is situated to be in such a condition, by reason of substances in, on or under the land, that*
>
> *(a) significant harm is being caused or there is a significant possibility of such harm being caused, or;*
>
> *(b) significant pollution of controlled waters is being caused or there is a significant possibility of such pollution being caused;*"

This definition was coined for Part IIA of the 1990 Act for the purposes of the identification, containment and decontamination of land which poses a significant threat to human beings or the natural world; however, it is not apt in connection with the determination of planning applications. This is not so much a matter of thresholds as such, but the distinct differences between the Part IIA regime and the planning regime. The contaminated land mechanisms within the planning regime are triggered, or should be triggered, where there is a reasonable and objective suspicion that a proposed development site might be affected by contamination and the test to be applied is whether or not such a site is, or will be, suitable for the proposed use. The "*remediation*"[1] mechanisms in Part IIA of the 1990 Act were inserted to provide for the treatment of sites to a point where significant harm is no longer a concern. The two approaches are completely different.

The Environmental Damage (Prevention and Remediation) (England) Regulations 2015 provide that "*Environment damage to land*" means: "*contamination of land by substances,*

---

[1]    See Section 78A(7) for the definition of "*remediation*" which is particular to this Act.

*preparations, organisms or micro-organisms, were that damage results in a significant risk of adverse effects on human health.*" Arguably, this definition is closer to one which is suitable for use in the planning regime.

Once one gets beyond these somewhat philosophical matters, one gets into the very mundane point of looking for the establishment of metrics which can be deployed in the real world in assessing whether land is suitable for its proposed use, regardless of the labels one may attach to it. This is not an easy matter.

Arguably, it could be reduced to the anthropomorphic notion that it is a condition of land which human beings do not like. This is to say, having little or no regard for impact on the environment. Hence, is it an aesthetic matter or does it involve measuring adverse impacts on human beings and/or biodiversity?

Truth be told, it is difficult to find anywhere in the world which is pristine; not even Mount Everest. On 26 June 2019 the BBC reported:

> "It's being described as the "world's highest rubbish dump". That's because Mount Everest, the tallest mountain in the world, has a problem with climbers leaving their waste on the slopes – both rubbish and poo." [2]

The Amazonian rainforest is not in the clear:

> "The pollution plume produced in the city of Manaus, northwest Brazil, tends to drift towards pristine areas of the Amazon rainforest, elevating up to 50 times the concentration of tiny, harmful particles in parts of the forest with near pre-industrial atmospheric conditions.
>
> This is one of the key findings of a team of researchers from the United States, Brazil and Germany studying how humans have affected the Amazon's atmosphere." [3]

This short extract has not been cherry picked but, when read in context, the research itself does not make it clear whether the said "*harmful particles*" are actually harmful to flora or fauna or both within the Amazonian rainforest and, if so, to what extent. To put it another way, for the purposes of this book, one has to read beyond broad strap lines and interrogate the base information which is presented to, as the case may be, planning officers, councillors and members of the public. This is a point which is discussed at greater length below.

In 2018, the Guardian reported:

---

[2]   https://www.bbc.co.uk/newsround/31711591.

[3]   https://www.scidev.net/global/environment/news/brazilian-pollution-spreads-to-untouched-amazon-rainforest.html - 15/03/19.

*"Plastic and traces of hazardous chemicals have been found in Antarctica, one of the world's last great wildernesses, according to a new study.*

*Researchers spent three months taking water and snow samples from remote areas of the continent earlier this year.*

*These have now been analysed and researchers have confirmed the majority contained "persistent hazardous chemicals" or microplastics.*

*The findings come amid growing concern about the extent of the plastic pollution crisis which scientists have warned risks "permanent contamination" of the planet."*[4]

Thus, it is unlikely that one will find any corner of the globe which is not, in some way, affected by man-made pollution.[5]

Then, inevitably, this brings us to the vexed question of carbon dioxide, methane, radon and other gaseous emissions.

Atmospheric carbon dioxide is, literally, everywhere and it is a necessary waste product of those life processes which utilise oxygen. This includes animals, plants[6] and even fish. The production of carbon dioxide could, rightfully, be called a natural process. Yet it is said to be a greenhouse gas, which traps heat in the atmosphere and will, therefore, impact on global temperatures. It dissolves in water to reduce oceanic PH levels and may interfere with marine organisms. Carbon dioxide is also introduced into the oceans through hydrothermal vents.[7] The potential for these effects begs the question of whether the outputs from these natural processes can be labelled "*contamination*". The position is complicated by the fact that some of these effects may be beneficial to, or tolerated by, certain organisms.[8] In

---

[4]    *Antarctica: plastic contamination reaches Earth's last wilderness* - Matthew Taylor - 6 June 2018 - https://www. theguardian.com/environment/2018/jun/06/antarctica-plastic-contamination-reaches-earths-last-wilderness.

[5]    Flying to the moon or Mars will not provide a respite because, of course, man-made artefacts have now been transported to them.

[6]    However, whilst plants exhale carbon dioxide, during photosynthesis, they actually absorb more than they release.

[7]    Lupton, J; Lilley, M; Butterfield, D; Evans, L; Embley, R; Olson, E; Proskurowski, G; Resing, J; Roe, K; Greene, R; Lebon, G (2004). *Liquid Carbon Dioxide Venting at the Champagne Hydrothermal Site, NW Eifuku Volcano, Mariana Arc*. American Geophysical Union. Fall. Meeting (abstract #V43F–08): V43F–08.

[8]    Fumio Inagaki (2006). *Microbial community in a sediment-hosted CO2 lake of the southern Okinawa Trough hydrothermal system*. PNAS. 103 (38): 14164–14169. Bibcode:2006PNAS.10314164I. doi:10.1073/pnas.0606083103. PMC 1599929. PMID 16959888. Videos can be downloaded at Supporting Information.

the Jurassic period, the atmospheric carbon dioxide concentration was possibly 4-5 times greater than today[9] but this was an era of abundant flora and fauna.[10]

Methane is, of course, a major component of landfill gas, albeit it arises in considerable quantities as a result of natural processes. Methane is a propellant and, as such, can be dangerous when it accumulates in a confined space, together with a source of ignition. The well-known case of an explosion within a bungalow in Loscoe is discussed below. Not surprisingly, a considerable part of this book is dedicated to the matter of landfill gas.

The same type of concerns can be deployed in respect of radon gas. It is a radioactive, colourless, odourless, tasteless gas and occurs naturally in the normal radioactive decay of thorium and uranium. Radon can also present in ground water. At natural temperature and pressure,[11] radon gas has a density of about 8 times the density of the Earth's atmosphere at sea level. This means that it can collect in buildings unless expelled by ventilation.

The answer is the same in respect of both carbon dioxide and radon gas. That is to say, they can be regarded as potentially pollutive because they can affect the ecological environment which is currently enjoyed by the flora and fauna of this planet. Arguably, the human interest is largely anthropic and has to do with not only the preservation of the species but also the continued maintenance of living standards. The altruistic interest is in the preservation of wildlife and natural habitats. Or, more to the point, the question of whether or not planning authorities, the Planning Inspectorate or, indeed, High Court judges are entitled to go beyond the so-called "*conventional wisdom*" which has it that not only is there "*climate change*" but that this phenomenon is being driven to some sort of man-made tipping point which is so immediate that it has been described with alarmist propaganda such as "*climate emergency*". This rhetoric has, inevitably, to be balanced against the very real need to provide housing, energy, food et cetera.

This discussion leads to four conclusions:

(1)     First, it is meaningless to speak of "*contamination*" in the land development context unless the subject of the conversation has the potential to have an adverse effect on mankind or the current environment.

---

[9]     *Climate and CO$_2$ in the Atmosphere*. Retrieved 10 October 2007. 80. Berner, Robert A; Kothavala, Zavareth (2001). *GEOCARB III: A revised model of atmospheric CO$_2$ over Phanerozoic Time* (PDF). American Journal of Science. 301 (2): 182–204. Bibcode:2001AmJS301.182B. CiteSeerX 10.1.1.393.582. doi:10.2475/ajs.301.2.182. Retrieved 15 February 2008.

[10]    Some commentators argue that the Earth was hot and humid. Others say that the Sun was less bright in those days, therefore the "*greenhouse*" effect might have been less than one would first imagine!

[11]    This matter of differential temperatures and pressures between sub-terranean gas deposits and the external atmosphere is an important component in the volume of gas which is emitted at any particular time. All other things remaining equal, a decrease in external air pressure will allow more gas to escape due to the increase in this pressure differential.

(2)     Secondly, nothing turns on whether the said *"contaminant"* occurs naturally or is man-made.

(3)     Thirdly, it is necessary to have ways of measuring the potentially adverse effects of a contaminant. Otherwise, one is engaging in the art of unjustifiable speculation as a component in the process of making a decision.

(4)     Fourthly, the question of *"how much"* has to be followed by the question of whether it is potentially harmful. An occasional puff of radon gas is unlikely to have any health impacts, but prolonged exposure can contribute towards cancer.

## 1.2     What is *"pollution"*?

As with *"contaminated land"*, recourse to the Environmental Protection Act 1990 is not helpful in defining *"pollution"* in the planning context, not least because the approach there is somewhat tortuous.

The DEFRA publication entitled Environmental Protection Act 1990: Part 2A Contaminated Land Statutory Guidance April 2012 states (p.4) that:

> *"The terms "contaminant", "pollutant" and "substance" as used in this Guidance have the same meaning – i.e. they all mean a substance relevant to the Part 2A regime which is in, on or under the land and which has the potential to cause significant harm to a relevant receptor, or to cause significant pollution of controlled waters. This Guidance mainly uses the term "contaminant" and associated terms such as "contaminant linkage". However it recognises that some non-statutory technical guidance relevant to land contamination uses alternative terms such as "pollutant", "substance" and associated terms in effect to mean the same thing."*

To put it another way, this is a jumble! Somewhat ironically, Section 4.4 (p.26) of the Guidance is then headed *"Significant pollution of controlled waters and significant possibility of such pollution"* and then goes on to use the word *"pollutant"* and derivatives thereof throughout.

As noted above, Section 78A(2) of the 1990 Act defines *"contaminated land"* as being:

> *"... any land which appears to the local authority in whose area it is situated to be in such a condition, by reason of substances in, on or under the land, that -*
>
> *(a) significant harm is being caused or there is a significant possibility of such harm being caused, or;*
>
> *(b) significant <u>pollution</u> of controlled waters is being caused or there is a significant possibility of such pollution being caused;"*(Emphasis added)

Under Section 78A(9), the phrase *"pollution of controlled waters"* means *"the entry into controlled waters of any poisonous, noxious or polluting matter or any solid waste matter."*

The problem with these definitions appears to be that, at least so far as the matter of pollution is concerned, they are (at least in part) circular in the same way as many dictionary definitions.[12] No doubt those who are heavily invested in the Part IIA regime might disagree; however, one wonders whether it is appropriate to disappear down this particular rabbit hole in the different field of town and country planning.

If one looks to the literature as a whole, then, generally, one gains the impression that the word *"contaminant"* appears to be used as a description of an element which adulterates something else. If the thing which is being adulterated is land, then it is apt to use the phrase *"contaminated land"* albeit that *"polluted land"* would be equally effective as a matter of ordinary usage. However, if one is referring to the contamination of a medium other than land (i.e. air or water), then it is apt to use the word *"pollution"*, albeit that *"contaminated air [etc]"* would be equally effective as a matter of ordinary usage. This is by no means a perfect analysis; however, it is the approach which will be taken in this book.[13]

---

[12] Hence, *"pollution of controlled waters"* means *"the entry into controlled waters of any ... polluting matter."* Per Tweedledee: *"If it was so, it might be; and if it were so, then it would be: but as it isn't, it ain't. That's logic."* (Lewis Carroll, *Through the Looking Glass* (1872)).

[13] *"When I use a word,"* Humpty Dumpty said in rather a scornful tone, *"it means just what I choose it to mean – neither more nor less."* *"The question is,"* said Alice, *"whether you can make words mean so many different things."* *"The question is,"* said Humpty Dumpty, *"which is to be master – that's all."* (Lewis Carroll ibid).

# Chapter 2

# Derelict And *"Brownfield"* Lands

## 2.1    Derelict land

The phrase *"derelict land"* has a wider meaning than *"land affected by contamination"* or *"contaminated land"*. Land may be derelict without necessarily being contaminated,[1] for example, where the site contains old buildings or deposits of inert spoil. The Derelict Land Act 1982 gave the Secretary of State for the Environment powers to advance Derelict Land Grants in respect of land which was *"derelict, neglected or unsightly"*, but did not define the word *"derelict"*. However, the publication entitled Scottish Vacant and Derelict Land Survey 2018 (Published 24 April 2019 by the Local Government and Communities Directorate) stated:

> *"2.8 Derelict land (and buildings) is land which has been so damaged by development, that it is incapable of development for beneficial use without rehabilitation."*

The publication *A Brown and Pleasant Land*[2] provided a useful illustrative diagram:[3]

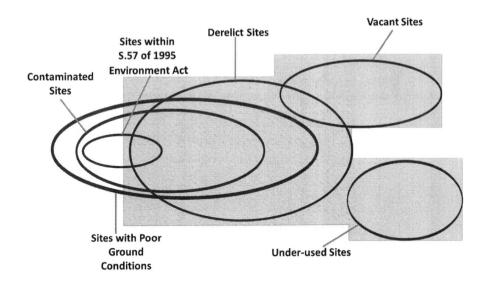

---

[1]    Albeit, it is reasonable to presume that such land has the potential for being contaminated: see below.

[2]    *A Brown and Pleasant Land*, Parliamentary Office of Science and Technology (Report 117). Reproduced by permission.

[3]    Reformatted from original for purposes of reproduction.

It is important to note that many sites which are not derelict may, nonetheless, be contaminated or the active sources of pollution; for example an existing petrol filling station with leaking underground storage tanks: see Paragraph 4.3.

## 2.2    Brownfield land

It has been the long-standing aspiration of a number of organisations and governmental departments to focus new development onto derelict or previously used land in order to spare as much greenfield land as is practicable. This is particularly the case in urban areas where derelict sites are unsightly, yet often stand in good proximity to social and transport infrastructure and, therefore, can be deemed to be *"sustainable"* once developed.

In 2011, Planning Policy Statement 3 said:

> *"40. A key objective is that Local Planning Authorities should continue to make effective use of land by re-using land that has been previously developed.*
>
> *41. The national annual target is that at least 60 per cent of new housing should be provided on previously developed land. This includes land and buildings that are vacant or derelict as well as land that is currently in use but which has potential for re-development."*

The Campaign to Protect Rural England had this to say in 2019:

> *"In order to provide enough housing in England for everyone who needs it, we must be creative within our finite land. By making use of suitable brownfield sites, the homes we need can be built in the places we need them, while our beautiful countryside is allowed to thrive. Brownfield sites are also often close to where people already work and live, with infrastructure such as public transport, schools and shops already in place."*[4]

Paragraph 119 of the current NPPF (2021) states:

> *"119. Planning policies and decisions should promote an effective use of land in meeting the need for homes and other uses, while safeguarding and improving the environment and ensuring safe and healthy living conditions. Strategic policies should set out a clear strategy for accommodating objectively assessed needs, in a way that makes as much use as possible of previously-developed or "brownfield" land."*

The statement *"previously-developed or "brownfield" land"* is a puzzle. One can highlight the *"or"* betwixt those two words and the question to be asked is whether this *"or"* is disjunctive or conjunctive, in the sense that previously developed land is something separate from brownfield land (with the disjunctive meaning), or (with the conjunctive meaning) that

---

[4]    Campaign to Protect Rural England, *State of Brownfield, 2019.*

previously developed land and brownfield land are one and the same thing. It is worth looking the glossary when one is so befuddled: see below.

Paragraph 120(c) adds that planning policies and decisions should:

> *"... give substantial weight to the value of using suitable brownfield land within settlements for homes and other identified needs, and support appropriate opportunities to remediate despoiled, degraded, derelict, contaminated or unstable land."*

Again, the relationship between the statements *"brownfield land"* and *"despoiled, degraded derelict, contaminated or unstable land"* is unclear. Again, it is necessary to go further into the NPPF in order to try and ascertain an answer (if answer there be).

Unfortunately, the situation is not as straightforward as the executive organs of ministerial departments and the CPRE might think or proselytise it to be. The first question is, of course, what is a *"brownfield site"*?

The glossary to the National Planning Policy Framework (2021) says that one must go to *"previously developed land"* for a definition of *"brownfield" land*[5]:

> *"Previously developed land: Land which is or was occupied by a permanent structure, including the curtilage of the developed land (although it should not be assumed that the whole of the curtilage should be developed) and any associated fixed surface infrastructure. This excludes: land that is or was last occupied by agricultural or forestry buildings; land that has been developed for minerals extraction or waste disposal by landfill, where provision for restoration has been made through development management procedures; land in built-up areas such as residential gardens, parks, recreation grounds and allotments; and land that was previously developed but where the remains of the permanent structure or fixed surface structure have blended into the landscape."*

This definition of *"previously developed land"* is often taken to cover brownfield land outside the NPPF, but it was created for policy purposes and is not adequate for the present context.

One problem is the statement: *"This excludes: ...land that was previously developed but where the remains of the permanent structure or fixed surface structure have blended into the landscape ..."* The problem is, of course, that this will, in many cases, encompass made ground. And, as discussed at Paragraph 4.2 below, made ground can be a source of concern in terms of whether or not some of its sub-soil constituents are potentially contaminative or pollutive. Thus, this definition is not referring to actual greenfield sites, but, instead, to sites which were formerly used for some form of industrial or other process where the buildings and other hard structures are then demolished and the remains then buried under topsoil,[6] followed

---

[5] Which begs the question of why the NPPF is using two different terms for the same thing?

[6] Indeed, the site might be made ground as the result of imported mixed fill, which is problematic in itself: see Paragraph 4.2.

by a covering of grass. Far from being satisfactory, this definition is, actually, misleading. Whilst it should not do so, it is bound to tempt those determining planning applications into equating this type of land with a greenfield site; which, of course, it is not. It is land which, by any measure, should be treated as potentially contaminated and, accordingly, treated in that way. Nor is it safe to say that this type of land can be treated as being suitable for activities such as public open space without understanding whether or not it is in need of some form of decontamination. This definition is, clearly, predicated on visual appearance which is, quite frankly, not fundamental to the exercise. To put it at its highest, the appearance of the site can be an indicator of its brownfield nature; however, it is far from being definitive and is simply one of the factors which will be taken into account. To put it another way, the approach taken in the NPPF can be very misleading.

Similar comments can be made about the statement *"This excludes: ...land that is or was last occupied by agricultural or forestry buildings ..."*

Agricultural and forestry buildings typically include machine storage and repair facilities which can, in many cases, be equated to general engineering operations. As with all general engineering operations, there is not only the possibility of oil spill during the course of works on machinery, but, also, the probability that deleterious chemicals and substances will be held on site. Hence, it makes no sense to exclude such buildings and, indeed, it is difficult to understand the thought processes which went into excluding them. Indeed, some commentators include agricultural land as being brownfield sites in any event, presumably on the basis that the cultivated areas will, in all probability, have been subject to pesticides and the like.

The Brownfields Handbook[7] examines this point in more detail:

> *"3.1 What is a brownfield?*
>
> *There are many definitions of what a brownfield is and understanding varies mainly between the American and European perception of it. The European perception sees brownfield land as derelict, under-utilised or vacant land that may or may not have environmental damage, on which previous use has ceased or subsided and which the market was not able effectively reuse without some sort of an intervention. What is and what is not a brownfield also depends substantially on local circumstances. What appears to be brownfield by one standard may be regarded as a budding enterprise by another. Also it is important to realise that some brownfield sites may still be partially in use. Although many brownfields are no longer in full use, the standard description "under utilised" implies that sites in this category are unlikely to be wholly in use. One example of this may be a commercial operation which is rationalising or reducing staffing levels. In such a case, that area of the site which is no longer used by the owner is classed as brownfield, even if other parts continue in productive use. The fact*

---

[7]   *Lifelong Da Vinci Project on Brownfields* – Brownfields Handbook (May 2006).

*that we cannot absolutely and exactly define what a brownfield is and what it is not, presents one of the barriers to their reuse. Here is a definition broadly now accepted in the European space. Brownfields are sites that:*

- *have been affected by the former uses of the site and surrounding land;*

- *are derelict or under used;*

- *have real or perceived contamination problems;*

- *are mainly in developed urban areas;*

- *require intervention to bring them back to beneficial use..."*

The following table shows one non-definitive classification by previous use:

| |
|---|
| • Industrial |
| • Military Railway and transport |
| • Agricultural |
| • Institutional (schools, hospitals, prisons) |
| • Commercial (shopping centres, offices) |
| • Cultural (culture houses, cinemas) |
| • Leisure (sports ground, parks, open space) |
| *(Adapted from Brownfields Handbook - Table 1: Brownfield type by previous use)* |

Whilst contamination is not a necessary precondition to treating a site as being brownfield, it is likely to be affected by contamination. The US Environmental Protection Agency had this to say:

*"A brownfield is a property, the expansion, redevelopment, or reuse of which may be complicated by the presence or potential presence of a hazardous substance, pollutant, or contaminant."*

The advice added that:

"*Brownfield properties are often overlooked for reuse or redevelopment due to fear of environmental contamination. Understanding the types of contaminants present (or potentially present) and how people may be exposed to those contaminants will help a community plan cleanup and site reuse options that limit exposure risk.*

*U.S. EPA, states and tribes have programs that can help communities identify properties that are brownfields, determine whether the property is environmentally-contaminated, address contamination when needed and plan for site reuse that will bring new benefits to the community.*"

Below are the contaminants most commonly reported from "*brownfields*" treated using US EPA grant funds, viz:

| Contaminant | Substance Type | Examples of Past Uses |
|---|---|---|
| 1. Lead (Pb) | Metals | Mining, fuel, paint, inks, piping, batteries, ammunition |
| 2. Petroleum | Oil, hydrocarbon compounds | Drill and refining, fuel, chemical and plastic production |
| 3. Asbestos | Fiber in rock | Mining and processing, piping, insulation, fire proofing, brakes |
| 4. Polycyclic aromatic hydrocarbons (PAHs) | Hydrocarbon compounds, combustion by-product | Coal tar, creosote, soot, fire, industry/ manufacturing by-product |
| 5. Other metals | Metals | Metal fabrication, plating, mining, industry/ manufacturing |
| 6. Volatile organic com- pounds (VOCs) | Manmade chemicals | Industry and commercial product solvents, degreasers, paint strippers, dry cleaning |

| 7. Polychlorinated Biphenyls (PCBs) | Manmade chemicals | Heat and electrical transfer fluids, lubricants, paint and caulk, manufacturing, power plant |
|---|---|---|
| 8. Arsenic (As) | Metals | Pesticides, agriculture, manufacturing, wood preservative |

## 2.3     Regeneration of brownfield sites and derelict sites

The Brownfields Handbook states (page 67) that:

> *"Conceptual models challenge conceptual thinking regarding the brownfield regeneration process and therefore help to broaden the way decisions are made about individual sites. CABERNET has been better able to assist national policy developments by the experiences gained through developing and considering the range of conceptual models available. The models have been used extensively in the CABERNET dissemination activities and notable positive feedback has been received. Using a conceptual model to characterise different types of site, in terms of their economic viability and highlighting how status can change based on variation in location standing, site treatment costs and other economic conditions, can help policy makers identify strategies that can improve the economic viability and status of sites."*

The following table classifies sites in accordance with their likely commercial viability in accordance with the broadly accepted model from the CABERNET[8] project:

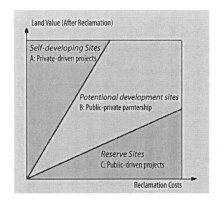

*(Adapted from The Brownfields Handbook – Fig 7.2 @ p.68: Brownfield type by likelihood of reuse)*

---

[8]     Concerted Action on Brownfield and Economic Regeneration Network.

13

The CABERNET ABC conceptual model identifies three types of sites according to their economic status (for example due to the cost of regeneration, the value of the land, etc). Sites are classified as:

- *"A Sites" – sites that are highly economically viable and the development projects are driven by private funding.*

- *"B Sites" – sites on the borderline of profitability. These projects tend to be funded through public private co-operation or partnerships.*

- *"C Sites" – are not in a condition where re generation can be profitable. Their regeneration relies on mainly public sector or municipality driven projects which are of low economic viability. Public funding or specific legislative instruments (e.g. tax incentives) are required to stimulate regeneration.*

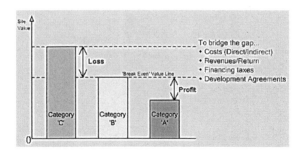

*(Adapted from The Brownfields Handbook – Fig 7.1 @ p.68: The Economic Components of the A-B-C Model (According to CABERNET 2005))*

The Brownfields Handbook states (page 68) that:

"*The A-B-C model highlights the funding drivers for brownfield regeneration. This conceptual model can be used to assist institutions that are responsible for regional development and investment by allowing then to characterise strategies for dealing with different types of brownfield land.*

*By identifying the type of site and considering the factors that are affecting a site's category,[9] ...both public and private bodies can examine intervention options and regeneration strategies. Using this conceptual approach to examine the factors that affect re-categorisation of a site, for example from a B Site to an A site, can result in the development of site-specific strategies which can also be useful.*"

---

[9]   i.e. if it is an A, B, or C site.

## 2.4     Inhibitions on redevelopment

In 2004, Syms reported[10] that, in spite of the fact that governmental policies are firmly in favour of redeveloping previously developed land in preference to greenfield development, there are still a number of developers, albeit probably reducing in number, who were reluctant to develop on previously developed land. The reasons they gave were many and varied but generally fell into one or more of the following categories:

•     Fear of the unknown;

•     Regulatory controls;

•     Delays;

•     Increased costs;

•     Stigma.

The Brownfields Handbook addresses the *"stigma"* problem which might arise when bringing, or proposing to bring, such sites forward for regeneration:

> *3.1.2 "... It is important to add that the term "brownfield" is appropriate when addressing and attracting national attention to the issue or making the issue a regional or local priority. However, once we are looking for investors it is inadvisable to continue to talk about brownfield land, as for many investors the term "brownfield" may imply polluted and difficult plots. At this stage it is advisable to drop the "brownfield" terminology altogether and to talk of, for example, "urban land reuse"."*

Not surprisingly, the matter of stigma is something which has to be conceded at an intuitive level, but there is a paucity of empirical evidence to show how this depressive perception might affect property values in practice and is there is little consensus in the reasoned hypotheses of researchers in the field.[11]

Notwithstanding all of this, the matters of fear of the unknown, stigma etc are very important for both developers and local planning authorities.[12] A developer should have regard to the uncertainties which attach to a site which is suspected of being contaminated, adjust this offer price accordingly, and provide for contingencies, in this economic viability assessment.

Turning to regulatory controls, it follows that a local planning authority should, when presented with such a viability assessment, accept that these matters are real concerns, in

---

[10]   See also Syms, P. (2004) - *Previously Developed Land*, pages 37 to 75.

[11]   See Wilshaw, D.G. (1998), *Stigma, Perception and the Remediation of Contaminated Land* - Journal of Property Research, vol.15, No.4, pages 285 – 303. See also Sims, P (2004) - *Previously Developed Land*, pages 36 to 56.

[12]   See Case study 2 below.

terms of both land acquisition values and the markup which should be attributed to meeting the uncertainty in possible future risk management costs. If the local planning authority fails to do so, then it runs the risk of causing this stigmatised land to remain undeveloped in perpetuity. Unfortunately, economic viability assessments are something of a dark art, but, nonetheless, it is essential for a local planning authority faced with such a site to seek to grapple with it, or, alternatively, to refer the matter to an external expert for advice.[13]

## 2.5     Due diligence

One would normally expect that the prudent purchaser would employ a valuer at an early stage in order to start framing an economic viability assessment for his or her project. However, a valuer must not dwell on matters which are the concern of specialists in contaminated land.

The overarching guidance for valuers is the *RICS Valuation – Global Standards*[14] together with the national guidance supplement for the UK.[15]

Paragraph 6.1[16] of the Global Standards provides that matters that will frequently require consideration and comment in a report prepared for secured lending include comment on environmental issues, such as flood risk potential and historic *(sic)* contamination.

Paragraph 1.2[17] states that many matters may, or will have, an impact on the market's perception of the value of the relevant interest, aspects of which may only become fully apparent during an inspection of the property. These can include non-natural hazards such as ground contamination where there are substances in, on or under the ground resulting from historic *(sic)* or current uses.

Section 2[18] mentions the aspects that are common to many valuations involving real estate, and often raise issues about the extent of investigation that is appropriate or about the nature of the assumptions that might validly be made. These include *"Sustainability, and environmental, social and governance (ESG)"* matters. The Global Standards go on to say that potential or actual constraints on the enjoyment and use of property caused by sustainability and ESG factors, *"may result from natural causes (such as flooding, severe storms and wildfires), from non-natural causes (such as contamination) or sometimes from a combination of the two (such as subsidence resulting from the historic (sic) extraction of minerals)."*

---

[13]   See Chapter 6 on the duplication of controls.

[14]   Effective from 31 January 2022 - Published by the Royal Institution of Chartered Surveyors (RICS).

[15]   *RICS Valuation - Global Standards 2017: UK national supplement* (Issued November 2018, effective from 14 January 2019).

[16]   Ibid page 20.

[17]   Ibid page 22.

[18]   Ibid page 127.

Despite the considerable diversity of circumstances, the key question is always the extent to which the factors which are identified might affect value, "*Particular care should be taken when assessing or commenting on ESG factors, as valuers may not have the specialist knowledge and experience required. In appropriate cases, the valuer may recommend making further enquiries and/ or obtaining further specialist or expert advice in respect of these matters.*" (Page 128, para. 2.6).

Para. 2.6[19] refers to "*these matters*" in more detail and (inter alia) lists "*...non-natural constraints, contamination and hazardous substances.*" The Standards go on to say that:

> "*A valuer may not be competent to advise on the nature or risks of contamination or hazardous substances, or on any costs involved with their removal. However, a valuer who has prior knowledge of the locality and experience of the type of property being valued can reasonably be expected to comment on the potential that may exist for contamination and the impact that this could have on value and marketability.*"

And:

> "*The valuer should state the limits on the investigations that will be undertaken and state any sources of information or assumptions that will be relied on. ...Sustainability and ESG Special assumptions may only be made if they can reasonably be regarded as realistic, relevant and valid for the particular circumstances of the valuation.*"[20]

The UK Supplement states:[21]

> "*No enquiries regarding contamination or other environmental hazards are to be made but, if a problem is suspected, the valuer should recommend further investigation. The valuer will not carry out an asbestos inspection and will not be acting as an asbestos inspector in completing a mortgage valuation inspection of properties that may fall within the Control of Asbestos Regulations 2012.*"

---

[19]   Ibid page 128.

[20]   Ibid page 129.

[21]   Page 93.

# Chapter 3

# *"Remediation"* As A Term Of Art

*'Term of art': a word having a particular meaning in a field (as the law) – called also 'word of art'.*[1]

Given that the challenge for any redevelopment scheme involving land which may be affected by contamination is to make it suitable for use, it follows that a bespoke approach is needed which will usually involve a mixture of outright decontamination and appropriate mitigation measures. It does not follow that any decontamination exercise involving the digging out of contaminated soils will result in the removal of these components from the site itself. It is acceptable to move such soils to a part of the site which may not, later, be used by a sensitive receptor; for example, buried under a hard surfaced car park or, even, a structural landscape feature which allows the contaminants to die down naturally over time.[2]

It might also be the case that the proposed development is capable of living with contaminated land provided that suitable mitigation measures are carried out. For example, there is extensive technical guidance on ways of allowing residential development to co-exist with landfill gas emissions, provided that appropriate mitigation measures are carried out and the correct administrative responses are followed. Indeed, the bulk of this book is dedicated to the multitude of responses which may be deployed when land is affected by contamination. Furthermore, none of this information is secret, but, rather, it is well understood by those skilled in this field.

Thus, it should come as a surprise to an experienced practitioner to find that an administrative body is, apparently, unaware of these techniques or, simply, eschews a proper description of them. At worst, it betokens lack of knowledge on the part of those administrators who deploy unschooled language. One such careless misuse is of the word *"remediation"* in many national and local policy documents when, as noted above, it is not always the case that the site as a whole will be *"remediated"* at all.

The Glossary to *Guidance for the Safe Development of Housing on Land Affected by Contamination – R&D66: 2008 Volume 2* defines *"remediation"* as:

> *"Action taken to prevent or minimise, or remedy or mitigate the effects of any identified unacceptable risks."*

This, clearly, goes beyond (whilst encompassing) the initial treatment process.

---

[1]   https://www.merriam-webster.com/dictionary/term%20of%20art.

[2]   Albeit a lending institution might not be too keen on such approaches and there is always the danger of stigma in any event.

The loose use of the word *"remediated"* without qualification can suggest that the site is (to use another misleading phrase) to be *"cleaned up"*, when, in fact, the object of the exercise is to make it suitable for the proposed development. As discussed elsewhere in this book, the emergence of a scheme which will meet the suitable for use objective is an iterative process which involves matching the evolving development to the many and various solutions which may be deployed – many of which are not aptly covered by a blank use of the expression *"remediation"*. It is important to note that this point goes way beyond mere pedantry, because the loose use of language may mislead those seeking to apply such policies. This is particularly so when the reader is not necessarily one who is skilled in the field of contaminated land (e.g. the average member of a planning committee).

As always, it is important to try to be clear as to the messages which language seeks to convey. This starts with defining the terms which are being used in discourse. Unfortunately, the unqualified use of the expression *"remediation"* is not helpful because, on analysis of the various contexts in which it is used, this does not lead to a consistency of meaning across various usages. To many, it may mean *"clean up"* of the subject site to some metaphysical and unspecified (and probably unattainable) standard, which allows for all conceivable (sometimes improbable) end uses. To others, it might, simply, be seen as a synonym for treatment.

In contaminated land and the planning process, the objective is to make a site suitable for the proposed use both now and in the future. Therefore, it should follow that the question of how one reaches this objective starts with site adaptation treatment as a discrete and first substantive step. The achievement of this objective is not, always, once and for all following treatment, because it is often necessary to provide for long-term monitoring and maintenance, and, where necessary, ongoing further treatments of the site in respect of emergent problems. It therefore further follows that the global notion of *"remediation"* may, if unqualified, encompass only site adaptation treatment to meet the suitable for use test in the first instance, but not ongoing responsibilities.

Hence, it is advisable, and sometimes necessary, to separate these sequential but discrete elements when discussing the overall notion of remediation. Thus, if one is seeking to discuss site adaptation treatment options, then the word *"treatment"* is more apt. One only needs to look to Appendix 3 of this book to see why this usage is, indeed, apt. There is the need to select a site adaptation treatment process which is bespoke to the site in question with the objective of meeting the suitable for use test when the treatment reaches an appropriate stage. This treatment will, again, as is clear from Appendix 3, not obviate all potential contamination due to the practical, financial and technical limitations which are also discussed in the Appendix against each mentioned technique. It is also clear, from Chapter 12, that monitoring and maintenance follow on from this initial site adaptation treatment and are addressed as sequential, but discrete stages, in making the site suitable at the outset and in the future.

It quickly becomes apparent that this concept of *"remediation"* should be an overarching generic notion which may include (depending on the case):

- Treatment;

- Mitigation;

- Validation;

- Monitoring;

- Ongoing maintenance.

Each element is the subject of the well-known technical guidance discussed in this book and, whilst they may overlap, each is a discrete exercise or topic area.

The options available for site adaptation treatment are many and varied. This can be readily gleaned by an examination of Appendix 3. None of these techniques provide remediation in an absolute sense, but, instead, will reduce the perceived contamination to levels which are deemed to be acceptable in terms of the relevant development. With town and country planning, this is whether the treatment renders the site suitable for its proposed use. Arguably, the prudent author will identify this stage as part of settling any policy, condition or obligation so as properly to identify the targets to be achieved in the development process and, also, to provide objective requirements in the event that enforcement action is needed. This is to say there should be, in the result, some form of *"treatment plan"*.

Validation is the subject of specific guidance. It is incumbent on authors to make the position clear so as to provide for *"metricated targets and measurable performance"* at each stage: see Chapter 11.

Ongoing monitoring and management is, almost axiomatically, something which does not fit within the expression of *"remediation"* per se, yet it is often shoehorned into global *"remediation plans"*. The problem is that any obligations or requirements which are intended to subsist for considerable periods of time must be settled with great particularity or they will fail. The developer who appeared to be liable at the outset might be reluctant to discharge their liabilities in the long term because the developer may have left the site and see no reason to impact their profit and loss account unless pressed to do so. Or the developer's company might have fallen into liquidation or have been wound up. As such, the prudent local planning authority should consider how these objectives will be secured. This will, usually, be by way of some form of bond or guarantee which is executed pursuant to Section 106 Agreement.

Simply wrapping these complexities into a vague *"remediation plan"* or *"remediation strategy"* is often a case of failing to match the reality to the expectation, and is made worse where, as is often the case, the said plan or strategy is not settled with forensic precision by lawyers. If one takes all of these factors into account, then, arguably, it should be clear that the expression *"remediation"* must be construed as a term of art for a class of possible actions which encompasses (as the case may be) treatment, mitigation, validation, mitigation, monitoring and management and ongoing treatment. Furthermore, simply relying on a phrase such as *"remediation"* or *"remediation plan"*, or *"remediation strategy"* is unhelpful at best and lazy draftsmanship at worst. It should be incumbent on those settling policies or planning documents to make the effort to separate them.

As to legislation, the traditional starting point is to say that the words in a statute are normally given that their ordinary or natural meaning. This is sometimes known as the *"golden rule"*. It is said that one should seek to understand the *"plain meaning"* of the words in question. There is, however, the difficulty where the subject matter of the statute is a highly technical one. For example, there is no *"plain meaning"* for the word *"remediate"*, because the phrase will have different meanings to different people and will vary according to the specific context within which it is used.

The problem here is that any canter through the literature shows that *"remediation"*, is not a phrase which can, reliably, be left to the service of a hypothetical *"reasonable reader"* (see below) because, in the context of contaminated land, it refers to a technical process, viz:

> *"If the language be technical or scientific and it is used in a matter relating to the art or science to which it belongs, its technical or scientific must be considered its primary meaning."* [3]

And:

> *"If it is a word which is of a technical or scientific character then it must be construed according to that which is its primary meaning, namely, its technical or scientific meaning. But before you can give evidence of the secondary meaning of a word, you must satisfy the court from the instrument itself or from the circumstances of the case that the word ought to be construed not in its popular or primary signification but according to its secondary intention."* [4]

The difficulty with the second extract is that statute is not, normally, construed purposively; and reverting extrinsic evidence of the intent of Parliament or the rule-making body is strictly controlled: see *Pepper v Hart* [1992] 3 W.L.R. 1032.

Whilst one should be very wary of placing weight on other regimes, it is interesting to note that Section 78A(7) of the Environmental Protection Act 1990 defines *"remediation"* as follows for the purposes of that Act:

> *"Remediation" means–*

> *(a) the doing of anything for the purpose of assessing the condition of–*

---

[3]  C., per Coleridge, J at p. 525; per Tindal, C.J at p. 555; per Jessel, *M.K Taylor v Corporation of St. Helens* (1877) 6 Ch D 264, 270.

[4]  Per Fry, J in *Holt & Co v Collyer* (1881) 16 Ch D 718 @ 720.

*(i) the contaminated land in question;*

*(ii) any controlled waters affected by that land; or*

*(iii) any land adjoining or adjacent to that land;*

*(b) the doing of any works, the carrying out of any operations or the taking of any steps in relation to any such land or waters for the purpose–*

*(i) of preventing or minimising, or remedying or mitigating the effects of, any significant harm, or any significant pollution of controlled waters, by reason of which the contaminated land is such land; or*

*(ii) of restoring the land or waters to their former state; or*

*(c) the making of subsequent inspections from time to time for the purpose of keeping under review the condition of the land or waters;*

*And cognate expressions shall be construed accordingly."*

This definition clearly goes beyond initial *"clean up"*.[5] The statutory guidance[6] goes further, viz:

*"6.6 Remediation may involve a range of treatment, assessment and monitoring actions, sometimes with different remediation actions being used in combination or sequentially to secure the overall remediation of the land.*

*6.8 Assessment or monitoring actions may also be required as part of remediation.*

*6.10 Remediation may require a phased approach, with different remediation actions being carried out in sequence or in parallel."*

The predecessor to the 2012 guidance (Circular 01/2006)[7] was more fulsome,[8] viz:

*"(a) a "remediation action" is any individual thing which is being, or is to be, done by way of remediation;*

---

[5]  See also the Environmental Damage (Prevention and Remediation) (England) Regulations 2015 – Schedule 3 para 9.

[6]  Environmental Protection Act 1990: Part IIA Contaminated Land Statutory Guidance (Department for Environment Food & Rural Affairs, April 2012).

[7]  Annex 3, Para. C.8.

[8]  Those settling policy or planning documents could, usefully, take heed of these definitions and hierarchical interaction when engaging in their own drafting.

*(b) a "remediation package" is the full set or sequence of remediation actions, within a remediation scheme, which are referable to a particular significant pollutant linkage;*

*(c) a "remediation scheme" is the complete set or sequence of remediation actions (referable to one or more significant pollutant linkages) to be carried out with respect to the relevant land or waters;*

*(d) "relevant land or waters" means the contaminated land in question, any controlled waters affected by that land and any land adjoining or adjacent to the contaminated land on which remediation might be required as a consequence of the contaminated land being such land;*

*(e) an "assessment action" means a remediation action falling within the definition of remediation in section 78A(7)(a) and 78A(7)(a) (as modified) (see paragraphs C.6 and C.6A above);*

*(f) a "remedial treatment action" means a remediation action falling within the definition in section 78A(7)(b) and 78A(7)(b) (as modified) (see paragraphs C.6 and C.6A above);*

*(g) a "monitoring action" means a remediation action falling within the definition in section 78A(7)(c) and 78A(7)(c) (as modified) (see paragraphs C.6 and C.6A above)."*

Turning to the use of *"remediation"* in policy and planning documents, it might be argued that those seeking to interpret such documents should apply a purposive approach; this is to say, to seek to understand what the authors were trying to achieve. However, the question of what the authors might or might not have intended when settling policy, planning conditions or planning obligations is not, normally, a matter of great weight; indeed, it is excluded in many cases.

As to policy, the guiding principle is that both national and development plan policy must be construed with purported objectivity. This is to say that it is not enough the determining body has reached an interpretation which might be reasonable, albeit not shared by another body.

There is ample case law to show that the subjective approach is wrong in law and that the correct legal approach is a different one.

In *Tesco Stores Limited v Dundee CC* [2012] UKSC 13, the Supreme Court held that the courts have the final word on the correct interpretation of local plan policy. This approach also applies to national policies: see *St Albans City & District Council v Hunston Properties Ltd* [2013] EWCA Civ 1610.

In *Redhill Aerodrome Ltd v Secretary of State* [2014] EWCA Civ 1386, Lord Justice Sullivan stated that the [NPPF] means what it says and not what the Secretary of State would like it to say.[9]

In other words, it is what the courts will say those words to mean in the event that they are in issue and brought before them. A subjective but reasonable interpretation of a policy which alludes to remediation of land affected by contamination, is, therefore, not enough. It must be one which will be deemed to be objectively sound by the courts.[10]

Likewise, the construction of planning conditions and planning obligations is, ultimately, a matter for the courts. In *Trump v Scottish Ministers* [2015] UKSC 74, the Supreme Court held that the proper approach was to interpret a planning permission as a *"reasonable reader"* would understand it in its context.[11]

In summary, the unqualified use of the expression *"remediation"* and its kin (whether the author intended it or not in their own mind) is better construed as relating to an overarching class which encompasses and, which can be analysed into, the discrete actions of treatment, mitigation, validation, monitoring and maintenance and re-treatment. If one is in a position to do so (perhaps when drafting planning conditions or planning obligations), then it is better to refer to the particular action which is being addressed directly rather than leaving it to the hope that this might or might not be implied. Thus, a purported *"remediation plan"* which goes to site adaptation treatment and validation only is better described as a *"treatment plan"*, but a scheme which covers treatment, validation, monitoring and ongoing maintenance can, perhaps, be described as a *"remediation plan"* (because this plan, or strategy, will be bringing together all of these discrete actions between two covers) albeit the phase *"risk management plan"* is perhaps a better description. However, in leaving details to the said *"remediation plan"* or *"risk management plan"*, the author should, it is suggested, ensure that the maxim *"Metricated Targets and Measurable Performance"* is observed at all levels. This means separating and dealing with each *"remediation action"* (see above) so that the garment is knitted in a tight stitch.

---

[9] See also *Forest of Dean DC v SSCLG* [2016] EWHC 421 (Admin) and *Barwood Strategic Land II LLP v East Staffordshire BC & Anor* [2017] EWCA Civ 893. For those interested in considering this topic in more depth, Alistair Mills provides a useful summary in his book *Interpreting the NPPF - The New National Planning Policy Framework* (Alistair Mills, Barrister, Landmark Chambers - Bath Publishing (2018)).

[10] Those who suggest that this smacks of Humpty Dumpty (in that an expression means exactly what the courts mean it to mean, neither more nor less) are, of course, expressing a valid concern for those advising developers and local planning authorities in the absence of case law which is on all fours with the matter in front of them.

[11] See also *R (Skelmersdale Limited Partnership) v (1) West Lancashire Borough Council (2) St Modwen Developments (Skelmersdale) Ltd* [2016] EWHC 109 (Admin). The problem here, of course, is that one is not dealing with the *"reasonable reader"*; the *"man on Twitter"*; the *"man in the pub"*; or the proverbial *"man on the Clapham Omnibus"*, but a highly complicated technical field. See *Metallic Protectives Limited v Secretary of State for the Environment* [1976] J.P.L.166; *R v Secretary of State for the Environment, exp Watney Mann (Midlands) Ltd* (1976) J.P.L. 368; and *Dudley Bowers Amusements v Secretary of State* (1986) 52 P. & C.R. 365.

# Chapter 4

# Causes Of Concern

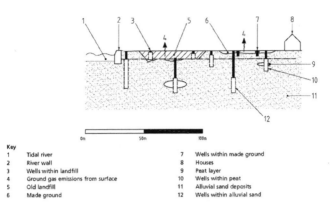

*Example of conceptual model cross-sections and targeted response zones for*
*potentially pollutive gases*

**Key**

| | | | | |
|---|---|---|---|---|
| 1 | Tidal river | | 7 | Wells within made ground |
| 2 | River wall | | 8 | Houses |
| 3 | Wells within landfill | | 9 | Peat layer |
| 4 | Ground gas emissions from surface | | 10 | Wells within peat |
| 5 | Old landfill | | 11 | Alluvial sand deposits |
| 6 | Made ground | | 12 | Wells within alluvial sand |

The purpose of this chapter is to outline some matters which might[1] have the potential of affecting land by contamination arising from activities which have occurred, or are occurring, on the subject site or nearby land, such as:

• landfill sites;

• made ground;

• underground storage tanks;

• abandoned mines; and

• industrial pollution.

## 4.1 Landfill sites
A development site might be of concern either because the proposed development will take place on a closed landfill site or because of reasonable concerns that a nearby landfill

---

[1] NB: It is always worth reading "*might*" as meaning "*might or might not*" to avoid journalistic hyperbole. Likewise, the even more nebulous "*may*".

site (closed or active) might be the cause of polluted emissions to the development site as a result of interconnecting pathways between them.

Whilst the discussion of potential pollution by way of landfill sites often centres on closed landfill sites, it is worth bearing in mind that, often, one has to have regard to active landfill sites which are, for some reason, operated in an irregular fashion, for example, the site of alleged illegal dumping at Arnold's field, Launders Lane in Rainham for a period of at least 12 years. Whilst the dumping has now ceased, the site is bedevilled by underground fires and the London Fire Brigade has, reportedly, responded to more than 70 incidents between 2018 and 2022. Not only this, but it would also appear that the site is generating air pollution, which includes particulate matter in violation of the World Health Organisation's threshold for $PM_{2.5}$.[2]

Modern landfill sites are constructed, filled and completed in accordance with technical standards which ensure that the site is suitably lined, capped and vented, but this has not always been the case. Many closed landfill sites were created many years ago when standards were either not as stringent as they are nowadays or such standards which applied were not managed and monitored in accordance with modern practice. Accordingly, there are many cases where the contents of known former landfill sites are unknown. This poses a particular difficulty and, unusually, sometimes forces investigators to resort to anecdotal evidence.[3]

The antiquity of an historical landfill site is no guarantee that it does not pose a present danger. As a rough rule of thumb, biodegradable deposits will have a half-life of about 30 years in anaerobic conditions. Thus, whilst the levels of emissions from biodegradable deposits will fall at an exponential rate the real impact is governed by the quantity of materials that were deposited in the first place.

Furthermore, of course, it might be the case that the deposits are not biodegradable. Taking an extreme example, the half-life of radioactive waste is, for all practical purposes, irrelevant because it is so extended that gamma ray emissions will not diminish to any noticeable extent during any lifetime or any dozen lifetimes. In between, one might find that the deposits include chemicals which have been dumped in robust and sealed containers, with the effect that any degradation will not take place until those containers have, themselves, eroded to such an extent that the chemicals are thus exposed.

Another important point (and it is developed elsewhere in this book) is that the quantification of the volumes and compositions of potential contamination across a site as a whole is very difficult because, of course, core samples, gas capture etc are proxies only. They

---

[2]  https://www.bbc.co.uk/news/uk-england-london-63156343. The term "$PM_{2.5}$" refers to particulate matter or droplets in the air which have a value two and one half microns or less. Particles in and below the $PM_{2.5}$ threshold can travel deeply into human respiratory tracts, reaching the lungs and causing, or worsening, respiratory illnesses: see Paragraph 10.2.

[3]  "*Unusual*" in the sense that anecdotal evidence is normally excluded for forensic purposes because it is deemed to be inherently unreliable.

provide information in respect of the volumes of subsoil which have been investigated but these results must then be extrapolated for the site as a whole. This process requires professional judgements and, ultimately, reports which are expressed in degrees of confidence as opposed to certainties.

If a proposed development site is close to a landfill site, then the point of concern usually relates to possible emissions of landfill gas[4] which might have been conveyed to the development site as a result of hidden pathways. This was the situation in relation to the well-known incident in Loscoe, Derbyshire where a dwelling house was destroyed as a result of an explosion which was caused by the ignition of the methane component of landfill gas which had entered the house. The relevant landfill site was close to the house and the landfill gas appears to have made its way under the house by way of subterranean pathways. The gas collected in a void under the house and then migrated into the house itself.

**Key**

**Ingress routes**
1  Through cracks and openings in solid concrete ground slabs if present due to shrinkage and curing
2  Through construction joints and openings at wall-foundation interface with ground slab if not sealed
3  Through cracks in walls below ground level
4  Through numerous gaps and openings in suspended block and beam floors or timber floors
5  Through gaps around service pipes and ducts or within the ducts
6  Through cavity walls

This figure is taken from Figure 3 in CIRIA Report R149 [9].

**Accumulation areas**
A  Roof voids
B  Beneath suspended floors
C  Within settlement voids below floor slab
D  Drains and soakaways (or similar voids)

*Key ground gas ingress routes and accumulation areas within buildings*

---

4    *"Landfill gas"* is a loose class term for gaseous emissions from venting petrochemical deposits or decomposing organic landfill deposits and which may include methane, volatile organic compounds or other substances.

If one applies the source – pathway – receptor approach to this type of situation, then, the putative source is already known; namely, the landfill site. The receptor is already known; namely, the development site.

The problem for the investigator is to ascertain whether or not there is a pathway which connects the two. If one applies the phased approach to site assessment and risk assessment then the initial screen will not involve any sample collection or intrusive site investigations, but will be based upon a desktop study, a site walk-over and, if available, a review of any pre-existing materials relating to sample collection. If, for example, both the development site and the landfill are within an area of extensive aquifers or mine workings then the resultant conceptual model and preliminary risk assessment should conclude that the Phase 2 Assessment should be carried out.

The point at which the Phase 2 Assessment should be carried out will vary from site to site and determined on a case-by-case basis. If the application is for an outline planning permission, then, it might be the case that the Phase 2 Assessment is left until the grant of the outline planning permission subject to a condition requiring that this assessment be carried out, a detailed risk assessment be formulated and a risk management plan (if needed) be prepared before the development is commenced. If the development will be delivered in phases, then the condition should cater for this approach.

## 4.2    *"Made ground"*

ISO 11074:2015 defines *"made ground"* as:

> *"...anthropogenic ground comprising material placed without engineering control and/
> or manufactured by man in some way, such as through crushing or washing, or arising
> from an industrial process."*

The phrase *"manufactured by man"* seems to include processed by man; hence, the later references to crushing or washing.

The term *"anthropogenic ground"* is further defined as meaning *"deposits which have accumulated through human activity"*.

Given that the materials which are of concern will, as the name *"made ground"* suggests, be hidden underground, the detection of them can be difficult. The use of map-based evidence is a useful starting point and is discussed at Chapter 7. For example, if an historical Ordnance Survey map shows a pond, former railway cutting, water course or other contoured depression which is not evident in a modern edition, then it is reasonable to ask whether or not the said depression was filled with materials which might be, in some way, contaminated.

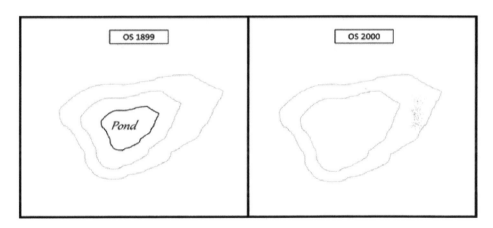

*Made ground*

Also, of course, if an historical Ordnance Survey map shows that an area was, many years ago, the site of heavy or pollutive industry, then it is reasonable to consider whether areas within it might have been used for the underground deposition of waste materials arising from those processes.

The importation of fill materials for structural landscaping might also be a problem, not least in connection with engineering works connected to *"sustainable urban drainage systems"* (SUDS), public open space or biodiversity net gain.

It is reported that, in 2023, Bellway Homes Limited undertook to pay £100,000 to environmental charities in the North East as redress for depositing soil contaminated with mixed waste at a site in Northumberland.[5] Bellway Homes imported 2,688 cubic metres of contaminated waste soil onto its St Mary's Park housing site near Stannington between 2017 and 2020. Bellway said the soil was shipped in to build a bund around an attenuation pond. The waste materials reportedly included wood, metal, wire cables, rubber, plastic and vehicle tyres and came from its developments at nearby Five Mile Park. As a result of action by the Environment Agency[6], Bellway Homes committed to a *"reactive"* Enforcement Undertaking to remove the waste from the site, to improve awareness of the law in relation to soils and waste and review its protocols. The company made a voluntary offer to pay £50,000 to Northumberland Wildlife Trust, £30,000 to Wear Rivers Trust and £20,000 to Tyne Rivers Trust.[7]

Perhaps one of the lessons which can be drawn from this example is that local planning authorities should be astute as to the implications in asking developers to engage in structural soil engineering, perhaps by requesting that details of the proposed fill material should be provided before the grant of planning permission. Arguably, a local planning authority could go further and impose an appropriate condition which allows them to be satisfied that the imported fill material will be examined for any possible contaminants before they are incorporated into the site. Clearly, such a solution would also encompass any relevant planning obligation under Section 106 of the Town & Country Planning Act 1990.

To give a practical example, it might be the case that the hypothesised remedy for the illegal use of contaminated materials for the purposes of ground engineering is the removal of those materials from site or, alternatively, some form of on-site treatment process. The all too common outcome of such proposed ex post facto action might be that the developer either does not have the financial resources to do so or, alternatively, has gone into liquidation. This will leave the executive bodies charged with resolving the problem with an even greater problem; namely, finding the money to carry out the works in the face of public pressure to do so.

## 4.3 Underground storage tanks

Disused underground fuel storage tanks raise significant concerns.

---

5   Construction Enquirer, March 2023 – Bellway dumped imported contaminated soil on its housing site | Construction Enquirer News.

6   The alleged offence was operating without or other than in accordance with an environmental permit (waste operation) – Regulation 38(1) of the Environmental Permitting (England and Wales) Regulations 2016.

7   See: https://www.gov.uk/government/publications/environment-agencys-use-of-civil-sanctions/enforcement-undertakings-accepted-by-the-environment-agency-1-june-2022-to-30-september-2022#environmental-permitting-england-and-wales-regulations-20102016 - Bellway Homes Limited (reference 911). Also: https://www.gov.uk/government/publications/environment-agency-enforcement-and-sanctions-policy/annex-1-res-act-the-environment-agencys-approach-to-applying-civil-sanctions-and-accepting-enforcement-undertakings.

The number of fuel filling stations had declined from more than 37,000 in 1970 to fewer than 9,000 in 2011, which represents closures in this period of more than 75% of all filling stations. The number of filling stations declined from 12,258 in 2001 to 8,677 in 2011, i.e. a 29% decrease.[8] The current trend towards the use of electric vehicles will, of course, lead to further closures in the future. To put it another way, this suggests that there might be a considerable number of underground fuel storage tanks which still contain residual fuel and are potential sources of leakages (due to rusting), yet are not necessarily recorded. This poses a considerable problem because leakages from petrol storage tanks can be a source of significant ground and groundwater contamination. Hence the expressions "*Magic Tanks*" and "*Leaking Underground Storage Tanks*" (LUSTS). The function of site investigations is, in part, to seek to identify those hidden underground tanks which may affect, or be affected by, a proposed development scheme.

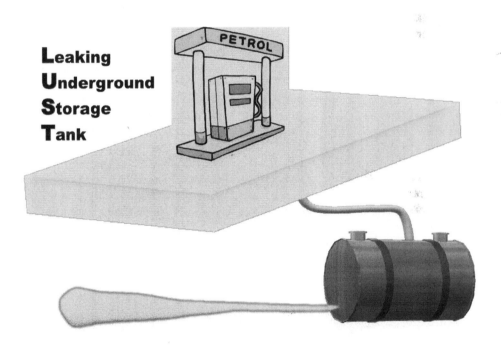

*"Magic Tanks" (LUSTs)*

If a scheme involves the redevelopment of a petrol filling station then, clearly, the local planning authority should require that appropriate surveys are carried out in relation to underground tanks.

---

8    Page 2, *Study of the UK petroleum retail market* (Deloitte, 14 December 2012 on behalf of the Department of Energy and Climate Change).

There are many examples of leakages. In 2007, BP was fined £8,000 for polluting ground-water near a service station in Hertfordshire. The company was obliged to remedy the problem, at a cost £320,000. The underground petrol storage tank in question had been installed in 1987 (ENDS Report, 25 March 2007). ENDS also reported that, in 2002, BP was fined £60,000 for a leak in Luton (ENDS Report 333, p.54) and Total Fina Elf was fined £54,000 for leaks from a site in Hampshire (ENDS Report 328, pp.59-60). In 2017 a leakage of 23,500 litres of fuel from a Tesco petrol station in Haslingden, Lancashire resulted in fuel entering the sewerage system, affecting local residents up to 1km away, forcing some to leave their homes, others to seek medical attention with headaches and sickness, and killing fish in the river Irwell. Tesco were prosecuted by the Environment Agency and fined £8 million (The Guardian, 16 June 2017). In August 2017, builders were forced to stop work on a house extension in Histon, Cambridgeshire when they discovered diesel contamination which originated from a nearby petrol station (Cambridge Live, 3 August 2017).

On 19 May 1993 evidence of substantial petrol pollution from leaking service station tanks was mentioned in a House of Commons debate.[9] During the debate, Mr Colin Pickthall MP observed that, in a recent incident, 17,000 gallons of petrol were recovered from the shell site at Longford Bridge in Warrington. He reported that a leakage in Lancashire affected 20,000m² of land and remedies included pumping gallons of petrol from domestic cellars, with 150 gallons being pumped from one home. He said that, in one case, on the A59 in Rufford Village, petrol leaked through the drains under the trunk road and into the cellars of the Hesketh Arms on the opposite side of the road. He noted that a Salford University student who worked for the Environmental Health Department of Warrington Borough Council, David Watson, had produced a study which showed that there were more than 280 cases of leakages from storage tanks across the country, although over an unspecified period of years. Mr Pickthall added that petroleum officers had informed local authorities of 216 cases in a 12-month period in just 29 local authorities and 54 cases were assessed as fire hazards. The worst case was in Braintree and involved between 20,000 and 25,000 gallons.

The detection of old hidden tanks is far from simple. Whilst the use of old ordnance survey maps can prove to be useful in seeking to locate the sites of disused filling stations, the reality is that filling stations were only recorded as such if they were discrete uses, as opposed to being part of a wider vehicle maintenance use. If a petrol filling station was being operated after 2000, then its operation would have required a licence for vapour recovery from the local authority.

### 4.4    Abandoned mines

Abandoned mines are a significant concern in respect of potential water pollution, ecological damage and ground contamination.

---

[9]    https://hansard.parliament.uk/Commons/1993-05-19/debates/0134c8da-a83e-40d3-ae3d-721dc3914f80/OppositionDay.

The Environment Agency report entitled *Abandoned mines and the water environment* (Science Project SC030136/41, August 2008) provided an overview in relation to water pollution. It stated that 9% of rivers in England and Wales, and 2% in Scotland, were at risk of failing to meet their Water Framework Directive targets of good chemical and technological status because of abandoned mines. These rivers were carrying some of the biggest discharges of metals such as cadmium, iron and copper and zinc to the seas around Britain. 72% of failures to achieve the cadmium quality standard in freshwater was limited to mining areas. In some areas, important drinking water supply aquifers were polluted or threatened by plumes of sulphate and chloride. Historical 13th century coal workings near Dalkeith in Scotland were still discharging acidic, iron rich waters into the River Esk in 1999 (Younger and Adams, 1999).

The report stated:

> *"We have estimated that 12,000 km² of river catchments in northern England are directly affected by historical metal mining. Over 90 per cent of surface and subsurface floodplain soils have heavy metal concentrations above background levels (Environment Agency, 2008). Similar results are expected for other metal mining catchments in northern England, Cornwall and mid-Wales."* [10]

*(Paragraph 2.3)*

Whilst the chemical reactions that cause water pollution may start when the mine is working, water levels in the mines are controlled by pumping. However, problems may arise when the mines close, the pumps are switched off and the groundwater levels rise until they reach the surface or discharge into aquifers (ibid @ paragraph 2.1). This may take a few months or many years. When the rebounding water finally reaches the surface, it may come out via old adits, springs, seepage through the ground or even through the bed of the river. In some deeper mines, water levels may never reach the surface but may connect with underground aquifers.

The problem is not limited to underground deposits of deleterious materials or the transmission of pollutants by way of disused mine shafts. Many underground collieries were the sites of surface deposits of mine wastes and these deposits could, in themselves, be the sources of pollution, for example, where rainwater infiltrates such deposits and then carries pollutant materials into groundwater and, sometimes, into nearby surface watercourses. This is, of course, leaving aside the ground contamination which could be the unenviable legacy of such surface deposits.

The report gave the example of pollution to the River Gaunless (paragraph 2.2.1). The environmental quality standards for iron were often exceeded in the river and this case demonstrated the respective problems of pollution from underground sources (i.e. *"point*

---

[10] NB: The mere fact that a concentration is above background levels does not, by itself, indicate a hazardous situation. The question to be answered is *"by how much"*?

*sources"*) and from *"diffuse sources"*, such as spoil heaps. There were six large point source inputs of mine water from former adits and shafts. Newcastle University investigated the impacts of pollution from, respectively, point sources and diffuse sources. Under low flow conditions, the diffuse sources accounted for about 50% of the loading. Under high flow conditions, this increased to more than 95%. The study showed that diffuse inputs from spoil run-off, re-suspension of previously deposited iron rich sediments and direct ground-water input through the riverbed are often more important than point source discharges.

The report also gave an example from Cwm Rheidol, Ceredigion (paragraph 2.2.3). The Cwm Rheidol complex of six inter-connected lead mines caused the Afon Rheidol to fail environmental standards for zinc and copper, whilst cadmium and lead concentrations were elevated. There were two major adit discharges as well as diffuse discharges from groundwater seepages and spoil heaps. More than a third of zinc, cadmium and copper loadings were from diffuse sources.

## 4.5      Industrial pollution

Pollution from industrial processes can also affect watercourses and groundwater. In the 1970s, a tannery caused the pollution of a public water supply borehole at Sawston, Cambridgeshire, by the chlorinated solvent tetrachloroethene. The borehole was a source of drinking water supply to 275,000 people. The Cambridge Water Company spent almost £1 million in carrying out rectification action, sued the tannery and obtained substantial damages.[11]

---

[11]   See *Cambridge Water Co Ltd v Eastern Counties Leather plc* (1994) 2 A.C. 264. The sequel is that the tannery went on to receive an award for responsible environmental management: https://www.endsreport.com/article/1577313/environmental-award-polluting-leather-company.

# Chapter 5

# Toxicity And Risk Management

- *I read it on Twitter*

- *I was talking to a man in the pub*

- *I saw it on the BBC*

One sometimes finds that a brownfield site may be described as "*toxic*" and that this alleged "*toxicity*" is put forward as a reason for inhibiting its redevelopment. As is often the case, the populist use of the word has little in common with its meaning in science. This chapter discusses the matter.

Those who correspond on sites which they headline as being "*toxic*" often provide a list of the portentous sounding chemicals which the site is said to contain or emit. These lists need to be taken with a pinch of sodium chloride because an inscrutable chemical label is no indicator of a potential for harm: see Case study 2 below.

For example, the hazard assessment for a particular mixture lists ingredients "*presenting a physico-chemical, health or environmental hazard within the meaning of the CHIP Regulations or which are assigned occupational exposure limits*" and they included naphtha (petroleum), calcium carboxylate and ethyl methyl ketoxime. If it was said that these chemicals were found on a site, then there might be cries of alarm. Certainly, one would not wish to have this substance in their house, which is unfortunate because it is a well-known brand of gloss paint!

Then consider diethanolamine, sodium hydroxide, diethylene glycol monobutyl ether or monoethanolamine. Again, this would sound worrisome if found on a site. In fact, these ingredients can be found in many oven cleaners.

The horror continues when a householder is told that their house is being bombarded with "*electro-magnetic*" radiation. They might, or might not, be relieved when they are told that this is, in fact, sunlight. Sunlight is, of course, safe is it not? This is right, at least up until the point it causes skin cancer. This gruesome example forms a neat segue into the principle point of this chapter; namely, that it is a matter of dosage. A little sunshine is a good thing, but too much can kill you!

Those who are interested in such things will know that the word "*toxic*" was named as the Oxford Dictionary's word of the year in 2018. For the purposes of this chapter, the dictionary defines "*toxic*" as "*poisonous*" with its roots derived from the medieval Latin term "*toxicus*" meaning poisoned or imbued with poison. The version of the Oxford Reference Dictionary which sits on my bookshelf defines it as "*of, caused by, or acting as a poison*".

Not surprisingly, the phrase *"non-toxic"* is defined as meaning *"not poisonous or not containing poisonous substances"* in the Cambridge English Dictionary. The Collins English Dictionary gives *"not of, relating to, or caused by a toxin or poison"*.[1]

Thus, *"toxic"* is equated with *"unsafe"* and *"non-toxic"* is equated with *"safe"*. Unfortunately, a toxicologist would not approach the matter in this way.

## 5.1    A sense of proportion

Landfill gas is often given as an example of a dangerous substance. In high concentrations it is an asphyxiant and explosive. However, the real-life incidents of actual harm are few and far between. Most textbooks on the subject refer to an explosion which destroyed a house in Loscoe, Derbyshire, but it is usually the only example they give. This is because such incidents are a rarity.

The situation is different with domestic gas supplies. Like landfill gas, it can be explosive and an asphyxiant in high concentrations. Given that the principal constituent of both landfill gas and domestic gas is methane, the similarities are to be expected. Yet millions of households willingly accept the supply of domestic gas for the purposes of heating and cooking. This is notwithstanding that (unlike landfill gas) there are many reported incidents of domestic gas explosions every year. Then, of course, there is the ever-present danger of carbon monoxide which results from the degradation of unburned domestic gas. This is despite the fact that gas appliances, and their installation, must be in accordance with very high safety standards. If one examines the situation objectively, then it must be the case that those who set and monitor those safety standards do so knowing that the importation of gas into the home brings with it a risk of harm. It must be the case that this risk of harm is deemed to be acceptable. These dangers can be mitigated by way of free-flowing ventilation; however, the principal means of room ventilation is by the windows which are, traditionally, closed at night. It is possible to install gas boilers in self-contained and well-ventilated enclosures, but this is not something one sees in modern housing estates. One answer might be to use electricity instead of gas. Unfortunately, the importation of electricity into homes brings with it its own dangers and, if adopted wholesale, would require a massive upgrade to the UK's electricity infrastructure.

The reality is that, so far as they consider the point at all, householders are willing to accept the benefits of domestic gas and electricity supplies notwithstanding any attendant dangers. Likewise, those who are responsible for setting safety standards must do so on the basis that the rewards exceed the risks.

It is right to say that landfill gas has the potential for harm, but one has to put this into perspective. The question is not whether it is harmful per se, but whether the risk is outweighed

---

[1]    The book also says that the word is derived from the Greek *"toxa"*, which means arrows. The origins of the term are best left to the philologists; however, neither definition is particularly accurate. The Merriam-Webster dictionary can be criticised for the same where it defines the word as meaning *"containing or being poisonous material especially when capable of causing death or serious debilitation"*.

by the reward. Where the risk of harm from landfill gas on a brownfield site is low, then this might be outweighed by the benefits of the development.

Those involved in the world of statistics are fond of pointing out that all activities involve an element of risk. Hence, the commonly cited example of crossing the road to get to the other side. The chicken crossed the road because the reward from doing so outweighed the risks, albeit of course, neither poultry nor humans normally consciously carry out a risk assessment before doing so. It is commonly pointed out that the risks of harm by flying are much less than those involved in driving a motor car. Notwithstanding, many people perceive flying to be an extremely hazardous activity. The perception of risk and its reality are not always the same thing. It therefore follows that decisions involving the development of contaminated land should, ideally, be based upon science and objective criteria rather than subjective perception or populist belief.

## 5.2    A word of warning

The warning is a relatively simple one, albeit often ignored. It has to do with the application of science to problems which arise in the real world and, in particular, the making of material progress in the real world notwithstanding the limitations of the scientific method.

Beware of the person who states that something is a matter of settled "*fact*". There is no such thing as an element of the scientific approach which accepts the notion of an immutable matter of "*fact*" and, so far as scientists are bold enough to say that things are matters of fact, they are often expressing a wisdom which, with the fullness of time, will usually fail to explain each and every aspect of a physical phenomenon.[2] Nor can one throw out the good in the pursuit of perfection, because this is a recipe for stultification. This warning is particularly apt in the context of land reputed to be affected by contamination.

Practical progress in this context (and many others) depends on adopting two things. First, the settings of parameters or tolerances which reflect the degrees of confidence which are appropriate to causing or allowing a certain thing to happen. Secondly, the adoption of an appropriate metric to ensure that this exercise can be framed with regard to the degree of confidence which is being sought.

Ultimately, this boils down to an exercise in risk evaluation. Thus, if an authority indicates that it wishes a contaminated site to be "*suitable for use*", then it is necessary to identify the tests which are going to be applied in order to make this determination. The outcome will not, however, be a matter of fact. In the real world, the assessment of a level of contamination starts with proxies which may or may not reflect the site as a whole. For example,

---

[2]   For example, in the 19th century, Newton's laws of motion were considered to be almost flawless; however, they failed to explain the orbit of the planet Mercury and it was left to Einstein's theory of relativity to provide an explanation. In turn, the theory of relativity does not mesh with quantum mechanics and so there is a well-known problem at this point. And, as we speak, the conventional wisdoms relating to the 'Big Bang' hypothesis are under challenge. Notwithstanding these problems, one has to make progress in the material world. Notwithstanding the difficulties with Newton's laws of motion, they were applied in the successful mission to place mankind on the moon.

a single standpipe in the middle of a 100ha site is a legitimate proxy (in the sense that it will gather materials within the path of the standpipe only or gases within the *"zone of influence"*[3] of the standpipe only), but it is unlikely to provide any determining body with an appropriate degree of confidence when assessing the proposed development or redevelopment of that site. Accordingly, if it is determined that it is necessary to carry out intrusive site investigations, then it will be necessary to settle a scheme which includes a prescribed pattern of boreholes (with or without standpipes), trenches, or both. Even then, the outputs from trenches or boreholes cannot be described as being matters of immutable fact because intrusive site investigations are not foolproof. This is particularly so when it comes to considering hypothesised zones of influence for standpipes or other gas capture equipment in relation to gaseous emissions.[4]

Even then, the sub-stratum of any site will almost never be entirely homogenous, thus this established pattern might miss a *"hot spot"*. The question for the determining body is not whether the site is *"suitable for use"* in an absolute sense, but whether or not the tests which have been applied are framed by reference to reaching a degree of confidence which is appropriate to the project and can be measured in accordance with an agreed or specified metric.

### 5.3 Toxic and non-toxic dosages

The notion of *"toxicity"* goes to the heart of a number of site assessment exercises and, so, it is necessary to gain a broad understanding of it.

*"Toxicity"* is the degree to which a chemical substance (or a particular mixture of substances) can damage an organism, and this is dose-dependent. For example, even water can lead to water intoxication when taken in too high a dose, whereas for a very dangerous substance (such as snake venom) there is a dose below which there is no detectable toxic effect. Paracelsus is said to have expressed the classic toxicology maxim, *"All things are poison, and nothing is without poison, the dosage alone makes it so a thing is not a poison"*. This is why public health standards specify maximum acceptable concentrations of various compounds in food and drink rather than seeking to impose unrealistic and unnecessary absolute embargoes on the use of these compounds.

A commentator may cite the mere presence of radioactive materials as their bull point in criticism of a proposed scheme; however, it is worth remembering that the self-luminous paint on those watch and clock dials which glow in the dark do so because of radio-luminesce. The paint consists of a small amount of a radioactive isotope which continually decays, emitting radiation particles as it does so. Indeed, continuing the theme, it is worth bearing in mind

---

[3]   For which see glossary to CIRIA C665 @ p.xv.

[4]   The matter of *"zones of influence"* has been the source of much debate over the years. See CIRIA Technical paper: *Risk and Reliability in Gas Protection Design – 20 years on: Part 2*. https://www.geplus.co.uk/technical-paper/technical-paper-risk-reliability-gas-protection-design-20-years-part-2-09-09-2019/.

that there is a world-wide back-ground level of radiation[5] which has existed throughout (at least) human history. This is harmless, although a trip to the now deserted city of Pripyat, near Chernobyl, would not be.[6]

Also, as the world has learned from the coronavirus pandemic, toxicity varies from subject to subject. Some people can absorb more of a virus or chemical than others. Typically, children are more vulnerable to potentially debilitating chemicals than adults.[7] And big young adults are usually less vulnerable than smaller older adults. Accordingly, those agencies which specify acceptable safe limits of absorption differentiate between different classes of subject.

One way of envisaging this concept is to consider that well-known poison, alcohol. If a person drinks small quantities throughout the year, then their body should be able to recover from any damage done, because it is given time to do so. If they consume a vast quantity in one sitting, then their body might be overwhelmed and they might suffer alcoholic poisoning. Thus, there is a relationship between dosage and recovery time. Furthermore, the effect of alcohol will vary according to sex, size and age. Thus, a dosage which might not affect a big young man beyond recovery might be fatal to a young child.

This approach underpins guidance such as Soil Guideline Values (SGV). Thus the Using Soil Guideline Values Better Regulation Science Programme Science report: SC050021/ SGV states:[8]

> *"SGVs are guidelines on the level of long-term human exposure to individual chemicals in soil that, unless stated otherwise, are tolerable or pose a minimal risk to human health. They represent "trigger values" – indicators to a risk assessor that soil concentrations above this level may pose a possibility of significant harm to human health (Defra, 2008b). Significance is linked to:*
>
> • *the margin of exceedance;*
>
> • *the duration and frequency of exposure;*
>
> • *other site-specific factors that the enforcing authority may wish to take into account.*
>
> *SGVs do not of themselves represent the threshold at which there is a significant possibility of significant harm (SPOSH)."*

---

[5] Levels typically range from about 1.5 to 3.5 millisievert per year but can be more than 50 mSv/yr. By comparison, regions around Chernobyl can have very high levels of radioactivity (up to 350 μSv/hr). To put it another way, one hour's exposure equates to the entire annual UK background dose in just one hour.

[6] Likewise, the Japanese city of Fukushima.

[7] Ironically, whilst it underpins the point about different doses for different people, it appears that children are less vulnerable to Covid-19 than adults.

[8] Page 4 – Published by the Environment Agency, March 2009.

## 5.4      Managing uncertainty

The only thing certain in science is uncertainty. The Glossary to *Guidance for the Safe Development of Housing on Land Affected by Contamination - R&D66: 2008 Volume 2* defines "*uncertainty*" as:

> "*A lack of knowledge about specific factors in a risk or exposure assessment including parameter uncertainty, model uncertainty and scenario uncertainty.*"

British Standard 8576:2013 (@ p.7) recognised that the management of uncertainty is inherent in risk assessments: "*One of the objectives of an investigation for ground gas is the <u>reduction of uncertainty in the conceptual model.</u>*" (Emphasis added)

British Standard EN ISO 21365:2020 recognises that a conceptual site model is a synthesis of all information about a potentially contaminated site relevant to the task in hand, with interpretation as necessary, and a <u>recognition of uncertainties</u>.

There is an inevitable margin of error in any risk assessment and the larger the margin of error, the less confidence one will have in the statistical output. The question goes to the tolerances which the model can absorb yet remain viable.

Tolerances are acceptance limits which are chosen for a process or a product. When a "*plus or minus*" figure is quoted, it may be called an "*uncertainty*", but can be given a numerical confidence level (e.g. 50%, 75%, 95% etc) expressing the degree of confidence in a results margin within which the notional "*true value*" being measured can be said to lie.

Likewise, threshold limits are "*bright lines*" which meet selected assessment criteria. Hence, the definition of "*site-specific assessment criteria*" in the Glossary to *Guidance for the Safe Development of Housing on Land Affected by Contamination - R&D66: 2008 Volume 2* is:

> "*Values for concentrations of contaminants that have been derived using detailed site-specific information on the characteristics and behaviour of contaminants, pathways and receptors and that correspond to relevant criteria in relation to harm or pollution for deciding whether there is an unacceptable risk.*"

And "*effectiveness*" is defined as:

> "*The extent to which a remediation treatment successfully reduces or controls unacceptable risks to a defined level.*"

## 5.5      The risk-based approach

The Glossary to *R&D66: 2008 Volume 2* defines "*risk assessment*" as:

> "*The formal process of identifying, assessing and evaluating the health and environmental risks that may be associated with a hazard.*"

And defines *"risk management"* as:

> *"The process involved in identifying, assessing and determining risks, and the implementation of actions to mitigate the consequences or probabilities of occurrence."*

The risk-based approach was summarised in *Contaminated Land Report 11: The Model Procedures for the Management of Land Contamination* (September 2004).[9] Paragraph 1.1 stated that for any individual site the land manager or other interested person faces two questions:

- Does the contamination matter? And, if so:

- What needs to be done about it?

The Glossary to *R&D66: 2008 Volume 2* defines *"site characterisation"* as:

> *"The process of gathering information about a site (or group of sites) and its setting(s) for the purpose of assessing and, where necessary, managing health and environmental risks."*

## 5.6     Costs and benefits

At several stages of the risk management process, judgements have to be made about the relative costs and benefits of particular courses of action or decisions. This *"cost-benefit analysis"* is an inherent part of the management of environmental risks in a sustainable way, and is a formal component of particular stages of regulatory regimes. It allows for the structured and transparent balance of the costs (usually, but not always, in financial terms) against benefits, which can be wide-ranging depending on the context – for example, enhanced health and environmental protection, increased commercial confidence in the condition of the land or simply greater certainty in ultimate decision making. The scope and particular criteria for any cost–benefit analysis will depend on the context.

Such considerations should not challenge the basic technical structure of the risk management process. However, they strongly influence the way in which it is put into practice – they can determine the level of detailed work carried out at any particular stage, the speed at which projects move through the process and the level of resource that may be available.

## 5.7     The *"suitable for use"* approach

Finally, how we deal with the problem. In a metaphysical ideal world, one could try to eliminate every whiff of pollutive gas, but the reality is that land is a very scarce resource in the UK, funding is not unlimited and so all development sites cannot be models of environmental perfection. It is necessary to evaluate risks and, if they exist at unacceptable levels, then to deploy commercially realistic treatment strategies to reduce them to acceptable

---

[9]     A now withdrawn (albeit useful) joint publication by the Environment Agency and the Department for Environment, Food and Rural Affairs (DEFRA).

levels. This is the crux of the pragmatic *"suitable for use"* approach which has been adopted for the purposes of town and country planning in the UK.

If one looked to the Netherlands in the late 1980s, then the approach was to try to achieve *"omni-functionality"* (aka the *"Dutch Standard"*) and to clean up all sites to what was perceived to be normal background levels. A similar approach was adopted in the USA in respect of their *"Superfund"* programme. These approaches have not been pursued because, of course, they were not financially viable. It is one thing to legislate that site adaptation treatment operations should meet the object of omni-functionality; however, it is another finding developers who are prepared to fund such treatment when it exceeds that which is necessary to carry out their developments and return a profit. The Netherlands now use a *"fitness for purpose"* approach which is, for all intents and purposes, similar to the UK's *"suitable for use"* approach.

English national guidance on the *"suitable for use"* approach is somewhat parsimonious.

In 1988, the then Draft BSI code of practice DD175:1988 '*Code of practice for the identification of potentially contaminated land and its investigation*' stated (at para 10.1, page 21):

> *"When assessing the suitability of a contaminated site for development, the central principle to be adopted is that the eventual users or occupiers of the site, buildings or building services, and plants and animals, ought not to be subjected to risks which could be avoided."* [10]

This type of comment must, of course, be conditioned by the fact that the pursuit of a completely unschooled risk-free environment is not only not necessary but also often not financially viable. Many risks are acceptable and a philosophy of the complete elimination of all risk is wholly unrealistic. As noted above, the assessment of risk is a balancing exercise which, in part, should turn on a cost benefit analysis.

In the consultation paper *Public Registers of Land which may be Contaminated* (1991) the Department of the Environment stated:

> *"3.1. The government shares the view of the Royal Commission on environmental pollution that contamination is not synonymous with pollution. The Commission regarded contamination as "a necessary but not sufficient condition for pollution", and also noted that "what today is regarded as no more than contamination may tomorrow be pollution, as a substance accumulates to ... harmful concentrations or as knowledge is gained of hitherto unsuspected effects".*

---

[10]   Now replaced by BS 10175:2011+A2:2017 Investigation of potentially contaminated sites - Code of practice + A1:2013.

*3.2. The Commission therefore used "contamination" to denote the presence in the environment of certain substances, without making a judgement on whether they are actually harmful. The use of the term in this paper follows this principle".*

Department of the Environment Circular 21/87 (Development of Contaminated Land) stated:

*"13. When it is known or strongly suspected that the site is contaminated to an extent which would adversely affect the proposed development, an investigation by the developer to identify any remedial measures required to deal with the hazards will normally be required before the application can be decided by the local planning authority…"*

The Report on the Environment (United States Environmental Protection Agency) said[11]:

*"Contaminated lands can pose a variety of health and environmental hazards. Some contaminated sites pose little risk to human health and the environment, because the level of contamination is low and the chance of exposure to toxic or hazardous contaminants is also low.*

*Other contaminated sites are of greater concern because of the chemicals that may be present and their propensity to persist in or move through the environment, exposing humans or the environment to hazards.*

*"Contaminated land": Land that has been polluted with hazardous materials and requires cleanup or remediation. Contaminated lands include sites contaminated as a result of improper handling or disposal of toxic and hazardous wastes, sites where improper handling or accidents released toxic or hazardous materials that are not wastes, and sites where toxins may have been deposited by wind or flooding."*

This distinction is observed by the Department for Environment, Food and Rural Affairs in its publication Environmental Protection Act 1990: Part IIA - Contaminated Land Statutory Guidance (April 2012) which states (@ para. 6):

*""Contaminated land" is used to mean land which meets the Part 2A definition of contaminated land. Other terms, such as "land affected by contamination" or "land contamination", are used to describe the much broader categories of land where contaminants are present but usually not at a sufficient level of risk to be contaminated land."*

This somewhat circular[12] definitional problem was caused by those drafting the 1995 Act who, instead of creating a particular term to describe the type of land covered by Part IIA, took the easy route of just calling it *"contaminated land"* without regard to the fact that it was, in fact, a subset of what had, up until that time, been described by that broad classification.

---

[11]   epa.gov/report-environment.

[12]   A banana is an object which looks and tastes like a banana!!

Needless to say, this does cause some confusion in the minds of advisers and commentators even up to the present day. Accordingly, it is important to focus very closely on the type of "*contaminated land*" which is being discussed in any particular context.

Paragraph 183 of the NPPF states:

> "*Planning policies and decisions should ensure that:*
>
> *a) a site is suitable for its proposed use taking account of ground conditions and any risks arising from land instability and contamination. This includes risks arising from natural hazards or former activities such as mining, and any proposals for mitigation including land remediation (as well as potential impacts on the natural environment arising from that remediation);*
>
> *b) after remediation, as a minimum, land should not be capable of being determined as contaminated land under Part IIA of the Environmental Protection Act 1990; and*
>
> *c) adequate site investigation information, prepared by a competent person, is available to inform these assessments.*"

The first point in this scant advice is very important. This is the concept of suitability for use and that the completed development site must be suitable for its proposed use. Clearly a residential use will be more sensitive to contamination than general engineering or a warehouse use etc and is the job of the developer and local planning authority to ensure that this is the case. This includes risks arising from natural hazards. The bulk of contaminated land commentary seems to focus on man-made hazards, but it is not clear why those commentators make this wholly arbitrary distinction. So at least it is helpful that paragraph 183 does (at least) recognise that natural hazards are something that have to be taken into account. The paragraph then goes on to refer to former activities which will clearly include mining, industry and similar potentially pollutive activities. Unfortunately, this wholly sensible inclusion of former activities leads to confusion when one attempts to reconcile the terminology of the NPPF in relation to previously developed land and brownfield land. According to the NPPF, a former industrial site which has been cleared and is now overgrown is not a "*brownfield*" or "*previously developed*" site: see the Glossary to the NPPF.

The reference to Part IIA of the Environmental Protection Act 1990 in Paragraph (a) is, arguably, unfortunate because it invites an overlap between two completely different regulatory regimes. This could cause problems in relation to the duplication of controls: see Paragraph 6.1 below. One initial response is, of course, that a site which has been declared to be suitable for residential use would, automatically, comply with Part IIA and, therefore, this proposition is otiose. Even with a general engineering development, it is hardly likely that any responsible local planning authority would grant planning permission for an operation which does not meet all modern standards in terms of preventing pollution. Again, this seems to make the cross-reference an otiose proposition.

Perhaps inadvertently, the inclusion of the particular proposition in Paragraph 183(b) does, at least, remind one that it is not enough to simply examine the problems of contamination within the arbitrary boundaries of a development site. It is equally important to ask whether the carrying out of the development will, itself, cause pollution elsewhere. This might, indeed, arise where cavalier treatment is carried out, thereby altering surface water run-off, drainage to aquifers, etc. Accordingly, it would be appropriate for the local planning authority to ask the developer to demonstrate that this is not going to be a problem, albeit without getting drawn into the unrelated complexities of the Part IIA regime. The obvious comment is that (a) refers to potential impacts on the natural environment arising from site adaptation treatment in any event.

Paragraph 183(c) is, of course, paternalistic!

This guidance is, unfortunately, nebulous in the sense that it gives no indication of the metric to be deployed in assessing matters of risk.

By contrast, Scottish guidance is more fulsome. Planning Advice Note 33: Development of contaminated land[13] advises that:

> *"The "suitable for use" approach consists of three elements:*
>
> *i) ensuring that land is suitable for its current use – in other words, identifying land where contamination is causing unacceptable risks to human health and the environment, on the basis of the current use and circumstances of the land, and returning it to a condition where such risks no longer arise ("remediating" the land); this is the role of the Scottish Environment Protection Agency (SEPA) in the case of "special sites 1" and local authorities in the case of any other type of site;*
>
> *ii) ensuring that land is made suitable for any new use, as planning permission is given for that new use – in other words, assessing the potential risks from contamination, on the basis of the proposed future use and circumstances, before permission is given for the development and, where necessary, to avoid unacceptable risks to human health and the environment, remediating the land before the new use commences; this is the role of the town and country planning and building control regimes; and*
>
> *iii) limiting requirements for remediation to the work necessary to prevent unacceptable risks to human health or the environment in relation to the current use or future use of the land for which planning permission is being sought – in other words, recognising that the risks from contaminated land can be satisfactorily assessed only in the context of specific uses of the land (whether current or proposed), and that any attempt to guess what might be needed at some time in the future for other uses, is likely to result either*

---

13    Published: 5 December 2017 (Directorate: Local Government and Communities Directorate).

*in premature work (thereby risking distorting social, economic and environmental priorities) or in unnecessary work (thereby wasting resources).*

*Within this "suitable for use" framework, it is important to recognise both that the use of any particular area of land may cover several different activities, and that some potential risks arising from contamination (particularly impacts on water and the wider environment) may arise independently of the use of the land. For example the current use of a site may be irrelevant if harm is being caused off-site e.g. the pollution of a nearby watercourse. In practical terms, the current use of any land should be taken to be any use which: (a) is currently being made of the land, or is likely to be made of it; and (b) is consistent with any existing planning permission, or is otherwise lawful under town and country planning legislation."*

Point (iii) is particularly pertinent to phased developments and the ongoing viability considerations which apply to them.

It is important to stress that different parts of a development site might have differing tolerances for contamination, consequently, the *"suitable for use"* approach might have to be applied on an area-by-area basis within the site. For example, a development which is described by the generic label *"residential"* will not be covered entirely by housing. There will be landscaped areas, hard infrastructure (such as roads and parking areas) and the like in addition to houses and gardens, and all of these will have different tolerances to the effects of contamination. Indeed, well placed hard infrastructure may provide impermeable capping for *"hot spots"*.

# Chapter 6

# Cognate Regimes And The Duplication Of Controls

## 6.1    Introduction

It is readily apparent that the planning system is not the only regime which seeks to regulate land affected by contamination, the most obvious example being, of course, that Part IIA of the Environmental Protection Act 1990 also provides a response to the most injurious parts of the problem. Accordingly, it is important that those in development control do not inadvertently take steps which duplicate or, even, contradict overlapping regimes. At best, this may lead to confusion and, at worst, it might put developers in the position where they cannot satisfy one body without upsetting another.

In 2004, Syms stated (para. 3.3)[1]:

> *"Some concern exists among developers as to which authorities are responsible for regulating redevelopment. At least one well-known housebuilder has made the mistake of agreeing a remediation plan with the Environment Agency, only to find that the proposed works were not acceptable to the local authority's environmental health officer, who recommended refusal of the application, resulting in a planning appeal."*

There is, also, the problem of the economic costs of the *"dead hand of bureaucracy"*.

Be that as it may, the general tenor of case-law and national guidance is that the local planning authority should presume that other regulatory regimes will operate effectively; however, one has to ask what this means in real terms on a regime-by-regime basis.

Fortunately, this should not be a problem for those developers and planning officers who deal with land affected by contamination provided that consideration is given to overlapping regimes at appropriate points in the process. In practice, the greatest potential for overlap will be in respect of active on-site treatment techniques which may involve processes which have the potential to emit to atmosphere, to pollute ground-waters or to produce controlled waste and which, therefore, may be the subject of separate permitting requirements. The prudent authority will, even if separate permits are not required, take advice from the appropriate statutory bodies as to the proposed methods of working.

## 6.2    Fettering discretion

A body which is vested with a statutory decision-making function is not entitled to surrender that function to another body, thereby abdicating responsibility for the discharge of its statutory duty. A failure to follow this principle can render its decision unlawful. The underlying principle is relatively straightforward; namely, that if Parliament had taken the

---

[1]    See Syms, P (2004); *Previously Developed Land* (Blackwell Publishing); pages 62 to 68.

trouble to vest a statutory duty in a chosen body, then that body does not have the right to, somehow, pass that duty over to this party. This action would, if allowed, overturn the intent of Parliament at the whim of the relevant executive body and undermine the Sovereignty of Parliament. The broad categorisation of this principle is known as the *"fettering of discretion"*. Nor is a body which is vested with a statutory discretion allowed to fetter that statutory discretion by adopting a rigid policy which precludes the consideration of each case according to the relevant material considerations.

In *R v Port of London Authority, ex. parte Kynoch* [1919] 1 K.B. 176, Bankes LJ said (@ p.184):

> *"There are on the one hand cases where a tribunal in the honest exercise of its discretion has adopted a policy and, without refusing to hear an applicant, intimates to him what its policy is and that after hearing him it will in accordance with its policy decide against him, unless there is something exceptional in his case. I think counsel for the Applicants would admit that, if the policy has been adopted for reasons which the authority may legitimately entertain, no objection could be taken to such a course. On the other hand there are cases where a tribunal has passed a rule, or come to a determination, not to hear any application of a particular character by whomsoever made. There is a wide distinction to be drawn between these two classes."*

In *British Oxygen v Minister of Technology* [1971] A.C. 610, Lord Reid, having cited this passage, continued (@ p.625):

> *"I see nothing wrong with that. But the circumstances in which discretions are exercised vary enormously and that passage cannot be applied literally in every case. The general rule is that anyone who has to exercise a statutory discretion must not "shut his ears to an application" ... I do not think there is any great difference between a policy and a rule. There may be cases where an officer or authority ought to listen to a substantial argument reasonably presented urging a change of policy. What the authority must not do is to refuse to listen at all. But a Ministry or large authority may have had to deal already with a multitude of similar applications and then they will almost certainly have evolved a policy so precise that it could well be called a rule. There can be no objection to that, provided the authority is always willing to listen to anyone with something new to say ..."*

*Lavender and Son Ltd v Minister of Housing and Local Government* [1970] 1 W.L.R. 1231 was a town and country planning case. The Minister's policy was not to release land for mineral working unless the Minister of Agriculture was not opposed to such working. The Minister rejected the plaintiff's appeal against a refusal of planning permission for the extraction of sand, gravel and ballast from some high-quality agricultural land, in view of the objection of the Ministry of Agriculture. The Minister's decision was quashed. Willis J stated:

> *"I do not think that the Minister after the inquiry can be said in any real sense to have given genuine consideration to whether on planning (including agricultural) grounds this land could be worked. It seems to me that by adopting and applying his stated*

> *policy he has in effect inhibited himself from exercising a proper discretion (which would of course be guided by policy considerations) in any case where the Minister of Agriculture has made and maintained an objection to mineral working in an agricultural reservation. Everything else might point to the desirability of granting permission, but by applying and acting on his stated policy I think the Minister has fettered himself in such a way that in this case it was not he who made the decision for which Parliament made him responsible. It was the decision of the Minister of Agriculture not to waive his objection which was decisive in this case, and while that might properly prove to be the decisive factor for the Minister when taking into account all material considerations, it seems to me quite wrong for a policy to be applied which in reality eliminates all the material considerations save only the consideration, when that is the case, that the Minister of Agriculture objects ..."*

The flaw in the *Lavender* case is often described as *"acting under a dictation"* or *"surrender of discretion"*, in the sense that the statutory decision-making body has, in fact, surrendered its statutory duty to another body instead of applying its own mind to the decision-making process on that particular point. The correct approach is for the authority to have regard to the responses of consultees and place appropriate weight upon those comments, but then to make its own mind up as to the point in question.

## 6.3    Planning policies

Paragraph 188 of the National Planning Policy Framework states:

> *"The focus of planning policies and decisions should be on whether proposed develop-ment is an acceptable use of land, rather than the control of processes or emissions (where these are subject to separate pollution control regimes). Planning decisions should assume that these regimes will operate effectively. Equally, where a planning decision has been made on a particular development, the planning issues should not be revisited through the permitting regimes operated by pollution control authorities."*

The National Planning Practice Guidance states:

> *"Are there any circumstances where planning conditions should not be used?*
>
> *Conditions requiring compliance with other regulatory regimes will not meet the test of necessity and may not be relevant to planning. Use of informatives to remind the applicant to obtain further planning approvals and other consents may be more appropriate."*
>
> *Paragraph: 005 Reference ID: 21a-005-20190723 - Revision date: 23 07 2019.*

*"Planning Practice Guidance for Onshore Oil and Gas (Department for Communities and Local Government"* (July 2013) relates to the exploration and extraction of the shale gas known as hydraulic fracturing (fracking). It contains some useful guidance on this point:

> *"What is the relationship between planning and other regulatory regimes?*

*29. The Planning and other regulatory regimes are separate but complementary. The planning system controls the development and use of land in the public interest and, as stated in paragraphs 120 and 122 of the National Planning Policy Framework, this includes ensuring that new development is appropriate for its location taking account of the effects (including cumulative effects) of pollution on health, the natural environment or general amenity, and the potential sensitivity of the area or proposed development to adverse effects from pollution. In doing so the focus of the planning system should be on whether the development itself is an acceptable use of the land, and the impacts of those uses, rather than any control processes, health and safety issues or emissions themselves where these are subject to approval under other regimes. Minerals planning authorities should assume that these non-planning regimes will operate effectively. What hydrocarbon issues can minerals planning authorities leave to other regulatory regimes?*

*31. Some issues may be covered by other regulatory regimes but may be relevant to minerals planning authorities in specific circumstances. For example, the Environment Agency has responsibility for ensuring that risk to groundwater is appropriately identified and mitigated. Where an Environmental Statement is required, minerals planning authorities can and do play a role in preventing pollution of the water environment from hydrocarbon extraction, principally through controlling the methods of site construction and operation, robustness of storage facilities, and in tackling surface water drainage issues.*

*32. There exist a number of issues which are covered by other regulatory regimes and minerals planning authorities should assume that these regimes will operate effectively. Whilst these issues may be put before minerals planning authorities, they should not need to carry out their own assessment as they can rely on the assessment of other regulatory bodies. However, before granting planning permission they will need to be satisfied that these issues can or will be adequately addressed by taking the advice from the relevant regulatory body:*

- *Mitigation of seismic risks – the Department of Energy and Climate Change;*

- *Well design and construction, well integrity during operation, operation of surface equipment on the well pad, well decommissioning/abandonment – the Health and Safety Executive;*

- *Chemical content of hydraulic fracturing fluid, final off-site disposal of water, mining waste - the Environment Agency."*

## 6.4    Case-law

Not surprisingly, there is case-law on the topic.

Arguably, the leading case is *Gateshead MBC v Secretary of State for the Environment and another* (1994) 67 P. & C.R. 179. This concerned a proposed clinical waste incinerator in a semi-rural location. Jeremy Sullivan QC (as he then was), sitting as a deputy High Court Judge, held that the environmental impact of emissions to atmosphere is a material consideration at the planning stage, but so also is the existence of a stringent regime under the EPA for preventing or mitigating that impact. The decision maker is entitled to be satisfied, having regard to the EPA controls that the difficulty is capable of being overcome, so there is no reason for refusing planning permission. Whether that point has been reached is a question for the decision maker on the facts of each individual case. Deputy Judge Sullivan said:

> *"Lest this judgement be misinterpreted, I stress that this decision is not carte blanche for applications for planning permission to seek to ignore the pollution implications of their proposed development and say "leave it all to the EPA"…"*

Indeed, the local planning authority, which surrenders its judgements on these matters to another body could, rightfully, be accused of *"acting under a dictation"* (see below).

*Hopkins Developments Ltd v First Secretary of State and another* [2006] EWHC 2823 (Admin) (George Bartlett QC (as he was then), sitting as deputy High Court Judge), concerned a concrete batching plant. Deputy Judge Bartlett said that the proposition that it was established that the impact of emissions to air from a proposed development is capable of being a material consideration but in considering that issue the planning authority is entitled to take into account the pollution control regime. Thus, in appropriate cases, planning authorities can leave pollution control to the pollution control authorities, but they are not obliged as a matter of law to do so. He went on to say that the Inspector in that case:

> *"… focussed on whether the development itself was an acceptable use of the land and the impacts it would have, rather than on the control of the processes or emissions themselves. In approaching the matter in this way, in my judgment, he acted in accordance with the law."*

He added:

> *"Planning authorities should focus on the impacts rather than the control of emissions, not that they must subordinate their judgment on the impacts to those of the pollution control authority."*

In *Harrison v Secretary of State for Communities and Local Government and another* [2009] EWHC 3382 (Admin), HH Judge McKenna (sitting as a deputy High Court Judge) said:

> *"The thrust of the decision in Hopkins … is that the planning decision maker was entitled to reach his own conclusions as to the impact of the proposed development on amenity and whether the site under consideration was the appropriate location for the proposed development. The fact that the impact might be capable of being regulated under a pollution control regime did not necessarily mean that the only possible option available to an Inspector was to leave everything to that regime. If the planning decision maker considered that there might be adverse consequences because of the effects*

> *of the proposed development on amenity and /or issues as to the appropriateness of locating the development on the site in question, he was entitled to have regard to such matters as material considerations in making his decision on the planning merits of the proposed development."*

Here, the matter in question was not public health per se, but residual adverse impacts on public amenity assuming that the relevant permit or licence schemes have been properly implemented.

## 6.5    Statutory nuisance
It is, hopefully, possible to deal with statutory nuisance quickly.

The Environmental Protection Act 1990 provides for the current iteration of *"statutory nuisance"*.

Section 79(1) provides that (subject to subsections 79(1A) to (6A)) *"statutory nuisances"* include:

• any premises in such a state as to be prejudicial to health or a nuisance;

• fumes or gases emitted from premises so as to be prejudicial to health or a nuisance; and

• any accumulation or deposit which is prejudicial to health or a nuisance.

The provisions have been amended to ensure that there is no overlap with the statutory scheme in Part IIA. Thus, it is stated that no matter shall constitute a statutory nuisance to the extent that it consists of, or is caused by, any land being in a *"contaminated state"*. By Section 79(1B), land is in a *"contaminated state"* if, and only if, it is in such a condition, by reason of substances in, on or under the land, that:

(a) harm is being caused or there is a possibility of harm being caused; or

(b) pollution of controlled waters is being, or is likely to be, caused.

This exclusion also appears to exclude the invocation of statutory nuisance by the environmental health department in connection with any complaints in respect of sites which are thus categorised as *"contaminated"*.[2]

## 6.6    The Building Regulations 2010
The Building Regulations 2010 contain provisions relating to the potential for contamination to buildings.

---

[2]    It also, of course, leaves a gap between those sites thus excluded and those which are actually captured by Part IIA, but this is another story.

In short (and for these purposes) the Regulations cover *"building work"* which include the erection or extension of a building, the material alteration of a building and certain work required by the Regulations relating to material change of use.

Regulation 4 sets out the requirements relating to *"building work"*:

*(1) Subject to paragraph (2) building work shall be carried out so that–*

*(a) it complies with the applicable requirements contained in Schedule 1; and*

*(b) in complying with any such requirement there is no failure to comply with any other such requirement.*

The Building Regulations are accompanied by Approved Documents. Approved Document C provides (page 5):

PART C SITE PREPARATION AND RESISTANCE TO CONTAMINANTS AND MOISTURE

Preparation of site and resistance to contaminants

C1. (1) The ground to be covered by the building shall be reasonably free from any material that might damage the building or affected its (stability, including vegetable matter, topsoil and pre-existing foundations.

(2) Reasonable precautions shall be taken to avoid danger to health and safety caused by contaminants on or in the ground covered, or to be covered by the building and any land associated with the building.

(3) Adequate subsoil drainage shall be provided, if it is needed to avoid-

(a) the passage of ground moisture to the interior of the building;

(b) damage to the building, including damage through the transport of water-borne contaminants to the foundations of the building.

(4) For the purposes of this requirement, *"contaminant"* means any substance which is, or may become harmful to persons or buildings, including substances which are corrosive, explosive, flammable, radioactive or toxic.

Thus, whilst the Building Regulations and Approved Guidance provide safeguards for land affected by contamination, there is no immediate and apparent conflict with a planning authority specifying, for example, that mitigation measures should follow a regime based on CIRIA 226. One should presume, of course, that those in the planning department of an authority would take guidance from its building control department in settling planning conditions or planning obligations.

Whilst there is a nominal overlap with the Building Regulations, it is clear that this should not inhibit a local planning authority in setting its own requirements.[3]

## 6.7    The Environment Agency

The Environment Agency protects water resources (including groundwater aquifers), ensures treatment and disposal of mining waste, emissions to air, and suitable management and treatment of naturally occurring radioactive materials. They issue permits for installations, medium combustion plant, specified generator, waste or mining waste operations, water discharge or groundwater activities, or work on or near a main river or sea defence. The Agency is, also, the body charged with the duty of enforcing various regulations relating to these matters.

Depending on the selected method of treatment, the developer might need to obtain such a permit. The local planning authority should not seek to prescribe treatment or mitigation measures which may conflict with the permitting regime.

This is not to say that the local planning authority is, in some way, precluded from taking prophylactic measures which are complimentary to the overlapping regime. One recent example is a case involving Bellway Homes Limited.

As noted above, it is reported that, in 2023, Bellway Homes Limited undertook to pay £100,000 to environmental charities in the North East as redress for depositing waste soil contaminated with mixed waste at a site in Northumberland.[4] As a result of action by the Environment Agency[5], Bellway Homes committed to a *"reactive"* Enforcement Undertaking to remove the waste from the site, to improve awareness of the law in relation to soils and waste and review its protocols. The company made a voluntary offer to pay £50,000 to Northumberland Wildlife Trust, £30,000 to Wear Rivers Trust and £20,000 to Tyne Rivers Trust.[6]

Hence, the prudent local planning authority might be well advised to request that details of the proposed fill material should be provided before the grant of planning permission.

---

[3]   It is notable that the appendix to the Approved Document provides a list of relevant guidance document, which tends to reinforce this conclusion.

[4]   Construction Enquirer, March 2023 – Bellway dumped imported contaminated soil on its housing site | Construction Enquirer News.

[5]   The alleged offence was operating without or other than in accordance with an environmental permit (waste operation) – Regulation 38(1) of the Environmental Permitting (England and Wales) Regulations 2010/2016.

[6]   See: https://www.gov.uk/government/publications/environment-agencys-use-of-civil-sanctions/enforcement-undertakings-accepted-by-the-environment-agency-1-june-2022-to-30-september-2022#environmental-permitting-england-and-wales-regulations-20102016 - Bellway Homes Limited (reference 911). Also: https://www.gov.uk/government/publications/environment-agency-enforcement-and-sanctions-policy/annex-1-res-act-the-environment-agencys-approach-to-applying-civil-sanctions-and-accepting-enforcement-undertakings.

Arguably, a local planning authority could go further and impose an appropriate condition which allows them to be satisfied that the imported fill material will be examined for any possible contaminants before they are incorporated into the site.

Furthermore, this could be the type of case which demonstrates that perceived constraints in connection with the *"duplication of controls"* need to be taken should be taken with a dose of pragmatism. Whilst it might be appropriate to say *"leave it to the Environment Agency"*, it, manifestly, makes more sense to seek to impose controls by way of the planning system at an early stage and, thereby, to ensure that problems do not arise in the future.

To give a practical example, it might be the case that the hypothesised remedy for the illegal use of contaminated materials for the purposes of ground engineering is the removal of those materials from site or, alternatively, some form of on-site treatment process. The all too common outcome of such proposed ex post facto action might be that the developer either does not have the financial resources to do so or, alternatively, has gone into liquidation. This will leave the executive bodies charged with resolving this problem with an even greater problem; namely, finding the money to carry out the works in the face of public pressure to do so.

### 6.8     The Health and Safety Executive

The Health and Safety Executive (HSE) regulates the safety aspects of all phases of extraction and is responsible for ensuring appropriate design and construction of a well casing for any borehole.

Depending on the selected method of treatment, the developer might need to obtain clearance from the HSE. Again, therefore, the local planning authority should not seek to prescribe treatment or mitigation measures which may conflict with the permitting regime.

### 6.9     Air quality

It might be said that matters relating to air quality are covered by the legislation which relates to air quality management areas and are not, therefore, the concern of local planning authorities. That is, to some extent, true. An examination of the UK and information resource which is published by the Department for Environment and Rural Affairs, shows that a number of urban areas are, indeed, the subject of air quality management areas. However, if matters of air quality management are not high on the agendas for local planning authorities, then it is arguable that they will be elevated as a result of the 2021 Act.

Section 17 of the Act sets out the *"environmental principles"* and those environmental principles include, in turn, the principle of *"preventative action"* to avert environmental damage and the adoption of the *"precautionary principle"* so far as it relates to the environment. As such, these principles are now given statutory force and the question for this chapter is how this will impact on day to day development control decision-making.

The starting point here is to consider the policy statement which has been adopted for the purposes of the Act, so as to crystallise the *"environmental principles"* as a matter of national policy. This is the document entitled *A Green Future: Our 25 Year Plan to Improve the Environment*. This document contains a clear commitment to reduce the emissions of five damaging air pollutants. The object is to halve the effects of air pollution on health by 2030. The gravamen of this policy statement will be carried into other government guidance and, in particular, the National Planning Policy Framework. It will, then, be carried forward into local development plan policies and, then, into day-to-day decision-making.

A local planning authority might be justified in asking why matters of air quality cannot be left to the Environment Agency and the emergent Office for Environmental Protection. One only needs to look at typical, relatively innocuous, site-specific applications for planning permission to see why this is not realistic in practice.

Take, for example a proposal to construct a fast-food takeaway. This is not an unusual application, but it raises concerns relating to air pollution. It is not, nowadays, the case that all patrons will drive to the car park and then walk to the restaurant. In many cases, they will use the drive-through facility, thereby starting and stopping cars or, alternatively, will present the sight of cars queuing to reach the service window. This will, of course, create a localised concentration of undesirable air pollutants. It is not a matter for the Environment Agency or the Office for Environmental Protection, but it is a matter for the local planning authority. This is particularly so if the proposed takeaway is located in an air quality management area. This is no different to the well-established use of the planning system to control the potential noise or odour effects of development proposals. Arguably, the local planning authority should look back to *"environmental principles"* set out in Section 17(5) of the Act and have particular regard to the principle of *"preventative action"* and the *"precautionary principle"* during the course of their deliberations. No doubt these principles will be carried through to emerging local plan policies in any event, in the fullness of time.

Furthermore, it is not a case of focusing on the actions of developers only. The fact of the matter is that the actions of local highway authorities and local planning authorities can have a deleterious effects air quality, however well meant they might be. Consider, for example the installation of traffic signals with a view to improving traffic management on the previously free flowing road. The operation of the signals will, in fact, create a localised concentration of air pollution. Vehicles which would have otherwise been cruising along the road would then be called upon to decelerate and stop at the lights, the net effect of this being that vehicles will be producing pollution whilst idling at the lights and when accelerating away once the lights have changed. The somewhat benign action of providing a pedestrian crossing will have exactly the same effect in terms of air pollution, as will the installation of road humps or any other traffic management mechanism, as a result of vehicles slowing down and accelerating.

These practical examples demonstrate that concerns about the duplication of controls can, sometimes, take on the appearance of being nice metaphysical points rather than matters which manifest themselves in the material world.

*Gladman Developments Ltd v Secretary of State for Communities and Local Government* [2019] EWCA Civ 1543 was a typical housing case where air quality was relevant. There Gladman applied for permission for 470 homes and 120 extra care units. In dismissing Gladman's appeals on non-determination, the Inspector concluded that it was likely that the developments would have an adverse impact on local air quality and the mitigation measures proposed were not sufficient to outweigh the negative effects. In the High Court, Gladman stated that, by making a decision based on air quality concerns, the Inspector was attempting to duplicate an *"air quality"* regime. The court held there was no relevant *"air quality regime"* for housing proposals.

# Chapter 7

# The Site Assessment Process

The site assessment process has, by custom and practice, been divided into the following basic stages:[1]

**Phase 1**: Hazard identification and assessment. A Phase 1 Environmental Site Assessment is often referred to as a *"Desk Study"* or *"Preliminary Risk Assessment"*.

**Phase 2**: Risk estimation and evaluation. The purpose of a Phase 2 Environmental Site Assessment is to quantify any land contamination on the basis of data collected from the relevant site, and will, normally, involve intrusive site investigations and/or gas collection. It will also inform a decision as to whether land treatment action is required.

**Phase 3**: Treatment; design, implementation.

**Phase 4**: Verification and monitoring.

This book will follow this relatively simple differentiation; however, it is worth noting that approaches vary between different guidance regimes.

The series of guidance documents named, generically, *"Land Contamination Risk Management"* (LCRM), set out an approach which tends to merge the Phase 1 and Phase 2 Assessments.[2]

## 7.1    Phase 1 Environmental Site Assessment

A Phase 1 Environmental Site Assessment involves research by a qualified environmental assessor into the current and historical uses of a property and its locality to assess if current or historical uses have, or may have, impacted the property and could pose a threat to the site, the environment or human health.

Paragraph 1.1.1 of *Guidance for the Safe Development of Housing on Land Affected by Contamination R&D66: 2008 Volume 1* describes the overall aim of this stage as being to assess the potential hazards that could be present on a particular site. Paragraph 1.1.2 lists the objectives for Phase 1 hazard identification stage as including the following:

•       To construct an initial conceptual site model.

•       To enable a preliminary risk assessment.

---

[1]    For example, see *Guidance for the Safe Development of Housing on Land Affected by Contamination - R&D Publication 66: 2008 Volume 1.*

[2]    Published 8 October 2020 (Last updated 20 July 2023): https://www.gov.uk/government/publications/land-contamination-risk-management-lcrm.

- To inform the need for and scope of further work (desk based or intrusive investigations).

Paragraph 1.1.1 stresses that:

> *"It is important to remember that there will always be some site specific factors which, in combination are particular to that site. Every site must therefore be considered unique and thus considered on its own merits."*

A Phase 1 Assessment should include a *"walk-over"* of the site and a visual inspection of the site, but does not include the collection and analysis of physical samples. It is, primarily, a desktop study with a non-intrusive site inspection, with the objective of gathering and assessing information from historical maps, the recorded geology of the area, potentially contaminative land uses (past and present) and hydrogeology.

Paragraph 1.1.1 of *R&D66: 2008 Volume 1* states that the process of hazard identification and assessment comprises:

- *A definition of objectives.*

- *A description of the site, in terms of location, extent, boundaries and current appearance.*

- *A determination of the history of the site land use.*

- *An identification of the current land use, including use/storage of hazardous materials etc.*

- *A description of environmental setting and establishment of site sensitivity.*

- *A description of the initial conceptual site model.*

The assessor will create a *"Conceptual Site Model"* which is used to make a provisional assessment of whether there is any potential risk to the environment or human health. This requires the consideration of whether a *"source-pathway-receptor"* pollutant linkage may exist (see below).

This should, then, be followed by a preliminary risk assessment based on the information then available.

It is submitted, perhaps boldly, that a local planning authority should seek the submission of a Phase 1 Assessment before the grant of a planning permission whenever there is objective and forensically robust evidence of possible contamination in the terms indicated above. The reason for this is that such an assessment should be neither expensive nor should it cause any undue delay to the planning process. Indeed, if the developer is not the current landowner, then he would, if prudent, have commissioned a Phase 1 Assessment as part of the due diligence process leading to the contract for sale.

The National guidance entitled "*Land Contamination Risk Management*" (LCRM)[3] is made up of 4 guides:

• LCRM: Before you start.

• LCRM: Risk assessment.

• LCRM: Options appraisal.

• LCRM: Remediation and verification

The LCRM uses a three-tiered approach to risk assessment. The three tiers are:

• Preliminary risk assessment.

• Generic quantitative risk assessment.

• Detailed quantitative risk assessment.

In order to meet the standards for land contamination and planning, the applicant must use a "*competent person*" within the meaning given by the glossary to the National Planning Policy Framework (NPPF)[4]. This is a person with a recognised relevant qualification, sufficient experience in dealing with the type(s) of pollution or land instability, and membership of a relevant professional organisation.

The assessor must always start with a preliminary risk assessment. This will establish whether there are any potentially unacceptable risks arising from contamination at the site. The advice in the LCRM on the conduct of a "*Tier 1: Preliminary risk assessment*" starts by advising that the applicant must assess the risks qualitatively to decide whether particular harm or pollution is unacceptable. This exercise needs to be based on:

• overall site objectives;

• qualitative assessment criteria; and

---

[3]   Published 8 October 2020 (Updated July 2023) - Land contamination risk management (LCRM) - GOV. UK (www.gov.uk).

[4]   https://www.gov.uk/guidance/national-planning-policy-framework/annex-2-glossary.

- type of receptor[5] which may be in play, such as human health, controlled waters, ecology or property.

The LCRM adds that:

> *"If appropriate, you can use a risk classification matrix to do qualitative screening to see what further action may be required.*
>
> *You must base your assessment on the potential severity that the risk poses to the receptors against the likelihood of it happening."*

As to a risk classification matrix, reference is made to Table 1.8 of *R&D Publication 66: 2008 Volume 1 – Guidance for the Safe Development of Housing on Land Affected by Contamination* as a useful example, viz:

### Table 1.8: Categorisation of risk

| | | Consequence | | | |
|---|---|---|---|---|---|
| | | Severe | Medium | Mild | Minor |
| Probability (Likelihood) | High likelihood | Very high risk | High risk | Moderate risk | Low risk |
| | Likely | High risk | Moderate risk | Moderate/ low risk | Low risk |
| | Low likelihood | Moderate risk | Moderate/ low risk | Low risk | Very low risk |
| | Unlikely | Moderate/ low risk | Low risk | Very low risk | Very low risk |

The LCRM goes on to say:

> *"To complete a preliminary risk assessment you need to:*
>
> - *define the overall site objectives;[6]*

---

[5] *"Receptor"* meaning *"something that could be adversely affected by a contaminant, for example a person, controlled waters, an organism, an ecosystem, or Part 2A receptors such as buildings, crops or animals."*

[6] E.g. whether industrial, residential etc.

- *do a desk study and site walk-over;*

- *develop an initial conceptual site model;*

- *identify potential contaminant linkages;*

- *decide whether to do an optional exploratory investigation;*

- *assess the risks qualitatively and update the conceptual site model;*

- *decide what further action is needed;*

- *produce a preliminary risk assessment report.*

The LCRM gives advice on the collection of information for the preliminary risk assessment:

*You will need to collect current and historical information about the site.*

*You can do this through:*

- *a desk study;*

- *a site walk-over;*

- *an optional exploratory investigation.*

*Use this information to:*

- *interpret historical, archived and current information to establish the location of previous site activities;*

- *understand the environmental setting of the site;*

- *identify areas or zones that may contain distinct and different types of contamination identify potential contaminant linkages;*

- *identify the types of contaminants likely to be present such as ground gases and vapours, solvents, metals;*

- *identify any potential health and safety requirements such as immediate risks to human health from ground gases and vapours or unexploded ordnance that could cause asphyxiation or explosion;*

- *develop an initial conceptual site model;*

• *scope out the likelihood and requirements of a detailed investigation if you progress to the next tier or stage.*[7]

The LCRM advises that one can find out the following from the desk study:

• site ownership and current status;

• location, national grid reference;

• size of the site – include any plans and maps;

• history and general description of the site;

• potential for unexploded ordnance;

• contact details of relevant organisations.

The assessor can get details of any:

• pollution incidents, spills, accidents or regulatory actions;

• current or past permits, licences or authorisations;

• proposed future changes to land use, such as planning applications;

• previous investigations or remediation;

• chemical or biological information from for example, previous site monitoring reports;

• natural background contamination information, such as for radon gas[8], if available;

• audit reports that may have been done.

The assessor should, also, find out the:

• location of historical landfill sites;[9]

• details of any reviews of coal or other mining related contamination hazards – current or historic;

---

7   See: Risk assessment - preliminary (INFO-RA1) (https://claire.co.uk).

8   https://www.gov.uk/government/collections/radon.

9   https://www.data.gov.uk/dataset/17edf94f-6de3-4034-b66b-004ebd0dd010/historic-landfill-sites.

- presence or proximity of sensitive ecological receptors such as Special Protection Areas;[10]

- location of any protected areas of countryside;[11]

- presence of any archaeological or heritage sites such as scheduled ancient monuments;

- details on other specific Part 2A[12] receptors such as property in the form of crops, livestock, buildings.

The assessor should also find geological, hydrogeological and hydrological information including:

- made ground, drift deposits, bedrock;

- geological features such as faults;

- presence of groundwater aquifers – unconfined, confined or a mixture of both aquifer types;

- principal, secondary or unproductive strata;

- sensitive groundwater locations such as source protection zones or safeguard zones;

- the vulnerability of the groundwater to pollution;[13]

- the likelihood of perched[14] groundwater;

- any abstraction points or wells on or close to the site including private water supplies;[15]

- the presence of and proximity to other controlled waters[16] such as surface water and coastal;

---

[10] https://magic.defra.gov.uk/MagicMap.aspx.

[11] https://www.gov.uk/check-your-business-protected-area.

[12] Of the Environmental Protection Act 1990.

[13] See: https://www.gov.uk/government/publications/protect-groundwater-and-prevent-groundwater-pollution/ protect-groundwater-and-prevent-groundwater-pollution#groundwater-vulnerability.

[14] "*Perched water*" is water that occurs above the main watertable or groundwater source, separated by an unsaturated or impermeable layer of rock or soil.

[15] See: https://www.gov.uk/government/publications/protect-groundwater-and-prevent-groundwater-pollution/ protect-groundwater-and-prevent-groundwater-pollution#sensitive-groundwater-locations See also the library at https://www.gov.uk/government/collections/groundwater-protection.

[16] For "*controlled waters*" see Section 104(1) of the Water Resources Act 1991. However, it should not, in environmental terms, make any difference whether waters are controlled or not.

- any available water quality information; and

- information on characteristics such as the likely groundwater flow direction.

The local authority may have useful information on suspected or confirmed contamination.

The investigator will look at various indicators of potential pollution. Gaps in vegetation may indicate the presence of toxic substances. One would normally expect to see vegetation (perhaps fauna as well) on long disused sites and its absence, or erratic distribution, indicates the need for further investigation: see paragraphs 3.2.3 and 3.2.4 of CLR 2 (volume 1). Unusual colours in surface materials may be due to the presence of chemicals; for example, yellow colouring may indicate the presence of chromium and black, orange or brown may indicate severe land gas contamination: see paragraph 3.1 of CLR 2.[17] In some cases, it may be possible to detect unusual smells or there might be objects on the site which may be indicative of past uses, for example old drums. The landform of the site may be an indicator. Contours may appear to be artificial or out of character with the surrounding area, thereby suggesting the possibility of tipping, quarrying and so on.

The difficulties start to arise where the Conceptual Site Model shows that there may be contamination. A Phase 1 Assessment will not, then, be enough and the next step should be a Phase 2 Environmental Site Assessment.

## 7.2    Phase 2 Environmental Site Assessment
The purpose of a Phase 2 Environmental Site Assessment is to quantify any land contamination based on data collected from the relevant site. It will also inform a decision as to whether land treatment action is required. The assessment will normally incorporate the following:

- A review of the Phase 1 Assessment.

- Consultation with regulatory bodies.

- Intrusive and non-intrusive site investigations for the collection of environmental samples to find and quantify pollutants in accordance with a specified national standard.

- A refinement of the Conceptual Site Model by further investigation of potential source-pathway-receptor pollutant linkages.

- A risk assessment to assess the potential risks to human health and environmental receptors in accordance with a specified national standard.

---

[17]    See also *R&D66: 2008, Vol 1* pp.21-32.

The intrusive site investigations can range from sampling by way of simple trial trenches to complex borehole matrices. The non-intrusive sampling can include gas capture chambers (*"flux chambers"*) or the like.

An accredited laboratory must undertake the analysis of samples taken from the site and an interpretative report should accompany the results.

An important point is that such in-depth investigations can take considerable time and may be very expensive. Also, it might be the case that the carrying out of intrusive site investigations is made difficult, or impossible, if the site is currently occupied in way which impedes such investigations (e.g. occupied by workshops, offices etc).

If the risk assessment shows that there are unacceptable risks to human health, property or the wider environment, then treatment to mitigate the risks will be required to make the site *"suitable for use"*.

The question for the local planning authority is when the Phase 2 Assessment should be carried out during the approval process. The easy answer is to say that it should be completed in every case before permission is granted, but this may be naïve for the following reasons:

- If the Conceptual Site Model produced by the Phase 1 Assessment does not suggest that a source-pathway-receptor linkage exists, then there is no intellectual imperative.

- If the developer is not assured that the principle of development is accepted, then he might, simply, walk away from the site rather than expending time, money and other resources on investigations which might prove to be otiose if permission is refused on other grounds.[18]

### 7.3     When is a site assessment necessary?
The Planning Practice Guidance website states:

> *"If there is a reason to believe contamination could be an issue, applicants should provide proportionate but sufficient site investigation information (a risk assessment) prepared by a competent person to determine the existence or otherwise of contamination, its nature and extent, the risks it may pose and to whom/what (the "receptors") so that these risks can be assessed and satisfactorily reduced to an acceptable level."*

> *Paragraph: 007 Reference ID: 33-007-20190722 - Revision date: 22 07 2019*

---

[18]   It is worth bearing in mind that some trial trenching can be very deep and require the services of heavy machinery. This may be an *"engineering operation"* requiring planning permission: see Section 55 of the Town and Country Planning Act 1990. In *Bedfordshire CC v Central Electricity Generating Board* [1984] EWCA Civ J0626-4, the Court of Appeal held that the drilling of three 2 inch diameter boreholes on a 400 acre site (to see if it was suitable for the disposal of nuclear waste) did not require planning permission, but the court seemed to assume that a more intensive investigation might.

The unqualified statement "*a reason to believe contamination could be an issue*" poses a problem because it does not indicate the level of evidence which should underpin this asserted "*reason*". First, it is not appropriate to speak of "*belief*" in the context of a scientific enquiry because science does not turn on subjective belief, but upon the objective analysis of hard evidence. Even within this context, it is necessary to formulate a working hypothesis from proper evidence rather than to rely on speculation. Secondly, any sound policy advice would, if tempted to use the word "*reason*" then, at least indicate whether it is a reason-ably held reason or not. As drafted, this advice would allow a local planning authority to demand a site investigation based upon flimsy evidence or, indeed, no real evidence at all.

The Guidance goes on to say:

> "*Unless this initial assessment clearly demonstrates that the risk from contamination can be satisfactorily reduced to an acceptable level, further site investigations and risk assessment will be needed before the application can be determined.*"

> *Paragraph: 007 Reference ID: 33-007-20190722 - Revision date: 22 07 2019*

As to outline planning applications, the Guidance states:

> "*The information sought should be proportionate to the decision at the outline stage, but before granting outline planning permission a local planning authority will, among other matters, need to be satisfied that:*

> • *it understands the contaminated condition of the site;*

> • *the proposed development is appropriate as a means of remediating it; and*

> • *it has sufficient information to be confident that it will be able to grant permission in full at a later stage bearing in mind the need for the necessary remediation to be viable and practicable.*"

> *Paragraph: 008 Reference ID: 33-008-20190722 - Revision date: 22 07 2019*

The problem with this advice is that it seems to incorporate terminology which is more appropriate to Part IIA of the Environmental Protection Act 1990. The objective of devel-opment is not to remediate land which is defined as "*contaminated land*" within the Part IIA regime, but to ensure that the development is "*suitable for use*", having regard to any concerns relating to possible contamination. If contamination is found, then simply stating that it must be "*remediated*" is overly simplistic because, of course, many developments are very resilient when it comes to land contamination and, more sensitive developments can be made suitable for use by way of appropriate mitigation and without the need for wholesale decontamination.

The NPPG, then introduces another, different, test by way of a flowchart; namely, whether the site is potentially affected by contamination and whether development of it could result in unacceptable risks, viz:[19]

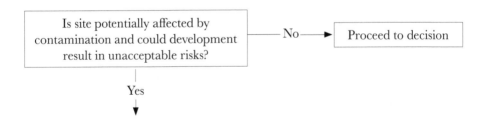

Unlike the narrative from the NPPG, this formulation is, perhaps, one which can be applied in practice, without doing too much violence to the words themselves. Taken as written, the question whether or not the site is potentially affected by contamination is something which has nothing to do with unqualified belief, but should turn on whether or not the evidence discloses potential contamination as a matter of observable fact. Furthermore, the reference to development resulting in unacceptable risks can encompass the *"suitable for use"* test, albeit a better drafting solution for this particular text would have been to refer to the *"suitable use"* test in terms.

### 7.4    When contamination is *"known"* or *"suspected"*

Some development plan policies suggest that certain measures should be taken when contamination is *"known or suspected"*. Leaving aside what is meant by the word *"contamination"*, the use of the unqualified subjective word *"suspected"* is not necessarily helpful because, in this context, it can be said that there are degrees of suspicion. They can range from very strong suspicions, which derive from robust evidence down to the merest whiff of a suspicion deriving from nebulous speculations.

The now withdrawn narrative to Circular 11/95 stated:

> *"74. If it is <u>known or strongly suspected</u> that a site is contaminated to an extent which would adversely affect the proposed development or infringe statutory requirements, an investigation of the hazards by the developer and proposals for remedial action will normally be required before the application can be determined by the planning authority. Any subsequent planning permission may need to include planning conditions requiring certain remedial measures to be carried out."* (Emphasis added)

This paragraph is, perhaps, a classic case of conflation and confusion. It is, perhaps, readily implied that the phrase *"known or strongly suspected"* excludes cases where there is a mere suspicion only and includes cases where the evidence is objectively robust to the extent that

---

[19]    Original reformatted for the purposes of publication.

the decision-making body can reasonably rely upon it. For example, it might be the case that a review of historical cartographical materials shows that the site was previously used for an industrial use. This, by itself, should raise a red flag because ground contamination is a well-known concomitant of such a use.[20]

Unfortunately, the passage then runs into difficulty. It refers to contamination, which would adversely affect the proposed development or infringe statutory requirements; however, it does not mention adverse impact on the environment or nearby land.

Further, it is stated that investigation of the hazards by the developer should be carried out. Whilst this proposition is not contentious, it is then followed by the ambiguous statement that proposals for *"remedial action"* will normally be required before the application can be determined by the local planning authority. There are a number of significant problems with this proposition. First, of course, it does not necessarily follow that the investigation will generate the need for invasive treatment. It might be the case that, instead, the investigation demonstrates that the site is suitable for its proposed use with mitigation. Secondly, this passage makes no mention of the position where an outline planning permission or a phased planning permission is granted when referring to planning conditions which require *"remedial"* measures to be carried out. Clearly, there is considerable difficulty in drafting such conditions, when significant aspects of the scheme remain to be decided.

The narrative went on to say:

> *"75. In cases where there is <u>only a suspicion</u> that the site might be contaminated, or where the evidence suggests that there may be <u>only slight contamination</u>, planning permission may be granted subject to conditions that development will not be permitted to start until a site investigation and assessment have been carried out and that the development itself will incorporate any remedial measures shown to be necessary."*
> (Emphasis added)

As noted above, the use of the unqualified word *"suspicion"* is not necessarily helpful because, in this context, it can be said that that are degrees of suspicion. Again, this passage makes no mention of the position where an outline planning permission or a phased planning permission is granted.

The problem with this type of subjective wording is, of course, that it is not accompanied by any form of objective standard which can be tested empirically and is inherently nebulous. Indeed, it could be argued that the wording of such guidance is not only incomplete in this particular but, also, should, at least, have attributed some form of objectivity to the narrative by adding the word *"reasonable"* in front of *"suspicion"*. This would import some degree of objectivity. It is possible to postulate a working baseline which is to ask whether there is a reasonable suspicion of a level of contamination which might make the site unsuitable for

---

[20]   See Case study 2 below. Likewise, a former tannery or the like.

its proposed use, in order to distinguish objectively sound suspicions from merely fanciful or ephemeral suspicions.

As to the use of the word "*known*", one needs to deploy the Socratic method and ask questions such as "*known by whom?*"; "*What method was used by that person in obtaining that putative knowledge?*"; "*What was that person's expertise and what methodology was deployed?*" Otherwise, simply adding the word "*known*" adds nothing to the guidance.

It is submitted that those faced with such policies must:

- Ask who must have this suspicion or belief.

- Ask whether such suspicion or belief is reasonable in the "*Wednesbury*" sense (i.e. based on sound evidence).

- Treat the establishment of a reasonable suspicion or belief as a threshold test which is separate from the evaluation of weight or risk.

Dealing with the first point first, the only suspicion which is relevant in this context is that of the decision-maker. The decision maker in almost all cases, will be the local planning authority. If a local planning authority is seeking to apply its mind to a material consideration, then it must do so in accordance with the "*Wednesbury principles*": see below.

To put it another way, any reference which turns on phraseology such as "*suspicion*" or "*belief*" is forced to be construed as a <u>reasonable</u> suspicion or a <u>reasonable</u> belief, because such phraseology is not at large in the context of public administration; but is conditioned by administrative law.

The greatest problem, for the decision-maker, is that of weight. What is the difference between "*slight suspicion*", "*suspicion*" and "*suspicion of slight contamination*" and all points in between? There would seem to be some form of sliding scale in play, and this is particularly so when these varying expressions are used together within a suite of statements within the same policy document. The problem is, of course, that if one is unclear about the polar extremes (which is certainly the case here), then it is impossible to plot points along some form of continuum.

Propositions relating to subjective beliefs or the like are dangerous in matters of science because, philosophically, science does not proceed by subjective belief, but by the formulation and testing of hypotheses based on observed and observable evidence. One tenet is that a proposition which cannot be falsified is not a fitting starting point for a hypothesis. To recite "*Hitchins Razor*", that which is advanced without evidence can be dismissed without evidence.

In this context, to "*believe*" has to be distinguished as having something to do with metaphysical or ideological assertions rather than the application of the modern scientific method.

The law is slightly different because there are many cases where statutes give administrative bodies discretion to take certain courses of action if they have cause to believe that a certain state of affairs may exist. For example, the Town and Country Planning Act 1990 allows a local planning authority to issue a temporary stop notice if it *"thinks"* that there has been a breach of planning control. However, such apparently subjective formulations are, of course, subject to the *"Wednesbury principle"* and can be reviewed by the courts if it is asserted that the body's belief is not soundly based, or is otherwise *"irrational"*. Furthermore, the decision-maker must avoid acting *"under a dictation"* or under a *"fettering of discretion"*. When these legal parameters are understood, then the local planning authority is bound to apply its mind to objective empirical evidence rather than to be swayed by speculative and subjective rhetoric from unschooled sources such as local media.

It is at this point that the science and administrative law come together. If the local planning authority is entitled or required to do something in connection with contaminated land and the trigger is *"reasonable suspicion"*[21], then the so called belief must be founded on objective evidence and not mere speculation. In most cases that objective evidence will derive from the consideration of expert opinion which, in turn, will be framed by reference to forensically sound evidence. Thus, the committee which makes its decision does so, based on the speculation in the media would not be on solid ground. It follows that one is able to draw the threads together under simple threshold formulations.

As to the matter of weight, this is not inherent in the establishment of a reasonable suspicion, but is, rather, the object of this suspicion; namely, the degree of contamination. This weighting should be set out with some particularity, rather than adding some form of conditioning phrase to the threshold concept of reasonable suspicion.

## 7.5     Matters of weight

Matters of weight are important because they tell the local planning authority and the developer how to approach the site investigations, planning conditions and planning obligations. The weight or seriousness of putative contamination is the part which is on a sliding scale. It consists of, at least, the following elements:

•     Impact on the development;

•     Impacts on nearby land;

•     Impacts on the environment.

Those charged with the task of advising the local planning authority must seek to identify whether such impacts may be present or arise and then to advise the authority as to levels of risk. The latter is a matter for expert opinion and those experts, in turn, are able to have regard to ample technical advice on the matter.

---

[21]   The *"reasonable"* being either expressed or implied.

It should follow that:

- The notion of "*reasonable suspicion*" (or similar formulation) is unfortunate but can be tackled in matters of policy provided that this is treated as a threshold which relates back to sound objective evidence.

- The administrative response should be conditioned by the weight which is attributable to the evidence and expert opinion.

Taken together, these paragraphs from Circular 11/95 suggested a dividing line.

If one starts with cases where there is only a "*slight suspicion*" that the site might be contaminated, or where the evidence suggests that there may be only "*slight contamination*", then it might be commercially imprudent to ask the developer to carry out extensive site investigations prior to the grant of planning permission when the evidence does not demand them. This may cause delay or cause the developer to drop the scheme and will have an adverse impact on cash flow.

As noted above, it is difficult to see how the word "*slight*" adds anything save for ambiguity. Accordingly, it is suggested that the better approach is to, as above, separate the threshold question of whether or not there is a reasonable suspicion of contamination from the following questions about the level of contamination and matters of risk. If the suspicion is soundly based, then a Phase 1 Assessment (see below) should be enough.

If this assessment indicates that further investigations are needed, then planning permission may, properly, be granted subject to conditions that the development will not be permitted to start until a Phase 2 Assessment has been carried out and that the development itself will incorporate any adaptation measures shown to be necessary.

If it is reasonably hypothesised, on the basis of robust evidence, that a site is contaminated to an extent which would adversely affect the proposed development, the environment (including groundwaters), nearby land or infringe statutory requirements, then an investigation of the hazards by the developer and proposals for site adaptation treatment can, properly, be required before the application is determined by the planning authority. It might be the case that the "*robust evidence*" is a Phase 1 Assessment which has shown that there are immediate and strong causes for concern.

Whilst not mentioned in the Circular, it is important to bear in mind that a large scheme will normally proceed in discrete phrases and, as such, any approach should reflect the commercial and practical realities of each proposed development.

If one takes, for example, a large residential development then it will be delivered over a period of years, sometimes decades. The scheme will normally start with the grant of an outline planning permission for the whole site and then each phase will be the subject of reserved matter approvals. It might be the case that the overall site is developed by more than one house builder. If the entirety of assessment and treatment costs are frontloaded, then those costs might have to be carried for many years into the future. Not only would these costs have to be reflected in any economic viability appraisal for the scheme but also the notional cost of borrowing over the requisite period. Furthermore, and very importantly, it is not possible to work up a treatment or mitigation strategy when the layout of the site has yet to be determined. Whilst it might be right to say that the scheme is *"residential"*, the reality is that the greater part of the site will not be used for housing. It will be used for infrastructure and such as highways, carparks, landscaping schemes etc. Whilst housing is a sensitive end use, this type of infrastructure is not. Thus, the carrying out of a treatment scheme which makes each and every part of the site suitable for housing is unnecessary, both in the practical sense and commercially. This is compounded by the fact that, in many cases, the answer for adapting a particular site might not entail treatment at all. It might be the case that pollutants can be managed by way of appropriate mitigation schemes; however, while such a scheme might be deemed to be appropriate in principle for a site, the actual implementation of the scheme will have to await the submission of reserved matters. It might, also, be the case that the layout of the scheme is changed as it evolves to alter the likelihood of receptors coming into contact with contaminants.

## 7.6      Generic Assessment Criteria

Generic Assessment Criteria are *"generic"* because they are settled by reference to broad assumptions which will not, normally, be replicated on a site-by-site basis. For example, the Contaminated Land Exposure Assessment (CLEA) guidance (see below) is based on a hypothetical generic site for which assumptions are made as follows:

•      Soil type;

•      Below ground level of contamination;

•      Width of source zone parallel to the wind direction;

•      Wind speed; and

•      For organic substances, that there is no free product.

A suite of *"Soil Guideline Values"* (SGVs) have been produced which are applied as nominal thresholds for treating the site or deciding that further investigations or actions are needed (see below).

Whilst taken from the long withdrawn ICRCL Guidance Note 59/83, the following diagram provides a useful representation of the approach:[22]

---

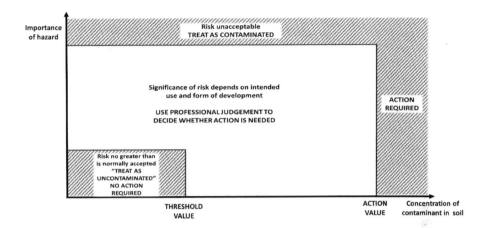

*Interpretation of "Trigger Concentrations"*

It is important to note at the outset that Generic Assessment Criteria are intended to provide a screening or sifting mechanism at an early stage in the process and are intended to field the need for a site-specific assessment for each potential contaminant until the scheme proposals are more advanced, both in terms of site knowledge and financial confidence. It follows that the criteria must be very conservative, otherwise undesirable contaminants may slip though the net because the thresholds are set too high. It also follows that later refinement of the site assessment reduces the extent of the management actions which would be required if the rude Generic Assessment Criteria were applied in an unrefined model.

If these basic rules are not understood then the particular threshold set out in model procedures can be taken to represent *"magic numbers"*. This is that the quantitative thresholds are taken to be definitive when this is exactly the reverse of the reasons for providing them.

### 7.7    The CLEA package
The CLEA package consisted of Contaminated Land Reports (CLRs) 7 to 10, the CLEA 2002 software, toxicological reports (TOX) and Soil Guideline Values (SGVs).

The modelling basis for the CLEA soil guideline values were set out in:

* CLR 9: *"Contaminants in soils: collation of toxicological data and intake values for humans"*.

* CLR 10: *"The CLEA model technical basis and algorithms"*.

*"Model Procedures for the Management of Land Contamination"* - Contaminated Land Report 11 (CLR 11) was published in 2003 and sought to draw the threads created by CLR 9 and CLR 10 and other documents together in an overarching document. It stated that the technical

approach presented in the Model Procedures was designed to be applicable to a range of non-regulatory and regulatory contexts. These included development or redevelopment of land under the planning regime.

CLR 11 was withdrawn in October 2020, in favour of the Land Contamination Risk Management (LCRM) model, but still remains a useful source of information for those interested in this topic.

The application of generic assessments within the overall risk management process was well illustrated by Figure 1 of CLR 11:

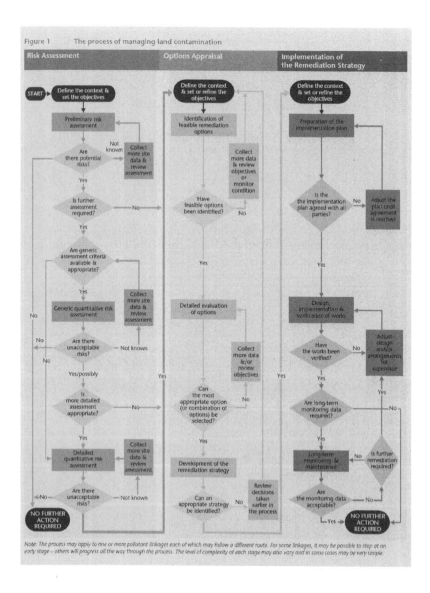

Figure 1    The process of managing land contamination

Note: The process may apply to one or more pollutant linkages each of which may follow a different route. For some linkages, it may be possible to stop at an early stage – others will progress all the way through the process. The level of complexity of each stage may also vary and in some cases may be very simple.

The basic risk management process in the Model Procedures has three main components:

- Risk assessment – establishing whether unacceptable risks exist and, if so, what further action needs to be taken in relation to the site.

- Options appraisal – evaluating feasible *"remediation"*[23] options and determining the most appropriate *"remediation"* strategy for the site.

- Implementation – carrying out the *"remediation"* strategy and demonstrating that it is, and will continue to be, effective. Figure 1 (reproduced above) sets out the process framework.

The Model Procedures provide a generic framework to show the key technical activities that may apply in each of these components, and identify the main decisions at each stage. They are not intended to present rigid technical requirements – the particular context in which the Procedures are applied, as well as the circumstances of an individual site, will determine both the specific technical details of the process and the criteria for making decisions.

The three tiers used in the Model Procedures for the specific context of land contamination are:

(1) Preliminary risk assessment.

(2) Generic quantitative risk assessment.

(3) Detailed quantitative risk assessment.

The overall process of risk assessment is often iterative – more detailed assessment may raise issues that require the earlier tiers to be revisited. Furthermore, the process within each tier may also be iterative, especially when information is evaluated and gaps are identified in the knowledge needed to make a particular decision. In this case, approaches taken earlier within the tier may need to be reappraised.

The above figure is not tailored to the *"Phase 1 Assessment"* and *"Phase 2 Assessment"* approach favoured in the planning regime; however, it is not a matter of great difficulty to integrate it, the preliminary risk assessment normally being part of the Phase 1 Assessment and following from the formulation of the Conceptual Model for the site.

The matter of generic risk assessment and soil value guidelines are discussed in more depth in Appendix 2.

---

[23] See Chapter 3 for *"remediation"* as a term of art.

## 7.8     Cartographical evidence

Map-based evidence can be essential when a person who wishes to develop a site seeks planning permission or is considering buying a site and wishes to ensure that it will not bring problems associated with ground contamination with it.

Paragraph 1.3.2 of *Guidance for the Safe Development of Housing on Land Affected by Contamination - R&D66: 2008 Volume 1* advises that historical plans can provide the following information:

- the history of industrial and other uses of a site and the surrounding area;

- the type of industrial activity undertaken (early Ordnance Survey maps often identify industrial uses such as acid works, gas works, or lead works whereas later (or large scale) maps often only label these features as "*Works*" or "*Factory*" etc);

- the layout of the site, including locations of buildings and tanks etc. at the date of the map; and

- evidence of excavations and infilling (e.g. mounds of material and earthworks).

The Guidance (para, 1.3.2) goes on to add that, when reviewing historical maps, there is often other relevant information to be gained from their study. For example:

- Distinctive names such as Gasworks Road, Clay Pit Lane etc. shown on maps indicate the former presence/proximity of such potential sources of contamination.

- The disappearance of cut features such as pits and quarries or water features such as canal basins or ponds can indicate land filling.

- Re-routed water courses will indicate linear areas of infilling.

The Guidance adds that care must be taken when interpreting slope marking symbols (which sometimes are not well defined) as it is very important to interpret spoil heaps or excavation features correctly. It also stresses that:

> "The identification of site history from historic [sic] maps must be undertaken diligently. It is wrong to assume that this is a simple task that can be undertaken by untrained staff."

The inspection of the site for contamination is unlikely to begin by carrying out very expensive site investigations, such as the drilling of boreholes. Instead, it usually begins with collating and seeking to interpret map-based evidence to see whether there is a potential source of contamination and, if so, then whether there is a possible pathway for pollutants between that source and the proposed development site. Two examples are set out below, namely closed landfill sites and "*made ground*".

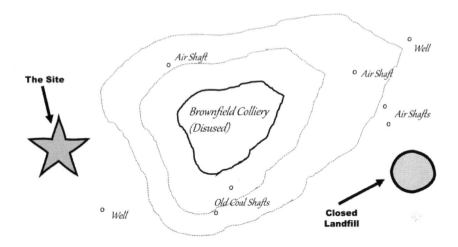

*Closed Landfill Sites*

Here, the development site is shown to be some distance from a closed landfill site. However, the OS maps show that there is a disused colliery between the two. The maps also show the presence of old air shafts which indicates that underground mining has taken place in the past. Furthermore, the map shows the presence of wells which, in turn, suggests that there is an underlying source of water which is probably in the form of an aquifer. This provides a strong suggestion that there could be one or more pathways between the closed landfill site and the proposed development site, viz:

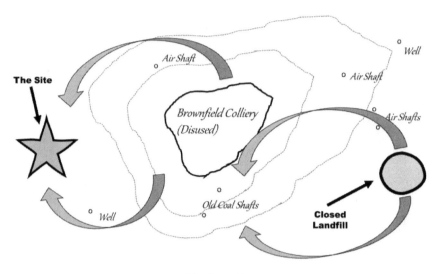

*Closed Landfill Sites*

This would suggest that it is necessary to move on to further, and more detailed, site investigations.

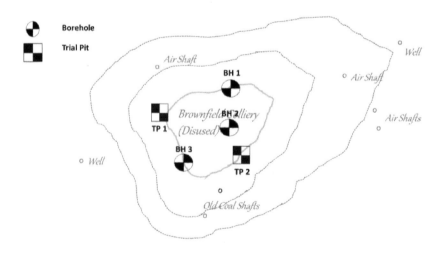

*Closed Landfill Sites*

Made ground is often very difficult to detect and so, again, map-based evidence might be helpful in seeking to describe a picture. An area of made ground is normally a depression which has been filled and then levelled. If the fill material was waste material or refuse then this could pose a problem, in that they could be a source of ground contamination.

*Made Ground*

It follows that the cartographer must seek to find historical depressions or holes which, for some obscure reason, appear to have been filled and levelled off. To give one example, it might be the case that an old ordnance survey map shows the presence of a pond or a water course, but then the feature appears to have disappeared in later versions of the OS and the ground has been, visibly, levelled off. This triggers the question of whether the fill material which was used in levelling the ponds or water course included contaminated materials.

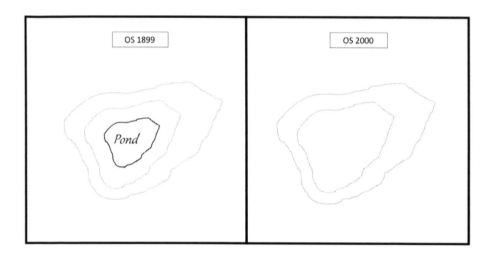

*Made Ground*

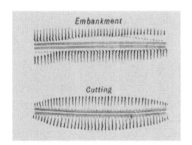

*Made Ground: Railway Groundworks*

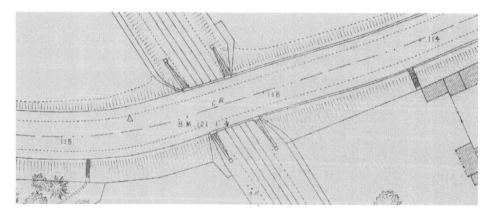

## 7.9    Geographical Information Systems (GIS)

A GIS can be described as a system for capturing, storing, checking and displaying data related to the positions of features on the Earth's surface together with their attributes. Thus the *"geographical"* component is that which shows the location of the feature, normally both visually and by way of the display of coordinates based on longitude and latitude. The *"infor-mation"* aspect is data which can be used to characterise and assess the particular attributes of the feature. The *"system"* is the interrelationship of data to provide an overall picture.

A computerised GIS package can be used to record and transform ostensibly analogue information into a more useful digital format, thereby making data more accessible and interchangeable. It also provides the ability to query that digital information by asking questions about geographic features, their attributes and relationships between them.

## 7.10    Paper maps as geographical information systems

It is wrong to suppose that digital geographical information systems exist in a universe which is completely separated from the world of paper mapping. Paper maps have always provided more than simple locational information, they have provided descriptive material as well.

If one examines the map extract below then it shows not only the geographical locations of the circled public facilities but also short descriptions of their functions.

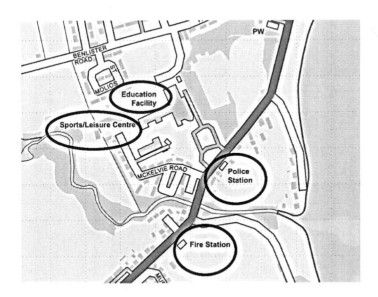

Thus, the map goes beyond merely providing geographical data. The descriptive content of the base map can then be expanded by adding a *"layer"* in a superimposed table which provides additional descriptive material for each identified feature, viz:

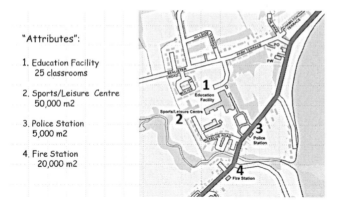

"Attributes":

1. Education Facility
   25 classrooms

2. Sports/Leisure Centre
   50,000 m2

3. Police Station
   5,000 m2

4. Fire Station
   20,000 m2

The paper map can, therefore, be the basis for the integration of qualitative, quantitative and locational data within a single overall model. It is, therefore, a *"geographical information system"*. Whilst, in modern times, the phrase *"geographical information system"* is taken to refer to computerised digital modelling, it has its basis firmly within traditional paper mapping. If one bears this in mind, the concepts behind digital geographical information systems become more readily apparent.

## 7.11    Computerised geographical information systems

The difference between paper mapping and digital GIS lies in the capacities of computer software to be used to store and manipulate more information than would be possible on a paper map. This software can store multiple layers and allows the reader to view separate layers within the digital GIS model, so as to focus on those which are of interest to them whilst momentarily removing otherwise less interesting layers from the display.

In computerised GIS, the stored *"digital data"* is information which has a geographical location as a starting point (called *"geographical data"*) and can be expressed and recorded by way of longitude and latitude in a *"Geographic Coordinate Reference System"*. This is supplemented by *"non-geographical data"*, which is, for present purposes, narrative information relating to the geographical data. Thus, it is possible to associate information about places (geographical data) with information about the characteristics of those places (non-geographical data). This latter is normally presented in a layer known as an *"attributes table"*. If one takes the figure on page 85, then the attributes layer shown on the map can be shown by way of a separate attributes table, viz:

| Attributes Table | | |
|:---:|:---:|:---:|
| 1 | Education Facility | 25 classrooms |
| 2 | Sports/Leisure Centre | 50,000m$^2$ |
| 3 | Police Station | 5,000m$^2$ |
| 4 | Fire Station | 20,000m$^2$ |

J Caduax-Hudson and D Lindsay had this to say[24] about Geographical Information Systems in connection with research relating to previously developed land:

> "These OS maps go back to the middle of the 19th century. Detailed analysis of historic [sic] maps is a laborious task and requires not only the sourcing of the maps, which are available from a variety of sources, libraries, in particular, but also requires the relevant features to be manually identified and logged and information moved from the old projection (Cassini) to the current map projection (Transverse Mercator)."

They go on to say:

> "An alternative to this is to obtain the data from commercial organisations that have undertaken both the scanning and capturing of these maps and associated information. These maps have proved useful as a basis for the analysis of land use information undertaken by local authorities to fulfil their obligations under Part IIA of the Environmental Protection Act 1990."

As to the types of information covered by GIS datasets, they said:[25]

> "The type of information contained within a GIS dataset enables the identification of filled and disturbed areas of land, for example, filled quarries or water features, potentially contaminative activities or industries such as refuse or slag heaps, tanks and energy facilities and past land use, such as gravel pits. Because the geographical information in a GIS is captured digitally, ...the information can be used for the purpose of automatically identifying any historical land use within any specified distance of the site."

As to the layers of information, they say:[26]

---

[24]  See *Previously Developed Land*, Symes et al, 2004, p.126.

[25]  Ibid p.134.

[26]  Ibid, p.130.

> *"In 1998 Landmark Land Information Group completed the creation of a unique database of Historical Land Use Data, and Potentially Contaminated Industries, linked to the guidelines set out in the Environmental Protection Act 1990 and the Environment Act 1995 ... The GIS database of historical land use contains seven layers of data covering the whole of England, Wales and Scotland; six contaminated use layers corresponding to specific time periods and one land use layer... Into the six potentially contaminated land -use layers, based on each time period or epoch,[27] potentially contaminated uses were categorised and digitalised ..."*

## 7.12 Data collection and sampling

Unless a generic risk assessment clears the site, then it might be the case that gas sampling and extensive intrusive site investigations are required.

There is a plethora of guidance on data collection and sampling.[28] For the purposes of this chapter, it is enough to refer to BS10175:2011+A2:2017 – Investigation of potentially contaminated sites – Code of practice.

It is important to remember that sites are rarely homogenous. They are normally heterogeneous and the situation is complicated by the fact that those carrying out the assessment need to try to picture a 3D model when, in fact, only two dimensions are immediately visible.[29] It is, therefore, necessary to formulate a sampling strategy.

There are a number of sampling techniques of which the principal ones are gas and vapour sampling, soil cores and trial pits. Each comes with its own advantages and disadvantages.

Gas and vapour samples can be drawn from boreholes by the use of vacuum pumps.

Soil cores are usually used for shallow soil sampling. The advantages of these techniques are relatively low costs and because sampling produces the least amount of disturbance to the site and neighbouring properties. The disadvantage of gas and vapour sampling is that the evaluation of the outputs has to rely on estimates of the zones of influence of the relevant boreholes. The *"zone of influence"* is the three-dimensional volume in the sub-soil from which it is presumed that the sampling technique is drawing its test materials. There is considerable literature on the estimation of zones of influence and it can be readily appreciated that the quantity and make up of a test sample can be heavily influenced by factors such as the sub-soil geology of the relevant site. For example, the presence of a nearby aquifer within the test area can complicate this process. The disadvantage of soil core sampling is that site conditions may be difficult to assess from a narrow, shallow core.

---

[27] It is not clear why the word *"epoch"* is used here.

[28] For example, BS 8576:2013 – Guidance on investigations for ground gas – Permanent Gases and Volatile Organic Compounds (VOCs). Published by BSI Standards Limited 2013.

[29] Potentially, a CAD model could provide a 3D visualisation.

Trial pits are useful in that they allow the assessor to view the strata within the section of the site where the trial pit is located. They are usually cost-effective and a relatively large area is exposed for inspection. Samples may be selected from specific features in the ground. The disadvantages are that it is sometimes difficult to work in confined spaces, they are generally limited to 3/4m in depth and cross contamination of samples can occur. The excavations for trial pits require areas for the hole, the excavator and the spoil heap. The pits can create considerable ground disturbance, disturbance to neighbours and allow substantial ingress of air into the soil. Odour or dust problems may be associated with spoil heaps.

Boreholes are deployed on a grid system, viz:

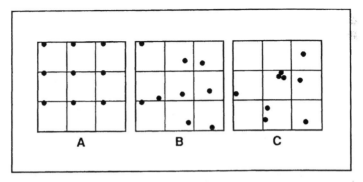

*Three sampling designs. A, regular square grid; B, stratified random; C, simple random*

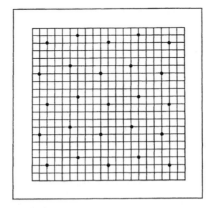

*Herringbone sampling design*

# Chapter 8

# Soil Contamination

## 8.1 The *"Characteristic Situations"*

The *"Characteristic Situations"* derive from Table 2 of BS:8485:2015 + A1:2019 and are:

| *"Characteristic Situation"* (CS) | Hazard potential |
|---|---|
| CS1 | Very low |
| CS2 | Low |
| CS3 | Moderate |
| CS4 | Moderate to high |
| CS5 | High |
| CS6 | Very high |

Residential buildings should not be built on CS4 or higher sites unless the type of construction or site circumstances allow additional levels of protection to be incorporated (e.g. high performance ventilation or pathway intervention measures, and associated sustainable systems of maintenance for the gas controls). Presumably, the *"sustainable"* in this case means capable of ongoing maintenance in the future.

For Characteristic Situations CS2 to CS4 a gas membrane will typically be incorporated into the building gas protection design as an effective way of meeting the scoring requirements for gas protection set out in the British Standard.

The CS are equivalent to the Characteristic GSV in CIRIA C665.

# Chapter 9

# Site Adaptation Treatment And Risk Management

Very few sites are so badly contaminated they cannot be redeveloped. The question is not so much the technical feasibility of making the site fit for use but the cost of doing so. This is a theme that runs throughout this book.

## 9.1  Why "*clean up*" is misleading

The primary aims of a risk management scheme are as follows:

- reduction of actual or potential environmental threats; and

- reduction of potential risks so that unacceptable risks are reduced to acceptable levels.[1]

> "*Consequently, the need for any remediation will depend on the degree of any actual or potential environmental threat or the level of any risk. Aspects of risk will in turn depend partly on the expected end-use of the site following remediation, as different at-risk targets can be associated with different end-uses.*"

In the case of town and country planning, this is expressed as meaning that the site should be made "*suitable for use*". To be more precise, the development should, when comprised of discrete uses within separate areas, be suitable for each differing use within the overall development.

*Land Contamination Risk Management (LCRM): Stage 3 remediation and verification*[2] advises that for "*Stage 3*" there are four steps to follow:

(1)  Develop a remediation strategy.

(2)  Remediate.

(3)  Produce a verification report.

(4)  Do long term monitoring and maintenance, if required.

It states:

---

[1]  Per "*Contaminated Land and its Remediation*", Hester and Harrison, Issues in Environmental Science and Technology 7 - Royal Society of Chemistry 1997 (@ p.47).

[2]  Updated 20 July 2023: see https://www.gov.uk/government/publications/land-contamination-risk-management-lcrm/lcrm-stage-3-remediation-and-verification.

*"For step 1, you will need to develop and then agree a remediation strategy that can be implemented in practice.[3] You will already have set your remediation objectives and criteria in step 1 of options appraisal. You will need to set monitoring objectives and criteria to track performance of the remediation. The remediation strategy is a record of how you will meet and carry out the remediation objectives.*

*You will need to produce a verification plan. This will be a part of the remediation strategy. It will need to set out all of the data requirements, including compliance criteria and monitoring details. This will establish a "lines of evidence" approach which will verify remediation is working or has worked."*

The advice that the parties should agree a *"remediation"* strategy that can be implemented in practice is important because this brings the matter of viability into consideration. The advised setting of monitoring objectives and criteria to track actual performance against the strategy is also important because this will inform the dialogue when one gets to the stage of settling planning conditions or obligations.

The LCRM guidance emphasises the need to develop a single strategy that will deal with the site as a whole:

*"The remediation strategy needs to include a clear set of remediation activities and how you will implement and verify them. It is a record of how you will meet and carry out the remediation objectives.*

*It needs to:*

- *clearly set out how the selected remediation option will mitigate the risks from the relevant contaminant linkages identified in the conceptual site model;*

- *meet the remediation objectives and criteria set in the options appraisal;*

- *meet any regulatory requirements such as to fulfil a planning condition, a Part 2A obligation or to comply with permit conditions;*

- *be compatible with other areas of work such as redevelopment or geotechnical aspects;*

- *state how it will protect human health, the environment, ecology and other receptors;*

- *provide a sustainable approach;*

---

[3] The said *"remediation strategy"* could, more accurately, be called a *"risk management strategy"* because the exact objective of the exercise is to (as per above) to reduce the risks to acceptable levels, rather than to obviate them entirely.

- *be practical, achievable, effective, durable and verifiable taking into account impacts of climate change and extreme weather events."*

Whilst this advice is very helpful, it needs to be borne in mind that it must be tailored to the details and critical path of each scheme. In particular, it is not realistic to provide a single detailed strategy for the whole of a scheme which is started with an outline planning permission. Here, the solution is to provide an overarching scheme which allows for the detail to emerge on a phase-by-phase basis.

The LCRM further advises that *"remediation"* strategy needs to (inter alia) include details of:

- *the monitoring objectives and criteria you will set for the site;*

- *the remedial actions that will be done;*

- *how you will implement remediation;*

- *how you will verify remediation is working by including a verification plan;*

- *any monitoring and maintenance requirements;*

- *any regulatory controls that need to be in place, such as permits and deployments.*

A prudent local planning authority should require the submission and approval of a remediation strategy prior to the commencement of any risk management work.[4]

*R&D66: 2008 Volume 1*[5] (para. 3.2.1) provides three *"remediation"* options:

*"...Conceptually, remediation action will involve breaking the pollutant linkage or linkages by use of one or more of the following methods:*

- *source control: technical action either to remove or in some way modify the source(s) of the contamination. Examples might include excavation and removal, bioremediation or soil venting;*

- *pathway control: technical action to reduce the ability of the contaminant source to pose a threat to receptors by inhibiting or controlling the pathway. Examples*

---

[4]   See also INFO-OA3: developing the remediation strategy (https://www.claire.co.uk/useful-government-legislation-and-guidance-by-country/200-developing-theremediation- strategy-info-oa3) on the CL:AIRE Water and Land Library.

[5]   *Guidance for the Safe Development of Housing on Land Affected by Contamination - R&D66: 2008 Volume 1.* Published jointly by the National House-Building Council, the Environment Agency and the Chartered Institute of Environmental Health.

> *would include the use of engineered cover systems over contaminants left in-situ or the use of membranes to prevent gas ingress into buildings;*

> • *receptor control: non-technical actions or controls that alter the likelihood of receptors coming into contact with the contaminants, for example altering the site layout."[5]*

*R&D66: 2008 Volume 1* also makes it clear that the *"remediation"* strategy is not once and for all, but may have to be evolved as knowledge of the condition of the site is refined:

> *"Short listing of the potential remediation options should take account of the available information and any associated uncertainties. For example, a technique may be initially identified as potentially suitable on the basis of its general effectiveness, but later, more site-specific evaluation may eventually lead to it being discounted.[7]*

Before requiring a developer to carry out a remediation strategy, the local planning authority should bear in mind that:

> *"Remediation of contaminated land can be an expensive and technically difficult process."[8]*

Annex D of The Homes and Communities Agency publication *"Guidance on dereliction, demolition and remediation costs"* (March 2015) provides two interesting case studies relating to residential schemes:

• Case Study A was an 8-hectare site in outer London. In the surrounding area historical gravel extraction and subsequent landfilling had taken place. There was a former sewage works 50m from the site and a former small gas works 100m from the site. The cost of the site preparation scheme was approximately £1.57 million equating to approximately £200,000 per hectare.

• Case Study B was a 6-hectare riverside site in the Yorkshire and Humberside region. The site had previously been used as a woollen mill, dye works and sewage works, and included some sludge and filter beds. A landfill was located less than 250m from the site boundary and used for the disposal of inert, industrial, commercial and household waste. The cost of the site preparation scheme was approximately £4.7 million, equating to approximately £790,000 per hectare.

In the case of Hertsmere Borough Council Elstree Film Studios in Borehamwood, the contractor, Sanctus Limited, treated approximately 34,000m³ of soil containing cement-bonded

---

[6]   Para.3.2.1. For landfill and other gases, see also CIRIA C665 – Assessing risks posed by hazardous ground gases to buildings (2007).

[7]   Para.3.2.1.

[8]   Defra Research Project Final Report Defra Project Code: SP1001 2010; p.6.

asbestos fragments and then removed the treated soils to landfill. The cost was £3,455,000 and the timescale was 9 months.

On a smaller scale, Lioncourt Homes prepared the 0.95ha site of a former scrap yard at Willenhall, West Midlands for a housing development. Historical contamination included, significant hydrocarbon impacted made ground, LNAPL[9] and dissolved-phase hydrocarbons in discontinuous shallow perched groundwater on-site. The contractor, Geostream UK, designed an integrated, in-situ treatment solution which eliminated on-site material handling and off-site disposal costs. The cost was £260,000 and the timescale was 10 weeks.

A wide range of different techniques can be used individually or in combination to achieve a break in a pollutant linkage. The options appraisal will consider a technique's effectiveness in dealing with the contaminants of concern, but will also give consideration to the wider circumstances of the site.

The range of issues to be considered include:

- costs and benefits (including finance considerations and liability);

- effectiveness of meeting *"remediation"* objectives (including site-specific criteria, timeliness);

- durability (risk-based and non-risk-based objectives);

- wider environmental effects (including disruption to amenity, emissions, and sustainability);

- regulatory requirements (meeting certain conditions or obtaining a licence or permit);

- practical operational issues (for example, site access, availability of services, agreed access); and

- aftercare issues (for example, the need to maintain and inspect *"remediation"* systems or to establish longer term groundwater or gas monitoring).

The publication *"Guidance on dereliction, demolition and remediation costs"*[10] advises (pages 12 and 13):

> *"Proposed end use; the sensitivity of the end use will dictate the level of remediation that is necessary, therefore cost may vary according to the nature of the proposed end*

---

[9]  Light non-aqueous phase liquid (LNAPL) is a groundwater contaminant that is not soluble in water and has lower density than water.

[10]  The Homes and Communities Agency, March 2015.

*use. It is therefore necessary to take a view about the likely future uses of the site; this will require the site to be placed within a broader regeneration and planning context.*

*Water risk; if the potentially contaminated site is in an area where there are sensitive water receptors on, adjacent to, or under the land, then it may be necessary to perform additional remediation of soils or water over and above that required to deliver a development suitable for the proposed end use ...*

*... Duration in use; The longer an area has been used for a particular historical purpose, there is likely to be a higher potential for contamination. Sites that are recent may be less contaminated than those used for similar purposes in earlier years. This is due to increased levels of environmental awareness and more stringent environmental regulations and control.*

*Geology; The risk to groundwater or surface water may be a primary driver for the remediation and the underlying geology will be relevant. If it is known, or can be easily established, that the site lies on areas where the underlying geology is of cohesive material (clays), then the potential for high remediation cost may reduce and lower cost.*

*Depth of contamination; The depth of the contamination will significantly affect the costs. The further below ground level the contaminated material is (i.e. that identified as requiring remediation), the greater the cost might be if it is in a sensitive setting. Notwithstanding it is unlikely that this will be known at an early stage, however, if it is known then the higher range might be selected. It is also possible that deeper contamination in low sensitivity settings may require less remediation if the surface layers sufficiently protected end users and, for instance, the site is located on unproductive strata.*

*Spread of contamination; The greater area of contamination the greater the cost of remediation will be. This may not be known at an early stage, however if there is a wide covering of previous uses then the higher range might be selected. For example, a small local gasworks on a corner of the site for 20 years will be different to a large producing gasworks over the entire site that has been in operation for over 100 years, often with a range of other supporting industries (tar works etc).*

*These differences may affect the range of costs selected, or may indeed indicate that a higher or lower category should be selected. Number and scale of previous uses; If the site has had more than one type of previous use it is possible that multiple contaminants maybe present that vary in nature. As a result this may increase the number of remediation options required and thus increase the cost. It would be prudent to select the higher range.*

*The scale of previous use will also be a factor.*

*Market conditions/remediation strategy/ contractor selection; The adopted remediation strategy will impact on the cost of the remediation. The amount of remediation, and therefore cost, is very sensitive to the level at which remediation targets are set and to a wide range of other variables. It is not unusual on one scheme, for several contractors to propose different remediation strategies and techniques to suit their operational capability, experience and preference. This may result in a range of costs for the site remediation."*

## 9.2    Source control
Generally, treatment methods are categorised into traditional excavation and removal (aka *"mass-transfer"* and *"landfill containment"*), in-situ treatment and ex-situ treatment.

## 9.3    Excavation and removal
The excavation and removal of contaminated waste to landfill[11] is not the most sustainable solution and is not encouraged by the Government. There are a number of principal problems:

- The movement of the waste is simply moving the problem from one place to another without solving it.

- The transportation of waste carries a *"carbon footprint"*.

- The removal of waste material may cause unforeseen environmental damage and may be disruptive for, or cause nuisance to, local communities.

- Biodegradable waste produces methane in landfill sites, and this is said to be a greenhouse gas.

The *"waste hierarchy"* ranks waste management options according to which is best for the environment and disposal is ranked as the last resort when recycling and other forms of recovery are not otherwise feasible.

The excavation and removal of waste to landfill is a costly exercise. Aside from excavation and transportation costs, it will entail the payment of landfill tax and a disposal fee.

If the developer cannot send his waste to landfill, then he must find another way to recover or dispose of it with reference to the waste hierarchy, for example incineration with energy recovery.

The great advantages of extraction and removal is that it can be done quickly and there should be no need for extended post-extraction monitoring.

## 9.4    In-situ treatments
SP1001 – Contaminated Land Remediation – CL:AIRE 29th November 2010 (*"SP1001"*) says:

---

[11]    Sometimes described as *"ex-situ"* remediation.

> *"In-situ methods are those that take place in the subsurface, without excavation of the contaminated soil or abstraction of groundwater. The main advantages of in-situ methods are that they can often avoid excessive environmental impacts and costs associated with excavation and abstraction and they can typically be implemented on operational sites. The major constraint is ensuring that the remediation technique can make effective contact with the contaminants in the subsurface (e.g. facilitating and optimising the mixing of reagents and contaminants or installing a permeable reactive barrier in the correct place)... Due to the complex nature of the subsurface and the level of understanding required, it can be difficult to verify the performance of in-situ techniques."[12]*

SP1001 provides commentary on twelve treatment profiles presented for in-situ treatment techniques and they are summarised below, albeit with some additions and with some extra narrative. They are:

(1)    Chemical oxidation and reduction;

(2)    Electro-remediation;

(3)    Enhanced bioremediation using redox amendments;

(4)    Flushing;

(5)    Monitored natural attenuation;

(6)    Permeable reactive barriers;

(7)    Phytoremediation;

(8)    Sparging;

(9)    Stabilisation/solidification;

(10)   Thermal treatment;

(11)   Venting; and

(12)   Vitrification.

These techniques are discussed in more detail in Appendix 3.

---

[12]    SP1001, Pages 9 and 10; Table 1.3.

## 9.5      Ex-situ treatments

Ex-situ techniques are those that are applied to excavated soil, or treatments of contaminated water or gaseous emissions that take place at the surface. The main advantage of ex-situ techniques, compared with in-situ, is that contaminants, being brought up to the surface, are made more accessible to treatment processes. This means that there can be a more intimate mixing of reagents and contaminants and process optimisation is more straightforward. Material that has been treated can be re-used on-site. Also, the verification process is typically simpler, as the treated materials are easier to access and sample. [13]

The indicative timescales for carrying out these treatments are broadly similar, at under 1 year. Therefore they tend to be faster than in-situ treatments.[14]

The main limitations of ex-situ treatment are the need for excavation and/or pumping which will increase costs and impact the ground environment. Consideration must also be given to material handling and exposure of workers to contaminants. Site adaptation treatments can involve intrusive ground works which may pose a risk on an operational site, and they may be conspicuous which will raise awareness of site works to the local community. Often additional land is required on site for the ex-situ operation.[15]

The treatment profiles mentioned in SP1001 are:

- Biological treatment;

- Chemical oxidation and reduction;

- Soil washing and separation processes;

- Stabilisation/Solidification;

- Thermal treatment;

- Venting; and

- Vitrification.

It is worth adding water and gas/vapour treatment to this list.

These techniques are discussed in more detail in Appendix 3.

---

[13]    Adapted from SP1001@ p.24, para 1.3.

[14]    SP10001, Table 1.4.

[15]    Ditto.

## 9.6　　Pathway control

Pathway control is technical action to reduce the ability of the contaminant source to pose a threat to receptors by inhibiting or controlling the pathway.

# Chapter 10

# Air Quality

## 10.1    What is *"air pollution"*?

Before looking at matters of law and policy, it is helpful to review some of the science behind this topic.[1]

The starting point to bear in mind is that what we describe as the *"air"* is, in fact, a mixture of discrete gases. The predominant gas is nitrogen, which is then followed by oxygen and smaller amounts of other gases. Air is, therefore, to some extent, a pre-existing chemical soup or cocktail.

It follows that exhaust emissions not only emerge as primary pollution when they leave vehicle exhausts but must, also, interact with the gases which comprise tropospheric air. Typically, a vehicular exhaust will emit nitrogen oxides and volatile organic compounds. Given a bit of help from sunlight, they will, in turn, produce nitrogen dioxide and ozone. Both are harmful to flora and fauna, including human beings.

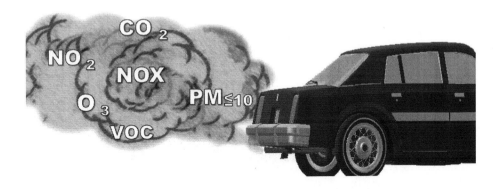

These vehicle exhausts will also emit particulate matter which is, again, harmful. Finally, of course, the emissions will include carbon dioxide, which is said to be a greenhouse gas.

Air pollution can come in many forms, but this chapter will focus on those forms which might become material considerations for the purposes of development control. In this connection, the main groups appear to be:

---

[1]    Much of the technical narrative in this section has been derived from *"What are the causes of air Pollution"* – Defra.

- Particulate Matter;

- Oxides of nitrogen;

- Benzene;

- 1,3-butadiene;

- Carbon monoxide;

- Ozone.

## 10.2    Particulate Matter (PM)

Particulate matter is a generic term for airborne particles. Primary particulate matter can come in the form of sand, dust, dirt, soot, or smoke and secondary particles can formed by chemical reactions in the air. The health concerns associated with particulate matter has to do with the fact that many such particles can be inhaled and work their way into the bloodstream.

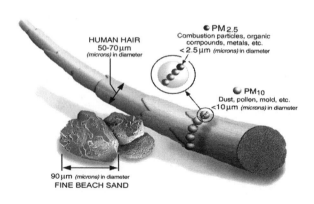

HUMAN HAIR
50-70 μm
*(microns)* in diameter

● PM₂.₅
Combustion particles, organic
compounds, metals, etc.
< 2.5 μm *(microns)* in diameter

● PM₁₀
Dust, pollen, mold, etc.
<10 μm *(microns)* in diameter

90 μm *(microns)* in diameter
FINE BEACH SAND

*Figure adapted from US:EPA original*

A particle with a *"diameter"* of about 10 micrometers (*"$PM_{10}$"*) and smaller can be inhaled.

These can get into the lungs and cause health risks. Fine inhalable particles with diameters of 2.5 micrometers (*"$PM_{2.5}$"*) and smaller pose the greatest risks, because they stand the higher chance of getting into the bloodstream.

It has been suggested that about two thirds of $PM_{10}$ emissions are $PM_{2.5}$ or below.

In the UK, the biggest human-made sources are fuel combustion and transport. Road traffic gives rise to primary particles from engine emissions, tyre and brake wear and other non-exhaust emissions. Secondary particulate matter is formed from emissions of ammonia, sulphur dioxide and oxides of nitrogen.

A report published in *"Cardiovascular Research"* (2020) 116, 2247-2253 argued that long-term exposure to air pollution had been linked to an increased risk of dying from Covid-19. The report suggested that, in Europe, 19% of deaths involving Covid-19 were influenced by air pollution. Professor Thomas Münzel's press statement is worth quoting at some length. He said:

> *"When people inhale polluted air, the very small polluting particles, the $PM_{2.5}$, migrate from the lungs to the blood and blood vessels, causing inflammation and severe oxidative stress, which is an imbalance between free radicals and oxidants in the body that normally repair damage to cells.*

> *"This causes damage to the inner lining of arteries, the endothelium, and leads to the narrowing and stiffening of the arteries. The Covid-19 virus also enters the body via the lungs, causing similar damage to blood vessels, and it is now considered to be an endothelial disease.*

> *"If both long-term exposure to air pollution and infection with the Covid-19 virus come together then we have an additive adverse effect on health, particularly with respect to the heart and blood vessels, which leads to greater vulnerability and less resilience to Covid-19.*

> *"If you already have heart disease, then air pollution and coronavirus infection will cause trouble that can lead to heart attacks, heart failure and stroke."*

### 10.3 Oxides of nitrogen ($NO_x$)

Nitrogen dioxide ($NO_2$) and nitric oxide (NO) are both oxides of nitrogen and together are referred to as $NO_x$. $NO_2$ is associated with adverse effects on human health. It is produced by those motor vehicle engines which use petroleum-based fuels.

At high levels $NO_2$ causes inflammation of the airways. Long term exposure may affect lung function and respiratory symptoms. $NO_2$ also enhances the response to allergens in sensitive individuals. High levels of $NO_x$ can have an adverse effect on vegetation. Deposition of pollutants derived from $NO_x$ emissions contribute to acidification and/or eutrophication of sensitive habitats leading to loss of biodiversity. $NO_x$ also contributes to the formation of secondary particles and ground level ozone, both of which are associated with ill-health effects.

Mr Justice Garnham put the matter pithily in *Client Earth (No. 2) v Secretary of State for the Environment, Food and Rural Affairs* [2016] EWHC 2740 (Admin):

> *"A recent analysis from Department for the Environment, Food and Rural Affairs ("DEFRA") estimates that the effects of exposure to nitrogen dioxide has "an effect on mortality equivalent to 23,500 deaths annually in the UK ...""*

### 10.4 Benzene

Benzene has a variety of sources, but primarily arises from domestic and industrial combustion and road transport. It is a recognised human carcinogen and no absolutely safe level can be specified in ambient air. Studies in workers exposed to high levels have shown an excessive risk of leukaemia.

## 10.5    1,3-butadiene

1,3-butadiene derives, mainly, from the combustion of petrol. It is a recognised human carcinogen and no absolutely safe level can be specified in ambient air. The health effect of most concern is the induction of cancer of the lymphoid system and blood-forming tissues, lymphoma and leukaemia.

## 10.6    Carbon monoxide

The largest source of carbon monoxide (CO) is road transport, with residential and industrial combustion making significant contributions. It substantially reduces capacity of the blood to carry oxygen to the body's tissues and blocks important biochemical reactions in cells. People with existing diseases which affect delivery of oxygen to the heart or brain, such as angina, are at particular risk.

## 10.7    Development plans and air quality

Paragraph 186 of the National Planning Policy Framework argues that opportunities to improve air quality or mitigate impacts should, so far as possible be considered at the plan-making stage, to ensure a strategic approach and limit the need for issues to be reconsidered when determining individual applications.

One problem is that it is optimistic to presume that measures of air quality will have a degree of stability throughout the plan period. It would appear that the DEFRA calculates projections for five-year intervals as a matter of routine and these are also the time intervals used by the European Commission.[2] As the lockdown imposed by response to the coronavirus pandemic has shown, such projections can be disrupted. For example, whilst the Covid lockdown softened some traffic patterns, it might have intensified others.

Furthermore, any presumption that the science will remain static throughout a plan period is not soundly based:[3]

> *"Traffic congestion increases vehicle emissions and degrades ambient air quality, and recent studies have shown excess morbidity and mortality for drivers, commuters and individuals living near major roadways. Presently, our understanding of the air pollution impacts from congestion on roads is very limited."*[4]

This would suggest that the science of multifactorial causation in this topic is still evolving.

---

[2]    See *Client Earth (No. 2) v Secretary of State for the Environment, Food and Rural Affairs* [2016] EWHC 2740 (Admin) at para. 57.

[3]    As to the science, see the criticisms of modelling methods at ibid para. 74.

[4]    *Air pollution and health risks due to vehicle traffic* - Kai Zhanga and Stuart Batterman - https://www.ncbi.nlm. nih.gov/pmc/articles/PMC4243514/.

One would intuit that the Covid lockdowns would have led to a demonstrable reduction in local air pollution levels, but reducing the recondite empirical evidence for this intuition to a clear cause and effect relationship is far from easy. A recent study by the University of Stirling found that a 65 per cent reduction in traffic on Scottish roads during the lockdown had no significant impact on outdoor air pollution.[5]

Dr Ruaraidh Dobson, who led the study, said:

> *"It has been assumed that fewer cars on the road might have led to a decline in the level of air pollution outdoors and, in turn, reduce the number of cases of ill health linked to this pollution.*
>
> *"However, our study - contrary to research from places such as Wuhan in China, and Milan - found no evidence of fine particulate air pollution declining in Scotland because of lockdown.*
>
> *"This suggests that vehicles aren't an important cause of this very harmful type of air pollution in Scotland, and people may be at greater risk from poor air quality in their own homes, especially where cooking and smoking is taking place in enclosed and poorly ventilated spaces."*

One of the problems is that the chemical components of air are "*messy*", in the sense that they fluctuate and a change in one component can precipitate unforeseen changes in others.

Clearly, it is not for lawyers or planners to second guess the scientists on this complex topic; however, this flags up the point that the opinions of scientists may change within discrete plan periods and may thereby change the assumptions which led to some development plan policies. It is, therefore, dangerous to be wedded to a policy statement simply because it is there.

The UK has internationally agreed targets to reduce overall national emissions of five air pollutants by 2020 and 2030.

In 2013, the WHO European Centre for Environment and Health stated:[6]

> *"Air pollution is an important determinant of health. A wide range of adverse effects of ambient air pollution on health has been well documented by studies conducted in various parts of the world. There is significant inequality in exposure to air pollution and related health risks: air pollution combines with other aspects of the social and physical environment to create a disproportionate disease burden in less affluent parts*

---

[5] *"Traffic is not a key contributor to air pollution, study finds"*: https://www.autoexpress.co.uk/news/353127/traffic-not-key-contributor-air-pollution-study-finds#:~:text=Road%20traffic%20is%20not%20a,improvement%20in%20outdoor%20air%20quality.

[6] Review of evidence on health aspects of air pollution – REVIHAAP Project Technical Report.

*of society. WHO periodically reviews the accumulated scientific evidence to update its air quality guidelines. The most recent update was completed in 2005. The guidelines address all regions of the world and provide uniform targets for air quality that would protect the large majority of individuals from the adverse effects on health of air pollution."*

In 2020, the Health Effects Institute and the Institute for Health Metrics produced a report[7] which led with two startling statements:

*"Air pollution is the fifth leading risk factor for mortality worldwide. It is responsible for more deaths than many better-known risk factors such as malnutrition, alcohol use, and physical inactivity. Each year, more people die from air pollution–related disease than from road traffic injuries or malaria."*

And:

*"More than 90% of people worldwide live in areas exceeding the WHO Guideline for healthy air. More than half live in areas that do not even meet WHO's least-stringent air quality target."*

The question for this book is whether these worrying statements impact on day-to-day development control decisions. Arguably, they have to do with public health as a whole and not town and country planning. The answers to these questions lie in whether the distribution of land uses by the planning system is a determinative factor in the propagation or control of pollution and, if so, whether these matters should, properly, be dealt with by other agencies.

## 10.8    The Environment Act 2021 and air quality
Not surprisingly, the Act contains a raft of provisions which go to air quality. As indicated above, it is necessary to determine how they relate to day-to-day development control; bearing in mind, in particular, the objective of seeking to avoid the duplication of regulatory controls.

So far as air quality is concerned, the provisions of the Act create a mix of statutory discretions and mandatory statutory duties and it is important to distinguish them.

Section 1 provides that the Secretary of State <u>may</u>, by regulations, set *"long-term targets"* in respect of any matter which relates to the *"natural environment"*, or people's (sic) enjoyment of the natural environment.[8] The use of the word *"may"* makes this a statutory discretion,

---

[7]    Citation: Health Effects Institute. 2019. State of Global Air 2019. Special Report. Boston, MA: Health Effects Institute. ISSN 2578-6873 © 2019 Health Effects Institute.

[8]    By Section 44, the *"natural environment"* means plants, wild animals and other living organisms, their habitats, land (except buildings or other structures), air and water, and the natural systems, cycles and processes through which they interact.

and not a duty; however, Section 1(2) then goes on to provide that the Secretary of State <u>must</u> exercise the power in subsection 1(1) so as to set a long-term target in respect of at least one matter within each "*priority area*", and this a statutory duty. By Section 1(4) a target set under this section must specify:

(a)    a standard to be achieved, which must be capable of being objectively measured (the "*specified date*"[9]); and

(b)    a date by which it is to be achieved (the "*specified date*"[10]).

A target is a "*long-term*" target if the specified date is no less than 15 years after the date on which the target is initially set: Section 1(6).

The "*priority areas*" are air quality, water, biodiversity, resource efficiency and waste reduction: Section 1(3). The phrase "*air quality*" is not defined[11] and so need not be limited to particulate matter, something which is covered in Section 2 in any event. This observation raises a significant matter of interpretation; namely, what might or might not be included under the rubric "*air quality*" within this section. The first point would appear to be that "*air quality*" should be construed as relating back to the overarching provision in Section 1(1); that is to say, it should relate to the natural environment, or people's enjoyment of the natural environment only and this begs the question of whether it should be construed to include gases and particulates which directly affect human beings or might impact on climate change. In particular, of course, there is the question of whether "*air quality*" in this connection includes emissions of carbon dioxide and other gases said to be associated with "*global warming*". Section 1(5) provides that regulations under this section may make provision about how the matter in respect of which a target is set is to be measured. This provision would seem to go to matters of quantification and measurement rather than allowing the Secretary of State to make regulations which define what is and is not to be measured.

Section 2(1) provides that the Secretary of State <u>must</u> by regulations set a target for particulate matter (the "*$PM_{2.5}$ air quality target*") in respect of the annual mean level of $PM_{2.5}$ in "*ambient air*"[12]. The use of the word "*must*" makes this a mandatory duty.

The key distinction between Section 1 and Section 2 on this point is that, in Section 2, the $PM_{2.5}$ air quality target may, but need not, be a long-term target unless it is selected as a priority area for Section 1(2): see Section 2(2). This duty is in addition to (and does

---

9      Section 1(8).

10     Section 1(8).

11     Likewise with "*biodiversity*". Nor, unfortunately, are these terms usually defined in planning conditions or planning obligations.

12     "*Ambient air*" will be defined by regulations: Section 2(4).

not discharge) the duty in Section 1(2) to set a long-term target in relation to air quality: Section 2(5).

By Section 2(3), "*PM$_{2.5}$*" means particulate matter with an "*aerodynamic diameter*" not exceeding 2.5 micrometres. The choice of the phrase "*aerodynamic diameter*" is unfortunate, because this may cause confusion with the way the term is used in other applications.[13] Ergo, it is in need of clarification either in guidance or in regulations.

The regulations setting the PM$_{2.5}$ air quality target may make provision defining "*ambient air*". The meaning of "*ambient air*" can be contentious because it will determine those areas which are within and outwith the input data for the specified target. The current definition is in the Air Quality Standards Regulations 2010 (S.I. 2010, No. 1001), viz;

> "... "*Ambient air*" means outdoor air in the troposphere[14] excluding workplaces where members of the public do not have regular access ..."

To put it another way, workplaces and construction sites are not included. This is despite the fact that they are major sources of air pollution. If the Secretary of State's regulations do not include construction sites, then it is arguable that local planning authorities may have to fill the gap, for example, where a house building site is proceeding in stages and incoming residents may be moving into dwellings as the state scheme is progressing.

It is the duty of the Secretary of State to ensure that targets set under Section 1 are met, and the PM$_{2.5}$ air quality target set under Section 2 are met: Section 5(3).

The Act sets up the Office for Environmental Protection (OEP). The UK currently has targets to reduce overall national emissions of five air pollutants by 2020 and 2030 these being imposed by European Directives and were enforced, in respect of public bodies, by the European Commission and applied by UK courts. The OEP will take on the role played by the Commission of monitoring the implementation of environmental law and taking enforcement action. Given that the OEP will be concerned with the achievement of national targets by public bodies, it is difficult to see how site-specific planning decisions will act so as to give rise to any duplication of regimes, this being similar in kind to the matters discussed in *Gladman Developments Ltd v Secretary of State for Communities and Local Government* [2019] EWCA Civ 1543.

---

[13] This is the notional diameter based on the application of a formula to the measured characteristics of a particle. This is not, in fact, the same methodology as that used in the application of the Air Quality Standards Regulations 2010.

[14] The troposphere is the lowest portion of the atmosphere. This layer contains most of the Earth's clouds and is the location where weather primarily occurs: https://www.britannica.com/science/atmosphere/troposphere.

The achievement of national air quality standards might be relevant to individual applications, where these standards are, themselves, relevant to them. The attempted site-specific application of broad-brush national standards is not without its own difficulties.

Moving from national to district, the Environment Act 1995 required local authorities to assess and manage the quality of the air in their areas. Where specified standards and objectives are not being met, they are required to declare Air Quality Management Areas and then prepare action plans. The Secretary of State has produced the National Air Quality Strategy, which specifies the standards and objectives that local authorities need to achieve. The Act is intended to strengthen these duties by giving greater clarity on the requirements of action plans enabling greater collaboration between local authorities and all tiers of local government, as well as with relevant public authorities, in the creation and delivery of those plans. It also requires the Secretary of State to regularly review the National Air Quality Strategy.

Paragraph 186 of the National Planning Policy Framework states (inter alia) that planning policies and decisions should sustain and contribute towards compliance with relevant limit values or national objectives for pollutants, taking into account the presence of Air Quality Management Areas and Clean Air Zones and that planning decisions should ensure that any new development in Air Quality Management Areas and Clean Air Zones is consistent with the local air quality action plan. Thus, the National Planning Policy Framework not only does not suggest any conflict of regimes, but also places these air quality strategies on the table when making planning decisions.

As discussed above, the 2021 Act (section 17) requires the Secretary of State to prepare a *"policy statement on Environmental Principles"*. This is, currently, the document produced in 2018 and which is (helpfully) called *"Policy Statement on Environmental Principles"*. The Environmental Principles are as follows:

(a)    environmental protection should be integrated into the making of policies;

(b)    the taking of preventative action to avert environmental damage;

(c)    the adoption of a precautionary principle so far as relating to the environment;

(d)    environmental damage as a priority be rectified at source; and

(e)    the polluter pays principle.

A minister must, when making policy, have regard to the Policy Statement on Environmental Principles: Section 19. This means that the National Planning Policy Framework will be prepared having regard to the Policy Statement on Environmental Principles currently in effect. In turn, the formulation of development plan policies must have regard to the National Planning Policy Framework. These development plan policies will, in turn, inform day to day development control decision-making. Accordingly, the Environmental Principles will trickle down to development control.

The Environmental Principles include preventative action to avert environmental damage and the adoption of the precautionary principle. These principles are of importance in connection with air quality.

As discussed above, the science is neither static nor certain. The science of causation is still evolving, and it has been argued that *"our understanding of the air pollution impacts from congestion on roads is very limited."*[15] Set against this, the threats are very significant. For example, the statement that air pollution is the fifth leading risk factor for mortality worldwide.[16]

Thus, if one applies the Environmental Principles to planning decisions, this represents a very significant shift in the burden of proof. If the applicant is unable to show that a reasonable and credible objection on air quality grounds cannot be made out, then this objection should stand as proved and weigh against the grant of planning permission. The decision-maker should apply the precautionary principle.

In 2000, the European Commission stated (para.4) that:

> *"Recourse to the precautionary principle presupposes that potentially dangerous effects deriving from a phenomenon, product or process have been identified, and that scientific evaluation does not allow the risk to be determined with sufficient certainty.*
>
> *The implementation of an approach based on the precautionary principle should start with a scientific evaluation, as complete as possible, and where possible, identifying at each stage the degree of scientific uncertainty."*[17]

### 10.9 Development control and air pollution

Paragraph 186 of the National Planning Policy Framework (2021) states:

> *"Planning policies and decisions should sustain and contribute towards compliance with relevant limit values or national objectives for pollutants, taking into account the presence of Air Quality Management Areas and Clean Air Zones, and the cumulative impacts from individual sites in local areas. Opportunities to improve air quality or mitigate impacts should be identified, such as through traffic and travel management, and green infrastructure provision and enhancement. So far as possible these opportunities should be considered at the plan-making stage, to ensure a strategic approach and limit the need for issues to be reconsidered when determining individual applications.*

---

[15] *"Air pollution and health risks due to vehicle traffic"* - Kai Zhanga and Stuart Batterman - https://www.ncbi.nlm.nih.gov/pmc/articles/PMC4243514/.

[16] See above.

[17] Communication from the Commission on the precautionary principle /* COM/2000/0001 final */.

*Planning decisions should ensure that any new development in Air Quality Management Areas and Clean Air Zones is consistent with the local air quality action plan."*

The emphasis appears to be on trying to resolve air quality matters at the plan-making stage, presumably on the basis that this will place less burden on the development control stage. The problem is, of course, that plan-making is not a speedy process and decisions must be made whilst they are being prepared. Furthermore, local development plan policies are not without their own difficulties, as discussed below.

The National Planning Practice Guidance website also contains advice on this topic:[18]

*"When could air quality considerations be relevant to the development management process?*

*Whether air quality is relevant to a planning decision will depend on the proposed development and its location. Concerns could arise if the development is likely to have an adverse effect on air quality in areas where it is already known to be poor, particularly if it could affect the implementation of air quality strategies and action plans and/or breach legal obligations (including those relating to the conservation of habitats and species). Air quality may also be a material consideration if the proposed development would be particularly sensitive to poor air quality in its vicinity.*

*Paragraph: 005 Reference ID: 32-005-20191101*

*What specific issues may need to be considered when assessing air quality impacts?*

*Considerations that may be relevant to determining a planning application include whether the development would:*

- *Lead to changes (including any potential reductions) in vehicle-related emissions in the immediate vicinity of the proposed development or further afield. This could be through the provision of electric vehicle charging infrastructure; altering the level of traffic congestion; significantly changing traffic volumes, vehicle speeds or both; or significantly altering the traffic composition on local roads. Other matters to consider include whether the proposal involves the development of a bus station, coach or lorry park; could add to turnover in a large car park; or involve construction sites that would generate large Heavy Goods Vehicle flows over a period of a year or more;*

- *Introduce new point sources of air pollution. This could include furnaces which require prior notification to local authorities; biomass boilers or biomass-fuelled*

---

[18] As is often the case with the NPPG, it is difficult to identify its target audience. If it is advice to experienced local planning authorities, then much of it appears to be of the "*teaching grandmother to suck eggs*" kind. Be that as it may!

*Combined Heat and Power plant; centralised boilers or plant burning other fuels within or close to an air quality management area or introduce relevant combustion within a Smoke Control Area; or extraction systems (including chimneys) which require approval or permits under pollution control legislation; ..."*

*Paragraph: 006 Reference ID: 32-006-20191101 - Revision date: 01 11 2019*

The National Planning Practice Guidance advises:

*"How can an impact on air quality be mitigated?*

*Mitigation options will need to be locationally specific, will depend on the proposed development and need to be proportionate to the likely impact. It is important that local planning authorities work with applicants to consider appropriate mitigation so as to ensure new development is appropriate for its location and unacceptable risks are prevented. Planning conditions and obligations can be used to secure mitigation where the relevant tests are met.*

*Examples of mitigation include:*

- *maintaining adequate separation distances between sources of air pollution and receptors;*

- *using green infrastructure, in particular trees, where this can create a barrier or maintain separation between sources of pollution and receptors[19];*

- *appropriate means of filtration and ventilation;*

- *including infrastructure to promote modes of transport with a low impact on air quality (such as electric vehicle charging points);*

- *controlling dust and emissions from construction, operation and demolition; and*

- *contributing funding to measures, including those identified in air quality action plans and low emission strategies, designed to offset the impact on air quality arising from new development."*

*Paragraph: 008 Reference ID: 32-008-20191101 - Revision date: 01 11 2019*

One of the key concerns for local planning authorities relates to air pollution arising from traffic movements, but there is something of a disjunction in the National Planning Policy Framework.

---

[19]    The planting of trees can also count towards *"biodiversity net gain"*.

Air quality is not, necessarily, a consideration confined to major new developments. New drive-through restaurants can become localised hotspots for air pollution.[20] A change in traffic signalling arrangements at a road junction could lead to longer queues of traffic with idling engines.

In both examples, the dangers are not simply limited to those in nearby properties. People waiting in cars are not protected because studies have shown that pollutants can accumulate within a car, often to higher levels than outside it.

The National Planning Practice Guidance goes on to add to its list of considerations, whether the development would:

- *Expose people to harmful concentrations of air pollutants, including dust. This could be by building new homes, schools, workplaces or other development in places with poor air quality;*

- *Give rise to potentially unacceptable impacts (such as dust) during construction for nearby sensitive locations;*

- *Have a potential adverse effect on biodiversity, especially where it would affect sites designated for their biodiversity value.*

*Paragraph: 006 Reference ID: 32-006-20191101 - Revision date: 01 11 2019*

The final bullet-point flags up that air pollution can have a deleterious effect on ecology.

Paragraph 110 of the National Planning Policy Framework states:

*"In assessing sites that may be allocated for development in plans, or specific applications for development, it should be ensured that:*

*a) appropriate opportunities to promote sustainable transport modes can be – or have been – taken up, given the type of development and its location;*

*b) safe and suitable access to the site can be achieved for all users; and*

*c) any significant impacts from the development on the transport network (in terms of capacity and congestion), or on highway safety, can be cost effectively mitigated to an acceptable degree."*

Paragraph 111 then adds:

---

[20]  *Drive-throughs are busier than ever during the pandemic – but they're hotspots for air pollution* - October 2020 - Anitha Chinnaswamy - Assistant Professor of Environment and Computing, Coventry University.

> *"111. Development should only be prevented or refused on highways grounds if there would be an unacceptable impact on highway safety, or the residual cumulative impacts on the road network would be severe."*

Therein lies a source of confusion, because there is nothing in paragraph 111 to say that a refusal based on the applicant's failure to promote sustainable transport modes is an acceptable ground of refusal. This would suggest that the mention of *"sustainable transport modes"*, in paragraph 110(a), is more aspirational than real and that paragraph 111 merely covers the considerations mentioned in paragraphs 110(b) and (c). Arguably, the Secretary of State should change paragraphs 110 and 111 by way of the duties imposed by the Act. This point is considered above in connection with the Policy Statement on Environmental Principles.

Paragraph 112(e) of the NPPF refers to designs which enable changing of plug-in and *"other low emission"* vehicles. This presupposes that the macro-electrical infrastructure to support these additional loads exist in the first place.

# Chapter 11

# Verification

## 11.1     The objectives of verification

The terms "*verification*" and "*validation*" are terms of art which the prudent authority should define in planning policy or planning documents. There is ample guidance on the meanings of these phrases.

The Environment Agency[1] states (page 1) that:

> *"The terms "verification" and "validation" are embedded in quality management standards for the evaluation of a product, service, or system. BS EN ISO 9000:2005 provides the following definitions:*
>
> *Quality – degree to which a set of inherent characteristics fulfils requirements;*
>
> *Verification – confirmation through the provision of objective evidence that specified requirements have been fulfilled; and*
>
> *Validation – confirmation through the provision of objective evidence that the requirements for a specific intended use have been fulfilled.*
>
> *Key aspects of both verification and validation are setting pre-defined requirements and the collection of evidence to show that those requirements have been met. This is also the case where evidence is needed to show that remediation of land contamination has met defined objectives, usually to ensure that risks to human health and the environment are insignificant."*

It follows that drafting which refers to BS EN ISO 9000:2005 (or its successor) will gain in robustness. The report adds:

> *"2.1 Verification of remediation*
>
> *For remediation, the fundamental purpose of verification is to evaluate whether identified risks are successfully managed over pre-defined timescales to meet the objectives of the remediation strategy, based on a quantitative assessment of remediation performance. Verification is an essential part of project closure, but its planning should not be left to the end. Indeed, its planning is a key part of developing the remediation strategy."*

---

[1]     Land Contamination: Verification of Remediation - Report: SC030114/R1 (Environment Agency, February 2010). See also INFO-IMP2: implementation, verification and monitoring (https://www.claire.co.uk/useful-government-legislation-and-guidance-by-country/189-implementationverification- and-monitoring-info-imp2) on the CL:AIRE Water and Land Library.

A "*verification plan*" is defined as:

> "*A document that sets out the requirements for gathering data/evidence to demonstrate that remediation meets the remediation objectives and remediation criteria. It includes monitoring, sampling and testing criteria, and identifies all those records that should be retained to demonstrate compliance within the specification (e.g., field monitoring data, laboratory data, level surveys above and below capping layers).*"[2]

A "*verification report*" is defined as:

> "*A document that provides a complete record of all remediation activities on site and the data collected as identified in the verification plan to support compliance with agreed remediation objectives and criteria. It also includes a description of the work (as-built drawings) and details of any unexpected conditions (e.g. contamination) found during remediation and how they were dealt with.*"[3]

There is a lot to be said for not only incorporating the terms "*verification report*" and "*verification plan*" into any drafting, but also to including these settled definitions (or any later iterations of them). The objective should be, in a Section 106 agreement or a planning condition, to specify metriculated targets which are defined by objective criteria and outputs which can be measured against these objective criteria.

The Glossary to *Guidance for the Safe Development of Housing on Land Affected by Contamination - R&D66: 2008 Volume 2* defines "*verification*" as:

> "*The process of demonstrating that the risk[4] has been reduced[5] to meet remediation criteria and objectives based on a quantitative assessment of remediation[6] performance.*"

Paragraph 3.6.1 to *Guidance for the Safe Development of Housing on Land Affected by Contamination - R&D66: 2008 Volume 1* states that the overall objective of verification activities is to demonstrate the achievement of the remediation objectives set out in the Remediation Strategy and Verification Plan and:

> "*It is also likely that verification will be required to provide evidence that:*
>
> • *planning/permit/licence conditions have been complied with;*

---

[2]   Ibid @ p.6.

[3]   Ibid @ p.6.

[4]   "*Risk*" is defined as "*A combination of the probability, or frequency of occurrence, of a defined hazard and the magnitude of the consequences of the occurrence.*"

[5]   Again, note the reference to the reduction of risk to acceptable standards rather than "*clean up*".

[6]   "*Remediation*" is further defined as "*Action taken to prevent or minimise, or remedy or mitigate the effects of any identified unacceptable risks*".

- *environmental management goals (e.g. dust generation, migration of run-off, soil gas and vapours, groundwater contamination) have been controlled."*

The advice goes on to say (para. 3.6.1) that some particular remediation activities take place over a prolonged period of time (e.g. bioremediation of soils, groundwater treatment, etc). In such circumstances:

*"...verification will provide data demonstrating whether the intended remediation action (such as reduction in contaminant concentration) is taking place at the expected rate. If the data is indicating that the remediation action is not occurring as predicted, action(s) must be carried out to react to that data (e.g. to increase the speed of the remediation, or the length of the remediation programme, or to decrease the remediation target etc.). Again any substantial change to the remediation objectives must be communicated to all relevant parties and agreed (as appropriate)."*

Thus, this is shown as an iterative process and one is left to consider whether an attempt to incorporate this approach might fall foul of the unhelpful *"tail-piece"* limitations on the drafting of effective condition: see Appendix 1. Again, this seems to steer one towards the use of planning obligations.

## 11.2 Common verification activities

Paragraph 3.6.2 of *R&D66 2008: Volume 1* explains that verification often involves the sampling and chemical analysis of soils on the site, using both in-situ test kits and off-site laboratories. This data will be used to:

- Determine the nature and extent of the residual contamination (together with its location);

- Ensure appropriate classification for waste disposal; and

- Confirm the chemical nature of soils imported to site (and thus to ensure compliance with both the remediation objectives and with the contract specification).

It goes on to advise that, similarly, sampling and chemical analysis of groundwater and surface waters (at an agreed frequency and at agreed locations) is commonly undertaken. This data should demonstrate that:

- The remediation treatment is achieving the required effect on contamination concentrations;

- That any authorised discharges or construction works are not impacting groundwater or surface water contaminant concentrations to unacceptable levels; and

- That treatment of soil gases/vapours has reduced their concentrations and/or that barrier/venting systems have managed the gas/vapour regimes to meet the remediation objectives.

## 11.3    The Verification Report

Paragraph 3.6.4 of *R&D66: 2008 Volume 1* states that the objective of the Verification Report is to document all aspects of the remediation works undertaken at the site and states that:

> *"In the past, many remediation projects were carried out without being properly or permanently recorded. Subsequent further work on such sites (e.g. for redevelopment etc.) inevitably has led to major programmes of site investigations, monitoring, risk assessments etc. all of which would have been unnecessary had proper records been kept and presented in a Verification Report."*

This advice is particularly apt where a larger scheme might be developed in phases and over many years.

Paragraph 3.6.5 states that the typical contents of a Verification Report will normally include:[7]

(1)    A description of the site background;

(2)    A summary of all relevant site investigation reports;

(3)    A statement of the *"remediation"* objectives;

(4)    A description of the *"remediation"* works;

(5)    The verification data (sample locations/analytical results);

(6)    Project photographs;

(7)    As built drawings;

(8)    Records of consultations with Regulators;

(9)    Duty of Care paperwork;

(10)    Environmental monitoring data;

(11)    A description of any residual contamination;

---

[7]    It also advises that the contents of a Verification Report are described in more detail in Figure 4B, Output 5 of DEFRA/Environment Agency, Model Procedures for the Management of Land Contamination (CLR 11) - 2004a.

(12) Any arrangements for post *"remediation"* management.

Again, there is a lot to be said for having regard to this advice in drafting planning documents and, as the case may be, making direct reference to it.

*R&D66* notes (para. 3.6.5) that it is important that the Verification Report is specific to the site and to the *"remediation"* actions that have been carried out (i.e. much in line with the maxim *"Metricated Targets, Measurable Performance"*).

The local planning authority should require that an up-dated qualitative risk assessment be provided to them by reference to the, then, current condition of the site. If the permission includes a relevant condition, then the authority should, if satisfied with the report, discharge the condition or ask for further detail before doing so.

# Chapter 12

# Long-Term Monitoring And Maintenance

Long-term monitoring and maintenance depend on the ability of interested parties to detect and (as the case may be) put right any problems which were not apparent when the initial treatment works and verification were carried out.

To a large extent, this turns on the accuracy and enforceability of planning conditions, planning obligations etc. Be this as it may, there is ample guidance on the subject.

*R&D66: 2008 Volume 1* (para. 3.5.1) advises that, where on-going monitoring and maintenance are required, such a programme must be defined in a monitoring/maintenance plan that describes:

- The scope and context of the monitoring and maintenance activities, including the remediation objectives and criteria that have yet to be achieved.

- The detailed specification of the work.

- The roles and responsibilities for carrying the work out.

- The locations, frequency and duration of monitoring.

- The detail of analyses to be performed (analytical suite, limits of detection, etc).

- The criteria for data evaluation, including when monitoring can cease.

- The proposals for review of monitoring and maintenance activities.

- The mechanics and format for recording, collating and reporting data.

One can usefully add:

- A contingency plan detailing a sequence of response actions if "*remediation*" criteria are not, or are not likely to be, met.

- The mechanism for making decisions about exceptional activities, for example replacement or repair, and communication with involved parties.

Monitoring or maintenance should continue until it is demonstrated that all the adaptive treatment objectives have been met. Monitoring may be needed to show that passive methods, natural attenuation or long-term source-control methods perform as predicted, for example:

- Monitored natural attenuation (Environment Agency, 2000).

- Permeable reactive barriers (Environment Agency, 2002a).

- Passive and active landfill gas control systems.

- Cover systems and containment walls.

- Phytoextraction or phytostabilisation.

- Pump and treat systems.

The objective of management is to ensure that the treatment and monitoring infrastructure continue to function and operate as designed. Activities may include:

- Inspection of monitoring boreholes, such as abstraction wells, pipework, pumps, surface condition of cover system.

- Servicing of equipment, such as sampling pumps and replacement of consumables.

- Replacement or rehabilitation of monitoring boreholes.

Monitoring and management reports will take the form of interim progress reports and a final report to show that all objectives and criteria have been achieved.

A management report should show:

- The scope of the work covered by the report.

- A schedule of regular activities since the previous report.

- Report on exceptional work items carried out since previous report.

- Information on use of consumables, energy etc.

- Requirements to action repairs or service plant.

- Recommendations for future routine or exceptional work items.

A monitoring report should include:

- The scope of the work covered by the report.

- A schedule of regular activities since the previous report.

- A report on visual inspection, monitoring and test results, including exceptional results recorded since the previous report.

- An assessment of compliance against previously agreed criteria.

- A report on any actions taken in response to exceptional results.

- Recommendations for future monitoring and any variations to the agreed monitoring programme.

- Supporting information, including sampling, analytical and quality assurance procedures used, type of equipment, calibration records, location and construction of monitoring points.

# Chapter 13

# Environmental Impact Assessment

Whilst it is neither the function of this book nor this chapter to provide an in-depth analysis of the environmental impact assessment process, it is necessary to consider that process so far as it is material to the determination of those planning applications which involve land affected by contamination.

## 13.1    The environmental impact assessment process

The requirement for the environmental impact assessment (EIA) of certain projects (EIA developments) derives from European Community law, in particular the EC Directive number 85/337 entitled The Assessment of the Effect of Certain Public and Private Projects on the Environment. The directive is, nowadays, implemented in domestic law by way of the Town and Country Planning (Environmental Impact Assessment) Regulations 2017.

Regulation 3 provides that the relevant planning authority, the Secretary of State or an inspector must not grant planning permission or subsequent consent for EIA development unless an EIA has been carried out in respect of that development. Regulation 2(1) distinguishes between two separate types of *"EIA development"*. First, *"Schedule 1"* development, for which an environmental impact assessment is mandatory. Secondly, *"Schedule 2"* development, for which an environmental impact assessment is required if the project is considered likely to give rise to significant effects on the environment by virtue of factors such as its nature, size or location (including location partly in a *"sensitive area"*[1]).

It is necessary to stress at the outset that *"environmental impact assessment"* is a process. It proceeds by way of a number of discrete stages. By Regulation 4(1) the process consists of:

(a)    the preparation of an *"environmental statement"*;

(b)    any consultation, publication and notification required by, or by virtue of, those Regulations or any other enactment in respect of EIA development; and

(c)    the steps required under Regulation 26.

---

[1]    *"Sensitive area"* means any of the following: (a) land notified under Section 28(1) (sites of special scientific interest) of the Wildlife and Countryside Act 1981; (b) a National Park within the meaning of the National Parks and Access to the Countryside Act 1949; (c) the Broads; (d) a property appearing on the World Heritage List kept under article 11(2) of the 1972 UNESCO Convention Concerning the Protection of the World Cultural and Natural Heritage; (e) a scheduled monument within the meaning of the Ancient Monuments and Archaeological Areas Act 1979; (f) an area of outstanding natural beauty designated as such by an order made by Natural England under Section 82(1) (areas of outstanding natural beauty) of the Countryside and Rights of Way Act 2000 as confirmed by the Secretary of State; (g) a European site: Regulation 2(1).

The EIA must identify, describe and assess in an appropriate manner, in light of each individual case, the direct and indirect significant effects of the proposed development on the following factors:

(a)    population and human health;

(b)    biodiversity, with particular attention to species and habitats protected under Directive 92/43/EEC1 and Directive 2009/147/EC2;

(c)    land, soil, water, air and climate;

(d)    material assets, cultural heritage and the landscape;

(e)    the interaction between the factors referred to in sub-paragraphs (a) to (d).[2]

Part of that process is the document known as an *"environmental statement"*. It is the environmental statement (and additions to it) which will be shown on the local planning authority's website as a background document and published in accordance with statutory requirements which include the requirement to consult with certain stipulated bodies. An environmental statement is a statement which includes at least:

(a)    a description of the proposed development comprising information on the site, design, size and other relevant features of the [proposed] development;

(b)    a description of the likely significant effects of the proposed development on the environment;

(c)    a description of any features of the proposed development, or measures envisaged in order to avoid, prevent or reduce and, if possible, offset likely significant adverse effects on the environment;

(d)    a description of the reasonable alternatives studied by the developer, which are relevant to the proposed development and its specific characteristics, and an indication of the main reasons for the option chosen, taking into account the effects of the development on the environment;

(e)    a non-technical summary of the information referred to in sub-paragraphs (a) to (d);

and

(f)    any additional information specified in Schedule 4 relevant to the specific characteristics of the particular development or type of development and to the environmental

---

[2]    Per Regulation 4(2).

features likely to be significantly affected.[3]

It is not, for present purposes, necessary to dwell on "*Schedule 1*" developments. These are, generally, large-scale developments which are unlikely to cross the desk of planning case officers on a regular basis. Schedule 2 developments can, however, present on a regular basis. The Schedule sets out tables which denominate the description of relevant developments and applicable thresholds and criteria, for example, motorway service areas where the area of the development exceeds 0.5ha. As noted above, the fact that the proposed project falls within a particular descriptor or threshold is not conclusive as to whether or not the environmental assessment process should be engaged. To do so it must be the case that the proposed development is likely to have a significant effect on the environment. Schedule 3 of the regulations sets out selection criteria which should be taken into account in assessing significant effects for Schedule 2 development:

## (1) Characteristics of development

The characteristics of development must be considered with particular regard to:

(a)   the size and design of the whole development;

(b)   cumulation with other existing development and/or approved development;

(c)   the use of natural resources, in particular land, soil, water and biodiversity;

(d)   the production of waste;

(e)   pollution and nuisances;

(f)   the risk of major accidents and/or disasters relevant to the development concerned, including those caused by climate change, in accordance with scientific knowledge;

(g)   the risks to human health (for example, due to water contamination or air pollution).

## (2) Location of development

(1)   The environmental sensitivity of geographical areas likely to be affected by development must be considered, with particular regard, to -

(a)   the existing and approved land use;

(b)   the relative abundance, availability, quality and regenerative capacity of natural resources (including soil, land, water and biodiversity) in the area and its underground;

---

[3]   Per Regulation 18.

(c)     the absorption capacity of the natural environment, paying particular attention to the following areas:

    (i)      wetlands, riparian areas, river mouths;

    (ii)     coastal zones and the marine environment;

    (iii)    mountain and forest areas;

    (iv)     nature reserves and parks;

    (v)      European sites and other areas classified or protected under national legislation;

    (vi)     areas in which there has already been a failure to meet the environmental quality standards, laid down in Union legislation and relevant to the project, or in which it is considered that there is such a failure;

    (vii)    densely populated areas;

    (viii)   landscapes and sites of historical, cultural or archaeological significance.

(3)     **Types and characteristics of the potential impact**

The likely significant effects of the development on the environment must be considered in relation to criteria set out in paragraphs 1 and 2 above, with regard to the impact of the development on the factors specified in regulation 4(2), taking into account:

(a)     the magnitude and spatial extent of the impact (for example geographical area and size of the population likely to be affected);

(b)     the nature of the impact;

(c)     the transboundary nature of the impact;

(d)     the intensity and complexity of the impact;

(e)     the probability of the impact;

(f)     the expected onset, duration, frequency and reversibility of the impact;

(g)     the cumulation of the impact with the impact of other existing and/or approved development;

(h)     the possibility of effectively reducing the impact.

If a proposed project falls within Schedule 2, then the question of whether or not an environmental impact assessment should be carried out is decided by a *"screening"* process. In the first instance, it is the function of the local planning authority to screen the application and consider whether the proposed project may have a significant impact on the environment. The developer is entitled to request a *"screening opinion"* from the local planning authority prior to making the application. Alternatively, the developer might (in order to save time) accept that an environmental impact assessment is appropriate and, thereby, submit an environmental statement along with his application. If the developer simply submits an application without screening opinion, or without an environmental statement, the local planning authority should produce a screening opinion in any event.

The case of *R (Swire) v SSHCLG* [2020] EWHC 1298 (Admin) is important in this context and in connection with *"made land"*. This was a judicial review of a decision that an environmental impact assessment was not required for a proposed development within the Kent Down Area of Outstanding Natural Beauty. The development involved the demolition of existing buildings and the construction of 20 dwellings. Whilst a relatively small development, the site involved a *"sensitive area"* and, accordingly, it was incumbent upon the council to provide a screening opinion. It was common ground that the site was contaminated due to the burial of carcasses infected with bovine spongiform encephalopathy (BSE). It had been disused for more than ten years; however, a permit for animal carcass rendering was still in force. The developer had commissioned site investigation and risk assessment reports which were submitted to the local authority in support of the application for planning permission. However, none of these reports made any reference to either the site's former use for BSE-infected animal carcass disposal from 1998 or any risk of contamination from such use. Indeed, the authors of the reports were not even aware of this former use. Notwithstanding, the council opined that an environmental impact assessment would not be needed because the redevelopment of the site for residential purposes was not likely to have any significant adverse effects on the environment, as a significant adverse effect could be overcome through the imposition of conditions at the reserved matter stage. The matter was then referred to the Secretary of State with a request for screening direction; however, the Secretary of State concluded that the development was not EIA development. The High Court quashed the Secretary of State's decision. Although the site was acknowledged to be a site burial ground, very limited evidence had been provided as to the nature of the contamination and the hazards which such contaminants might present for the homes and gardens to be constructed and as to any safe and effective methods for detecting, managing and eliminating such contamination and hazards. The reality was that the original risk assessment and site investigation reports did not mention BSE. Certain correspondence had been exchanged, but this was unsupported by any research. It was held that the Secretary of State had purported to adopt the precautionary approach, in accepting that there was a need for BSE risks to be assessed; however, he simply assumed that the approach conveyed in the conditions would successfully safeguard against BSE without sufficient information to support that approach.

Lang J said:

"In my view, the reports were very inadequate in this regard. The information was available in the public domain, the BSE crisis had occurred within living memory, and it was well-known in the locality, as demonstrated by the objections made by the Claimant and others to the planning application."

Her Honour added:

"There was a lack of any expert evidence and risk assessment on the nature of any BSE-related contamination at the Site, and any hazards it might present to human health. The measures which might be required to remediate any such contamination and hazards had not been identified. This was a difficult and novel problem for all parties to address. It was acknowledged by the Council in its screening opinion, acting on the advice of the Environmental Health Practitioner, that specialist advice would be needed to consider the remediation of prions associated with CJD/BSE. Therefore condition 21 merely referred to the requirement that a written method statement for the remediation of land and/or groundwater would have to be agreed by the Council without any party knowing what the remediation for BSE-related infection might comprise. The Defendant adopted the Council's approach in his screening opinion. But because of the lack of expert evidence, the Defendant was simply not in a position to make an "informed judgment" (per Dyson LJ in Jones,[4] at [39]) as to whether, or to what extent, any proposed remedial measures could or would remediate any BSE-related contamination. It follows that when the Defendant concluded that "he was satisfied that the proposed measures would satisfactorily safeguard and address potential problems of contamination" and that "the proposed measures would safeguard the health of prospective residents of the development", he was making an assumption that any measures proposed under condition 21 would be successful, without sufficient information to support that assumption. As Pill LJ said in Gillespie[5], at [41], "the test applied was not the correct one. The error was in the assumption that the investigations and works contemplated in condition VI could be treated, at the time of the screening decision, as having had a successful outcome". Whilst "not all uncertainties have to be resolved" (per Dyson LJ in Jones at [39]), on the facts this case was not one "where the likely effectiveness of conditions or proposed remedial or ameliorative measures can be predicted with confidence" (per Pill LJ at [34]). As the Site was proposed for residential housing, a higher standard of remediation would be required than if it were intended to adapt it for an industrial use, or merely to decontaminate it and return it to woodland (some sites will never be suitable for residential housing, because of industrial contamination)."

Whilst specific to EIA, this passage exemplifies the approach to be taken when proposing conditions in respect of sites affected by contamination.

---

[4]    *R (Jones) v Mansfield DC* [2003] EWCA Civ 1408.
[5]    *Gillespie v First Secretary of State* [2003] EWCA Civ 400.

A developer may, also, request a *"scoping opinion"* from the local planning authority. The scoping opinion will provide local planning authorities opinion as to the information to be included in the environmental statement. If the local planning authority fails to provide the opinion, then the developer has the ability to apply for one to the Secretary of State.

**13.2    Schedule 4 - information for inclusion in environmental statements**
An Environmental Statement should include the following:

(1)    A description of the development, including in particular:

(a)    a description of the location of the development;

(b)    a description of the physical characteristics of the whole development, including, where relevant, requisite demolition works, and the land-use requirements during the construction and operational phases;

(c)    a description of the main characteristics of the operational phase of the development (in particular any production process), for instance, energy demand and energy used, nature and quantity of the materials and natural resources (including water, land, soil and biodiversity) used;

(d)    an estimate, by type and quantity, of expected residues and emissions (such as water, air, soil and subsoil pollution, noise, vibration, light, heat, radiation and quantities and types of waste produced during the construction and operation phases.

Comment: If treatment works are anticipated, then items (b) to (d) will be of particular importance.

(2)    A description of the reasonable alternatives (for example in terms of development design, technology, location, size and scale) studied by the developer, which are relevant to the proposed project and its specific characteristics, and an indication of the main reasons for selecting the chosen option, including a comparison of the environmental effects.

(3)    A description of the relevant aspects of the current state of the environment (baseline scenario) and an outline of the likely evolution thereof without implementation of the development as far as natural changes from the baseline scenario can be assessed with reasonable effort on the basis of the availability of environmental information and scientific knowledge.

Comment: In most cases, this information should be available from a concurrent assessment of the pre-development baseline for the purposes of calculating biodiversity net gain.

(4)    A description of the factors specified in regulation 4(2) likely to be significantly affected by the development: population, human health, biodiversity (for example fauna and

flora), land (for example land take), soil (for example organic matter, erosion, compaction, sealing), water (for example hydromorphological changes, quantity and quality), air, climate (for example greenhouse gas emissions, impacts relevant to adaptation), material assets, cultural heritage, including architectural and archaeological aspects, and landscape.

(5) A description of the likely significant effects of the development on the environment resulting from, inter alia:

(a) the construction and existence of the development, including, where relevant, demolition works;

(b) the use of natural resources, in particular land, soil, water and biodiversity, considering as far as possible the sustainable availability of these resources;

(c) the emission of pollutants, noise, vibration, light, heat and radiation, the creation of nuisances, and the disposal and recovery of waste;

(d) the risks to human health, cultural heritage or the environment (for example due to accidents or disasters);

(e) the cumulation of effects with other existing and/or approved projects, taking into account any existing environmental problems relating to areas of particular environmental importance likely to be affected or the use of natural resources;

(f) the impact of the project on climate (for example the nature and magnitude of greenhouse gas emissions) and the vulnerability of the project to climate change;

(g) the technologies and the substances used.[6]

Comment: Again, the exhaustion of a number of the items on this list should be in parallel with the acquisition and assessment of information for the purposes of biodiversity net gain. Also, of course, these considerations will apply to the treatment phase for land contamination.

---

[6] Paras. 6–10 include further improvements.

# Chapter 14

# Contaminated Land And Viability

*R&D66: 2008 Volume 1* makes it clear that a treatment strategy is not once and for all, but may have to be evolved as knowledge of the condition of the site is refined:

> *"Short listing of the potential remediation options should take account of the available information and any associated uncertainties. For example, a technique may be initially identified as potentially suitable on the basis of its general effectiveness, but later, more site-specific evaluation may eventually lead to it being discounted."*[1]

> *Before requiring a developer to carry out a remediation strategy, the local planning authority should bear in mind that "Remediation of contaminated land can be an expensive and technically difficult process."*[2]

Annex D of The Homes and Communities Agency publication *Guidance on dereliction, demolition and remediation costs* (March 2015)[3] provided two interesting case studies relating to residential schemes:

- Case Study A was an 8 hectare site in outer London. The total cost of the treatment works was approximately £1.57 million equating to approximately £200,000 per hectare.

- Case Study B was a 6 hectare riverside site in the Yorkshire and Humberside region. The cost of the treatment works was approximately £4.7 million equating to approximately £790,000 per hectare.

Also worth noting:

- In the case of Elstree Film Studios in Borehamwood, the cost was £3,455,000 and the timescale was 9 months.

- On a smaller scale, Lioncourt Homes treated and made good the 0.95ha site of a former scrap yard at Willenhall, West Midlands for a housing development. The cost was £260,000 and the timescale was 10 weeks.[4]

Whilst not primarily concerned with the planning process, the former guidance in CLR 11[5] alluded to the need to balance costs and benefits in the broader context of site remediation:

---

[1]  Para.3.2.1.

[2]  Defra Research Project Final Report Defra Project Code: SP1001 2010.

[3]  Now withdrawn.

[4]  https://www.remediation.com/pdf/case-stuides/geostream-willenhall-case-study-september-2018.pdf.

[5]  Page 8.

> *"At several stages of the risk management process, judgements have to be made about the relative costs and benefits of particular courses of action or decisions. This "cost–benefit analysis" is an inherent part of the management of environmental risks in a sustainable way, and is a formal component of particular stages of regulatory regimes. It allows for the structured and transparent balance of the costs (usually, but not always, in financial terms) against benefits, which can be wide-ranging depending on the context – for example, enhanced health and environmental protection, <u>increased commercial confidence in the condition of the land</u> or simply greater certainty in ultimate decision making. <u>The scope and particular criteria for any cost–benefit analysis will depend on the context.</u>"* (Emphasis added)

## 14.1    The zero-sum problem and financial viability

Those who have studied economics might be familiar with the expression *"zero-sum"*. This expression seems to have derived from game theory and seeks to represent a situation where the gain or loss of each participant is (within the rules of the game) exactly balanced by the gains and losses of other participants with the result that, when all gains and losses are totalled up, they amount to the overall starting value of the pot. One way of imagining this is by way of the proverbial pie which can be cut into any number of slices, albeit that the total volume of the pie remains the same throughout, notwithstanding the distribution of shares between those who have the pleasure of eating it.[6] The translation of this concept into economic theory is, thus, discernible. If the sum total of money on the table in a particular game is fixed, then there will be winners and losers; however, this will be by way of a redistribution of the fixed total sum within the initial pot. The simple fact of the matter is that, when it comes to land development projects, one is often dealing with the zero-sum game.

This is to say that a particular project will yield a particular financial outcome and this is, for all practical purposes, the fixed pot of money which is on the table. It is out of this pot that all of the costs of bringing forward the project must be brought. There is no other money in the game. If the total cost of the projected project exceeds the anticipated financial income then the project is not viable. This excursion into economics and game theory is not, therefore, an academic one. If a local planning authority is seeking certain adjustments or benefits in a scheme, and they will cost money, then the money must be found out of the finite resources which are available within the financial model for the scheme. Unless there is some form of external government support, this is an exercise in the redistribution of costs within a closed zero-sum model.

To put it another way, one has to rob Peter to pay Paul. Thus, if the members of the planning committee take the view that the developer should provide certain provisions within a scheme, then, they should also recognise that the money for doing so might be taken from other planning benefits within the scheme, for example affordable housing.

---

[6]    Another analogy is to think of the First Law of Thermodynamics: i.e. the total energy of an isolated system is constant; energy can be transformed from one form to another, but can be neither created nor destroyed.

To put it another way, the pursuit of planning benefits within a scheme must be an itera-tive process which takes account of the financial viability assessment for the scheme. It is pointless asking for a benefit when the developer will, palpably, not to be able to afford it. Furthermore, this iterative process must take into account the cash flow model for most development schemes. This is to say, a model which will normally be heavily reliant on negative cash flow for a significant part of the early stages of the development process. For example, a housebuilder will not start making money until it actually starts selling houses. This could be some significant period of time from the date of commencement of the devel-opment, during which the developer is having to finance construction operations et cetera out of capital.[7] This means that, in terms of the cash flow model for a typical residential development, the loading of the costs of benefits onto the early stages of a scheme by the local planning authority is going to be unnecessarily detrimental when, in practice, it might be possible to defer those costs until a later stage, preferably when houses are being sold and income is flowing into the financial model.

Having discussed what might be described as the *"meta-narrative"*, it is now possible to go on and think about how this might be reflected in day-to-day development control transactions.

Take, for example, the situation where a large residential scheme is in front of members for approval. Both members and officers seem to be happy with the scheme; however, Councillor Brown suddenly proposes an additional planning condition. He suggests that all of the houses within the development should be provided with charging points for electrical vehicles. All members agree that this sounds to be eminently sensible and so the application is approved subject to this additional condition. There is, however, a significant problem in this scenario; namely, that no one has taken the trouble to consider how much these electric vehicle charging points are going to cost. Patently, no one has given any consideration to the impact that this additional cost may have upon the cash flow model for the scheme in question. Not only are these in the overall costs of the scheme, they will, also, have a sig-nificant impact on the cash flow model. They will, of course, need to be picked up during the construction process. If so, then it is not simply the costs of providing these charging points but also the notional cost of financing those construction costs until such time as they can be met out of the income flowing from the scheme. It might be doing Councillor Brown a disservice, but it is doubtful whether he re-ran the economic viability assessment for the scheme before venturing to propose his additional condition. Put it another way, if one supposes that the additional cost of a charging point will be £300 per dwelling, and it is proposed that the scheme will deliver 100 houses, then the overall base costs will be £30,000.[8] Given that the scheme is a zero-sum model, then this money must come from somewhere within the scheme. Unless the developer releases some of his anticipated profit,[9] money must be drawn from elsewhere. It might be the case that the developer then reverts saying that he cannot, now, provide all the affordable housing he initially promised or that

---

[7]   This is what financiers sometimes call a high *"burn rate"* of initial capital.

[8]   Plus financing costs!

[9]   In which case he might just walk away and put his money into a less troublesome investment.

the budget for affordable housing must be trimmed by £30,000. The ultimate question for Councillor Brown, in reality, might come down to whether or not he prefers affordable housing to electric vehicle charging points.

It is, therefore, suggested that one of the considerations which needs to flow through the minds of those within local planning authorities at the outset is whether proposed benefits are financially viable and, if so, whether the realisation of those benefits will be at the expense of other benefits.

Property development can be described as being capital intensive and cash-flow poor, particularly residential schemes. The typical model involves the following typical expenditures before any income is derived from the completion and sale of buildings:

• land acquisition;

• planning costs and fees;

• ecology surveys[10] and environmental impact assessments;

• architects fees;

• construction;

• marketing; and

• finance.

Even then, the developer is taking a risk that his financial model for the site will stand up over the months, or years, before an income stream is realised. Clearly, one way of closing the gap between outgoings and income is to split a large site into phases, so that the income stream from earlier phases goes to cross-finance the outgoings on later phases. This may mean keeping the costs of later phases down until they become viable.

It is submitted that one cannot treat town and country planning as isolated from the commercial realities of everyday property development. If the scheme is not financially viable, or if it is too risky, then it will not go ahead and, if financial viability is compromised in some way, then it might be the case that the scheme may go ahead but without benefits which are being sought by the local planning authority (for example affordable housing). The way in which concerns about possible land contamination are approached can have a significant effect on investor confidence and also the cash-flow model for the scheme. These are very important and central matters and should be taken into account in formulating a strategy for the site. Simply arguing that the whole site should be *"remediated"* or *"cleaned*

---

[10]    Particularly bearing in mind the *"biodiversity net gain"* provisions in the Environment Act 2021.

*up*" before any development takes place might sound impressive in an ideal world; however, it might prove commercially unrealistic with the result of the scheme is compromised or never goes ahead at all.

This matter of timing is important because it goes to the question of whether a developer might be deterred by the prospect of "*front-loading*" his application with the costs of full site investigations when the principle of the development has not been established. This might be one risk too many for some developers or investors.

Having mentioned matters of viability, CLR 11 went on to say:[11]

> "*Such considerations should not challenge the basic technical structure of the risk management process. However, they strongly influence the way in which it is put into practice – they can determine the level of detailed work carried out at any particular stage, the speed at which projects move through the process and the level of resource that may be available.*" (Emphasis added)

This, it is submitted, flags up a very important (perhaps vital) material consideration when one comes to the planning process. If a permission is granted which conditions the delivery of a risk management programme until the reserved matters stage, then this gives the developer the confidence to invest in the detailed design of the scheme and further site investigations. If the LPA insists on the carrying out of all this work before the principle of development is established, this may act as a disincentive to the development of brownfield sites, which runs counter to the notion of sustainable development. It would, almost certainly, considerably slow the delivery of residential sites to no demonstrable practical purpose. The weight to be attributed to the latter point is enhanced where the local planning authority does not have the advantage of a "*5-years' supply*" of deliverable housing land and cannot afford to deter potential housebuilders.

## 14.2    The planning process
The planning process has evolved in a way which reflects the commercial realities of real estate development. To put it bluntly, if it were commercially viable for all schemes to be progressed via full planning permissions only, outline permissions would not exist. They exist because the alternative would be that many would be investors would shy away from the expenses and uncertainties of a less flexible system in favour of more robust investments. Outline permissions are necessary to provide investors with confidence that the principle of development has been accepted before ploughing more money into their schemes. There is no need to provide empirical evidence to support this proposition because it is well-known, embedded in the system and plainly trite.

If the principle of development is accepted by the grant of an outline permission, then one of the details which remains to be settled is the distribution of uses across the site. The

---

[11]    Page 8.

net developable acreage always falls far short of the gross acreage because of the need to provide infrastructure such as roads, open space, structural landscaping and, nowadays, sustainable drainage (e.g. balancing ponds) and biodiversity net gain land. Whilst the general distribution of these uses might be foreshadowed in the Design and Access Statement and illustrative layouts, the devil of the reality will be in the detail. This is important in the present context because each discrete use will have different sensitivities to contaminants and what is *"unsuitable"* for one area might be *"suitable"* for another. Thus, dwellings will be sensitive uses whereas hard infrastructure (such as roads, car parks etc) will not only be more robust but also may act as mitigation measures in themselves. For example, a hard-surfaced car park will act to cap sub-surface emissions (e.g. landfill gas). It follows that it is not realistic to consider the adaptive treatment of a large site until matters of detail are brought forward at the reserved matters stage. Furthermore, it might be the case that mitigation measures are part of the built development itself, for example, passive ventilation measures to counter landfill gas or radon gas emissions.

## 14.3    *R (Judson) v Amber Valley Borough Council*

*R (Judson) v Amber Valley Borough Council* [2020] EWHC 517 (QB) was the judicial review of the grant of an outline planning permission for the construction of up to 220 houses at Nether Farm, Somecotes by Amber Valley Borough Council. The site was within 100 metres of the estimated boundary of a former landfill site. Amber Valley Borough Council is located in the Nottingham coal fields and so considers applications for the development of brownfield sites on a regular basis. Not surprisingly, it is reasonable to suspect that some may be subject to contamination, either from mine-workings or from the re-use of mines or quarries for other purposes. Hence, the council is experienced in dealing with sites which might be contaminated. Notwithstanding, some local residents objected to the application and, when permission was granted, they chose to challenge the council's decision in the High Court. The challenge was not successful.

The council was provided with a Phase 1 Assessment and, having regard to it, determined that *"Grampian"* type conditions would be imposed on the permission to ensure that any pollution would be detected and (if need be) managed as part of the development scheme. The issue for the court was, having regard to local and national policies, whether this was the correct approach.

The development plan was the Amber Valley Local Plan. The relevant policy was EN18 which provided:

> *"Planning permission will be granted for the reclamation and re-use of derelict, unstable and contaminated land, providing that where it is suspected or known that land is contaminated, a detailed and independent assessment is undertaken to identify the nature and extent of contamination and any remedial or mitigating measure which need to be undertaken.*

> *"Conditions may be attached to any planning permission to ensure that effective remedial or mitigating measures are taken to treat, control or contain any contamination so*

*as not to expose the occupiers of development and neighbouring land to unacceptable risk, or lead to the contamination of any water course or aquifer."*

It is worth pausing here to note that the policy did not say whether the *"suspicion"* should be a strong one; hence, whether it could be triggered by a mere suspicion only.[12] As noted above, it is arguable that the weight and reasonableness of a suspicion may be a factor in determining the weight of the administrative response.

The claimant submitted that, on a proper interpretation, Policy EN18 required a full assessment of potential contamination before outline planning permission was granted.

The council submitted that Policy EN18 properly interpreted did not require potential contamination issues to be resolved prior to the grant of outline permission rather than by way of conditions. Lewis J stated that counsel for the council:

*"... submitted that the claimant's approach would involve a radical departure from the usual way of dealing with such matters and would deter developers who might wish to know that a proposed development was acceptable in principle, subject to detailed investigations of certain matters before the development could be commenced ..."*

As noted above, the notion that a developer should provide a complete set of site assessments before the principle of development is established would compromise many otherwise beneficial schemes due to front-loading the (sometimes very expensive) costs of a complete suite of assessments. The further notion that a full and detailed risk management strategy could be composed before outline permission is granted would be wholly unrealistic and, frankly, naïve.

Lewis J stated that the wording of EN18 did not support the view that it required any questions of the potential presence of pollutants on the site to be investigated and resolved prior to the grant of outline permission with conditions only being used to deal with methods of *"remediation"* or mitigation. It did not impose any particular framework or timetable for carrying out the detailed investigation. It simply recognised that planning permission should be granted for development on contaminated land provided that a detailed assessment is undertaken and treatment or other adaptive measures are carried out. The second paragraph of Policy EN18 recognised that conditions may be attached to ensure that effective measures are taken. That cannot reasonably be read as meaning that conditions can only deal with *"remediation"* and mitigation and cannot in any case deal with investigations or assessment.

Lewis J stated:

---

[12] Or, as counsel for the Interested Party put it at the Permission hearing, a mere *"suggestion"*. NB: The author appeared for the council at that hearing!

> *"[24] The wording of Policy EN18, therefore, is consistent with an interpretation whereby detailed investigations to assess the nature and extent of any possible contamination may be dealt with by conditions requiring such matters to be investigated prior to the development being commenced if the defendant reasonably considers that to be appropriate way of proceeding in a particular case."*

He added:

> *"[25] Furthermore, that approach is consistent with the policy underlying Policy EN18. The aim is ensure that land can be brought into use provided that any risks to the occupiers of the development are identified and addressed. That may be done, in appropriate cases, by conditions requiring investigations to be done, and any necessary remediation undertaken, prior to the commencement of the development."*

Paragraph 121 of the then extant version of the NPPF provided that planning policies and decisions should ensure that:

- *The site is suitable for its new use taking account of ground conditions and land instability, including from natural hazards or former activities such as mining, pollution arising from previous uses and any proposals for mitigation including land remediation or impacts on the natural environment arising from that remediation;*

- *After remediation, as a minimum, land should not be capable of being determined as contaminated land under Part IIA of the Environmental Protection Act 1990; and*

- *Adequate site investigation information, prepared by a competent person, is presented.*

Lewis J stated:

> *"[31] ... There is nothing in paragraph 121 of the Framework to require that information to be provided, in all cases, prior to the grant of outline planning permission. A local planning authority may, in appropriate cases, require that information to [sic] be prepared pursuant to a condition attached to the grant of outline planning permission. For those reasons, the grant of outline planning permission here does not involve any failure to have regard to a material planning consideration, namely the provisions of paragraph 121 of the Framework."*

# Chapter 15

# Planning Obligations And Contaminated Land

The phrase *"planning obligation"* arose as a result of amendments made to Section 106 of the Town and Country Planning Act 1990 by the Planning and Compensation Act 1991.

Planning obligations are of importance because they can be used to overcome the doctrine of *"privity of contract"*. This legal doctrine means in essence, that, generally, the terms of a contract are binding only upon the parties to that contract – they are not binding on a party's successors. Thus, a landowner who enters into an ordinary covenant relating to development on their land could sell the land and the new owner might escape the covenant because they were not a party to the contract. Some types of restrictive covenant may run with the land and bind successors in title, but some do not. Positive covenants (e.g. to carry out works on the land) do not. This situation is manifestly unhelpful to bodies seeking to impose restrictive or positive obligations on the land (in the public interest) because they need to be sure that such obligations cannot be avoided by a sale of the land.

A planning obligation may be created either by a planning agreement or a unilateral undertaking. As its name implies, a planning agreement is a deed entered into between the persons interested in the land and the local planning authority. By contrast, a unilateral undertaking is a deed executed by the persons interested in the land only and delivered to the local planning authority.[1]

## 15.1    Section 106 of the Town and Country Planning Act 1990

It is imperative that the terms of Section 106 are borne in mind at all times when negotiating and settling planning obligations because Section 106 imposes a number of limitations on what can and cannot be done under its aegis.

Section 106(1) states:

> *"Any person interested in land in the area of a local planning authority may, by agreement or otherwise, enter into an obligation (referred to in this section and sections 106A and 106B as "a planning obligation"), enforceable to the extent mentioned in sub-section (3):*
>
> *(a) restricting the development or use of the land in any specified way;*

---

[1]   The Glossary to the National Planning Policy Framework (2021) defines a Planning Obligation as a *"legal agreement entered into under Section 106 of the Town and Country Planning Act 1990 to mitigate the impacts of a development proposal."* This is wrong because, of course, it fails to include Unilateral Undertakings – which are not *"agreements"*.

(b) *requiring specified operations or activities to be carried out in, on, under or over the land;*

(c) *requiring the land to be used in any specified way; or*

(d) *requiring a sum or sums to be paid to the authority on a specified date or dates or periodically."*

A planning obligation may be created either by a planning agreement or a unilateral undertaking.

## Section 106(13)

Before moving on to consider Section 106 in detail, it is necessary to pause and consider the impact of Section 106(13) on sub-clauses (a), (b) and (c), all of which use the word *"specified"*. The word *"specified"* has a particular effect within Section 106 and it is defined by Section 106(13):

> *"In this section "Specified" means specified in the instrument by which the planning obligation is entered into..."*

The apparent effect of Section 106(13) is that a requirement in a planning obligation may be defective if it leaves essential items to be settled by a later document. This begs the question of whether a requirement to carry out a scheme in a document which is approved after the date of the obligation is valid.

If the scheme approach is adopted via Section 106(1)(a), then it is difficult to see a problem. This restricts the development or use of the land *"in any specified way"* and the *"specified"* restriction should be articulated in the document itself, namely, that the commencement of development is subject to a clear embargo unless and until the relevant scheme (e.g. a treatment scheme or an aftercare scheme) is approved.

## Section 106(1)(a)

Section 106(1)(a) allows the imposition of restrictive covenants, for example *"no buildings on open spaces"*. However, subsection (1)(a) can also allow for positive actions if phrased in the negative or *"Grampian"* form i.e.:

> *"No part of the Development shall be begun unless and until a [ risk management scheme] has been submitted to and approved by the Council.*

> *"No part of the Development shall be begun unless an Aftercare Management Plan has been submitted to and approved by the Council."*

Indeed, it might be the case that the planning obligation sets out a specification for the said Aftercare Management Plan, for example, that the outputs meet standards which may be measured by way of an approved metric. It should, also, go on to provide that the approved

Plan shall then be carried out by reference to a timetable and might provide that long-term financial security is provided by way of a bond or fund of some description.

### Section 106(1)(b)
Requirements under Section 106(1)(b) can underpin the carrying out of on-site works (but not off-site works on land not controlled by any party to the development).

Section 106(1)(d) can then also be used to underpin long-term care requirements and requirements might be secured by bonding arrangements, guarantees etc (see below).

### Section 106(1)(c)
This is a relatively straightforward provision and, effectively, is the obverse of Section 106(1)(a). It allows for requirements that land shall be used in a particular positive way e.g. public open space etc.

### Section 106(1)(d)
This allows a variety of payment arrangements. It could encompass payments towards the achievement of identified objectives or a bond.[2]

Section 106(1)(d) does not use the word *"specified"*, therefore Section 106(13) does not appear to apply.

Section 106(2)(c) allows any payments under this provision to be calculated by reference to a formula.

Section 106(1)(d) would also appear to allow payments calculated by reference to enhanced land values resulting from the development.

Arguably, Section 106(1)(d) allows for *"roof tax"* payments. Section 106(1)(d) would also appear to allow payments calculated by reference to enhanced land values resulting from the development.

Some local planning authorities seek financial contributions by reference to the size of the development or by way of a *"roof tax"*. This type of contribution is often sought as part of a fund that is being built up for a future infrastructure works which will be only partially funded by the particular project. For example, the local planning authority may anticipate that the full fund will be generated by a series of separate developments in the locality over a particular period. Each separate developer will then be expected to make payments into the *"pot"* as their development progresses. Clearly there are problems with this approach. The final sum in the fund might not be sufficient to cover the costs of the project because anticipated developments might fail to come forward. This creates uncertainty as to whether the developer's payment will ever be used. Thus, the prudent developer will ensure that, if

---

[2]    It would be necessary to settle the bond so that the bondsman becomes a *"person interested"* in the land: per Section 106(1).

their contribution is not used, then it will be repaid. A properly worded repayment clause will provide for repayment if the specified work is not commenced within a defined period or is subsequently abandoned, and the developer should also ensure that interest upon the sum is also paid to them.

This practice was examined by the Court of Appeal in *R v South Northamptonshire District Council and Another ex parte Crest Homes Plc and Others* [1994] 3 P.L.R. 47, but Circular 1/97 commented on the *Crest Homes* case as follows:

> "On the facts of the case, the planning obligations were held to be lawful, but this should not be interpreted as providing a justification for similar arrangements in other circumstances. As Lord Justice Henry explained, the facts of the case were crucial "because they legitimise a formula which, if used in other factual contexts, could be struck down as an unauthorised local development land tax" (page 12, footnote 3)."[3]

The *Crest Homes* case indicates that advance payments need to be based on an accurate pre-estimate of the proposed expenditure and the better course of action, for local planning authorities, would be to try and ensure that any payment arrangements are by reference to accurate pre-estimates.

## 15.2    The Community Infrastructure Levy Regulations 2010

These Regulations place limitations on the use of planning obligations. Regulation 122 provides:

> *122.–(1) This regulation applies where a relevant determination is made which results in planning permission being granted for development.*
>
> *(2) A planning obligation may only constitute a reason for granting planning permission for the development if the obligation is–*
>
> > *(a) necessary to make the development acceptable in planning terms;*
> >
> > *(b) directly related to the development; and*
> >
> > *(c) fairly and reasonably related in scale and kind to the development.*
>
> *(3) In this regulation -*
>
> *"planning obligation" means a planning obligation under section 106 of TCPA 1990 and includes a proposed planning obligation; and*

---

3    A more fundamental question is whether a *"roof tax"* is a breach of the Bill of Rights 1688/1689.

*"relevant determination" means a determination made on or after 6th April 2010 -*

*(a) under section 70, 76A or 77 of TCPA 1990 of an application for planning permission which is not an application to which section 73 of TCPA 1990 applies; or*

*(b) under section 79 of TCPA 1990 of an appeal where the application which gives rise to the appeal is not one to which section 73 of TCPA 1990 applies.*

*"determination" means a determination -*

*(a) under section 70, 76A or 77 of TCPA 1990 of an application for planning permission which is not an application to which section 73 of TCPA 1990 applies, or*

*(b) under section 79 of TCPA 1990 of an appeal where the application which gives rise to the appeal is not one to which section 73 applies.*

It is important to consider the impact of regulation 122 when determining whether or not a planning obligation is an appropriate approach to the site which is affected by, or may be affected by, contamination.

The first precondition is that the planning obligation may only constitute a reason for granting planning permission for the development if the obligation is necessary to make the development acceptable in planning terms. The central test in respect of this precondition is, therefore, that of *"necessity"* and this must be distinguished from that which is merely desirable. It may not be *"necessary"* to require that a developer should provide for measures which goes beyond the specific requirements of the particular site in question. Whilst it might be considered desirable to require levels of *"remediation"* which go beyond that which is *"suitable for use"*, this additional burden is not necessary.

The second precondition is that a planning obligation may only constitute a reason for granting planning permission if it is directly related to the development. Thus, for example, it would normally be wrong to expect a developer to provide off-site measures which have no bearing on the condition of the relevant development site. Likewise, it would normally be wrong to impose a *"roof tax"* to fund the treatment of land outside a development site because this would be unlawful taxation (see above). The exception to these two examples would be if part of the income from a proposed development is put forward as *"enabling development"*: see Paragraph 15.7 below.[4]

---

[4]    Arguably, a charge of this kind should be by way of a separate Community Infrastructure Levy requirement.

Finally, the obligation must be fairly and reasonably related in scale and kind to the development. Again, this test would not be met if a developer is required to provide for measures which go beyond the specific requirements of the particular site in question. Nor would this test be met where the local planning authority has adopted a prescribed formula which fails to consider each development proposal on its own site-specific merits. Indeed, given the very different circumstances of each site on a case-by-case basis, it is difficult to see how any rational or lawful formula could be thus contrived.

### 15.3    Conditions or planning obligations?

The starting point is that it is not unlawful to have a planning obligation which secures matters which could have been secured by planning conditions: *Good v Epping Forest DC* [1992] E.G.C.S. 64. Consequently, any objection to the use of a planning obligation, as opposed to planning conditions, will be based on policy only.

In typically Delphic terms, the National Planning Practice Guidance website states:

> *"Planning obligations, in the form of section 106 agreements and section 278 agreements,[5] should only be used where it is not possible to address unacceptable impacts through a planning condition."*

> *Paragraph: 003 Reference ID: 23b-003-20190901 Revision Date: 01-09-2019*

The words *"not possible"* make no sense because, of course, the real test is whether a planning obligation is a better mechanism for searching the objectives sought by the LPA. No explanation is given as to the reasons for this unhelpful mantra; but the more useful (now withdrawn) narrative to Circular 11/95 stated:

> *"12. It may be possible to overcome a planning objection to a development proposal equally well by imposing a condition on the planning permission or by entering into a planning obligation under section 106 of the Act. The Secretaries of State consider that in such cases the local planning authority should impose a condition rather than seek to deal with the matter by means of a planning obligation. This is because the imposition of restrictions by means of a planning obligation deprives the developer of the opportunity of seeking to have the restrictions varied or removed by an application or appeal under Part III of the Act if they are or become inappropriate or too onerous."*

The modern reality is that this objection is not a strong one. As the Circular went on to say:

---

[5]    En passant, the reference to Section 278 Agreements makes no sense whatsoever. They have to do with carrying out works on the highway (usually outside the site and on land outside the control of the developer) and, therefore, provide for the necessary licence to carry out the works, the specifications for the works and for financial security etc. None of these are remotely relevant to planning conditions and are, certainly, not *"planning obligations"*. One is left to wonder as to the author of this text!

> *"It should be noted, however, that section 106A of the Act allows a developer to apply to the local planning authority to discharge or modify a planning obligation after the expiry of five years after the obligation is entered into ..."*

Furthermore, it is now commonplace to find that a developer will approach the local planning authority with a request to modify a planning obligation where the costs of discharging it will have an adverse impact on the viability of their scheme. This, also, presupposes that the planning obligation in question does not, in any event, contain its own internal mechanisms for the variation of documents which have been produced pursuant to the obligation. For example, it might be the case that a planning obligation provides that a scheme shall be submitted to and approved by the local planning authority before the development is commenced. However, it might equally be the case that the obligation allows for the scheme to be varied from time to time in writing by the parties. Accordingly, it would not be necessary to invoke Section 106A save in circumstances where the developer is suggesting that the whole notion of an approved scheme should be dropped from the obligation in toto. In the vast majority of cases, proposed modifications will relate to matters of detail such as changes in housing mix, plot distribution et cetera.

Thus, the policy case for preferring conditions is not persuasive, particularly given the paucity of objective reasoning. The practical and logistical reasons for the use of planning obligations in particular cases may, however, be compelling.

Planning obligations (especially bilateral planning agreements) offer a number of considerable advantages over conditions. A planning obligation can:

- include complex bonding/guarantee arrangements by way of security for performance;

- include expert determination/arbitration clauses;

- provide for the payment of money; and

- include obligations entered into by third parties e.g. mortgagees.

It is worth considering a worked example at this point. A condition might provide:

> *"No part of the development shall commence unless a Risk Management Plan incorporating the recommendations in the [****] report has been submitted to and approved by the local planning authority."*

This condition might, on the surface, appear to be perfectly unexceptional; however, there are a number of hidden problems.

First, one needs to consider a situation where there is a dispute between the parties as to the detailed content of the management plan. It might become necessary to resolve a dispute; however, the only dispute resolution mechanism available to the parties would (unless they can agree a mediation approach) be by way of an appeal to the Planning Inspectorate. Needless to say, this will take a considerable period of time. However, if the requirement is, instead, provided by way of a planning obligation, then the obligation should include a standard dispute resolution mechanism, hopefully by way of provisions requiring that disputes be resolved by an independent expert.

Secondly, it is not enough to consider the condition in isolation. It might be the case that the planning obligation for the scheme includes requirements relating to other matters. Thus, matters of treatment and future management of land affected by contamination may be intermingled with provisions in a planning obligation relating to sustainable drainage systems (SUDS), the provision of estate roads, public open space, the provision of strategic alternative natural green space (SANGS), biodiversity net gain land or the like by way of an overarching management strategy, perhaps involving the use of a management company. Accordingly, one might find that the matters mentioned in the condition are best drawn into the planning obligation so as to ensure an integrated approach and simplify enforcement.

## 15.4    Drafting planning obligations
### *"Trigger"* clauses

It is important that the parties are clear as to the date when the requirements in a planning obligation actually come into force. In the majority of cases, the date of grant of the relevant planning permission might not be the appropriate date because the planning permission might not be triggered for a considerable period of time – indeed it might not be used at all. In many cases there is little point in bringing a covenant into force when the planning permission which is the basis of the obligation is lying dormant and may well expire or be superseded by a later permission.

One common way of dealing with the point is by way of a *"trigger clause"*, e.g.:

> *"This planning obligation shall not come into force until and unless there is commenced*[6] *on the Land a material operation (as defined by section 56(4) of the Town and County Planning Act 1990) pursuant to the Planning Permission."*

The legal meaning of *"material operation"* is well settled by case-law and can include such minor operations as the pegging out of a highway or the digging of a trench: *Malvern Hills D.C. v S of S* [1982] J.P.L. 439. Section 56(4)(aa) includes demolition works as a material operation – something which could easily catch the unwary. It could be that the developer would prefer to have the obligation triggered by more substantial works or needs to carry out infrastructure works before starting the development itself (e.g. where an access will serve two or more separate sites). In that case the *"trigger"* could provide:

---

[6]    Some draftsmen say something like: *"This planning obligation shall not come into force until and unless a material operation is implemented [or carried out] on the land."* How do you judge when material operation is *"implemented"* or *"carried out"*? Ergo, keep it simple and refer to *"commencement"*, which should be easy to spot.

*"This planning obligation shall not come into force until and unless the construction of the foundations of the proposed [****] has been commenced."*

Another way of dealing with this is to narrow the meaning of *"material operation"*:

*"For the purposes of this clause [****], the phrase "material operation" shall not include any works or operations (including the creation of necessary access arrangements) for or in connection with:*

    *(a) site clearance or demolition;*

    *(b) site security;*

    *(c)˙ any site investigation or survey whether involving bore-holes or trenching or otherwise;*

    *(d) the diversion and laying of services; or*

    *(e) the display of advertisements."*

## Release clauses

It is important that the position of the parties on any future transfer of the land is addressed (so far as is possible) in the planning obligation itself.

The original landowner(s) might have no intention of carrying out the construction of the project. The landowner(s) may (as is often the case) simply obtain outline planning permission and then sell the site or parts of the site to developers who will finalise the planning position and construct the development. As such, the vendor(s) may not wish to be saddled with ongoing liability once the transfer is complete. Yet, having been a signatory to the planning obligation, the landowner(s) will remain liable in contract notwithstanding that a transfer has taken place. The purchaser will become liable as a successor in title under Section 106(3) of the 1990 Act, therefore the local planning authority will be able to sue either or both the vendor or the purchaser in the event of breach of the obligation. Effectively, they are jointly and severally liable. So how should the original landowner deal with the point?

Whilst Section 106(3) makes a planning obligation enforceable against successors in title, Section 106(4) states that the obligation may provide that a person shall not be bound by the obligation in respect of any period during which they no longer have an interest in the land.

Therefore, the usual approach is to require that the planning obligation contains a release clause along the following lines:

*"No person or body shall be bound by any obligation in this Deed in respect of any period during which that person or body no longer has an interest in the Land but without prejudice to liability for any subsisting breach of covenant prior to parting with such interest."*

Finally, it is important to think about the ultimate purchaser. In many cases, the intended final purchaser should not be saddled with any unacceptable liabilities. The classic example is the purchaser of an individual dwelling in a residential development. An appropriate clause in this case might be:

> *"No person or body shall be bound by any obligation in this Deed:*
>
> > *(a) in respect of any period during which that person or body no longer has an interest in the Property but without prejudice to liability for any subsisting breach of covenant prior to parting with such interest; or*
> >
> > *(b) "if that person or body is the owner of a single[7] dwelling within the Development."*

or if the scheme involves retail provision:

> *"if that person or body is the owner of a single[8] Retail Unit within the Development."*

Herein lies a dormant problem which becomes obvious when it is pointed out.[9] This occurs where the planning obligation not only requires that certain requirements be carried out after the new properties are occupied but also that those requirements must be discharged on the land which has just been sold to the said occupiers. In many cases, it may be politically undesirable to enforce against otherwise innocent occupiers, yet the original developer has put themselves out of the firing-line by their sale of the freehold. Thus, for example, requiring that certain treatment works take place after occupation might prove fruitless. Hence, the solution, in many cases, might be to ensure that the relevant measures are carried out before occupation or that the relevant land is excluded from plot sales.

## 15.5 *"Metricated Targets and Measurable Performance"*

It is essential that any clause which provides for the performance of any specified objective should be clear as to the objective which is being sought and should provide a measure of performance to show when the objective is been achieved. It must provide for defined metricated targets and measurable outputs. If it fails to do so, it is difficult to see how it will operate in practice. Take, as a simple example, the following:

> *"The Owner shall construct changing rooms on land to the north of the sports pitches with 6 months of the date that the sports pitches are substantially completed."*

One should see the problem immediately, namely that no specification is provided for the changing rooms. It is, therefore, impossible to glean from the agreement whether the changing rooms are going to be the size of a small garden shed or something more palatial.

---

[7] The word *"single"* prevents unintended releases on block purchases.

[8] Ditto.

[9] *"You have been in Afghanistan, I perceive"*: Mr Sherlock Holmes, *A Study in Scarlet* (Conan Doyle: 1887).

This clause is, by itself, largely unworkable and it is difficult to see what a court would make of it in the event that there is a dispute as to the character of the changing rooms to be erected. It might be argued that it is referring to changing rooms which will be reasonable having regard to the use to be made of them; however, even if this argument were to work, it does not absolve those who are drafting the agreement from the responsibility of doing so properly in the first instance.

Now take another example:

> *"The Owner shall identify two areas of land to the west of the Site (which shall be used for the deposit of spoil) for the approval of the Council and the said land shall then be used for the said deposits and maintained for the period of 25 years."*

It might well be the case that, leading up to the negotiation of the agreement, the parties had in mind the two particular areas of land. However, simply drafting on the basis that, at some future date, the, then, parties to the agreement (who might be completely different) will have the same images in their mind is somewhat optimistic. This type of drafting (which is not unusual) is badly flawed.

In this example, nothing is said about the respective sizes of the areas of land in question. It could be the case that the owner offers up two postage stamp sized areas of land and then asserts that they are required to do no more. It might be argued that one would then look to the background documents such as an illustrative masterplan. This, of course, presupposes that such documents will have survived to this later date. It is also posited on the perilous assumption that a court will have regard to extrinsic evidence in the interpretation of what should have been a self-contained legal document. The better alternative, it is suggested, is that, instead of storing up problems for the future, those drafting the agreement should attend to this point at the outset and provide some spatial parameters. Certainly, something will need to be said about the anticipated size of the areas in question. It might, also, be possible to annex drawings showing the indicative locations of these areas.

The next question, of course, is whether those drafting the agreement have attended to the matter of performance indicators. Here, again, there is a significant lack of particularity. The agreement gives no indication as to what maintenance means in this context. It is essential that some form of specification is indicated in the agreement, even if this is in a relatively simplified form at the outset.

Consider, also, the following definition:

> *""Remediation Strategy" means a written strategy for the management of long-term remediation across the Land."*

In analysing this clause, it is, again, necessary to break it down into whether there are defined targets and, if so, whether those targets are accompanied by measurable indicators of performance against them.

Whilst the clause provides for a written strategy for the management of the *"remediation"* exercise, it does not give a clear indication of the contents of the strategy. An alternative, and it is suggested better, approach would be to provide some heads of terms for the proposed strategy. These will not need to be voluminous; however, they would provide useful guidance for those who become charged with the task of providing the strategy.

A further problem relates to the situation where the discharge of risk management obligations is delivered in tranches which are tied to the different phases of a phased development. If this is going to be the case, then the planning obligation should specify, with precision, exactly how much treatment or adaptation is going to be tied to each particular phase. There is a danger that the parties might take the easy route of providing, in the obligation, that this phased delivery will be the subject of a scheme to be agreed after the date of the grant of planning permission, often once the development has been commenced. However, a difficulty is that a loosely drafted *"scheme"* requirement will be devoid of any indication of the benchmarks which could, in most cases, have been marked out in advance. As to the argument that the prescription of such benchmarks would result in an overly rigid approach, the short answer is, of course, that the *"scheme"* requirement can be tailed with the proviso that the scheme (including such benchmarks) could be *"modified from time to time by agreement between the developer and the local planning authority"*[10].

## 15.6    Practical enforcement of planning obligations
Subsections 106(5) and 106(6) provide the statutory enforcement mechanisms:

> *"(5) A restriction or requirement imposed under a planning obligation is enforceable by injunction.*

> *(6) Without prejudice to subsection (5), if there is a breach of a requirement in a planning obligation to carry out any operations in, on, under or over the land to which the obligation relates, the authority by whom the obligation is enforceable may –*

>> *(a) enter the land and carry out the operations; and*

>> *(b) recover from the person or persons against whom the obligation is enforceable any expenses reasonably incurred by them in so doing."*

It is important to consider the way in which these mechanisms might apply in real-life situations.

An elegantly drafted planning obligation is of little use to a local planning authority if it is either unenforceable or involves the expenditure of a disproportionate amount of powder and shot in the enforcement process. Yet many authorities fail to recognise that the provision

---

[10]    Unlike a planning condition.

of straightforward and efficient enforcement mechanisms is at the heart of the process. Take, for example, the following clause:

> *"If required by the Council by giving to the applicant at any time within 3 months from the date of the Commencement of Development at least 28 days written notice requiring the Applicant to enter into a contract with the Council or person of the Council's nomination for the transfer of an area of land within the Site of not less that 0.3 hectares ("the Donee Land") to the Council or said other person."*

This example is adapted from the real-life planning obligation, yet (leaving aside the grammar) it is fundamentally flawed because:

(a)   it involves the transfer of land, which does not fall within Section 106 (see Paragraph 15.1 above);

(b)   if it is outwith Section 106 then it is doubtful whether the clause is effective as an ordinary agreement to transfer under conventional property law principles because it does not appear to comply with the Law of Property (Miscellaneous Provisions) Act 1986;[11]

(c)   even if (a) and (b) can be overcome, the enforcement of such a clause would be time-consuming and difficult because it would involve forcing an unwilling applicant to execute a contract and transfer; and

(d)   nothing in the clause prevents the carrying out of the development whilst the applicant is in breach.

All of these criticisms could be avoided by the simple mechanism of planning an embargo upon progress of the development by way of a negative obligation:

> *"The Development shall not commence until the Donee Land[12] has been transferred to the Council or a person nominated by the Council PROVIDED that this clause shall be discharged and cease to be of effect in the event that the Council or its nominee fails to accept a transfer of the Donee Land when tendered by the Applicant in accordance with the following terms of this clause ..."*

If the Applicant fails to offer the transfer of the Donee Land in accordance with the terms of the planning obligation then the solution is straightforward; the council can apply for an injunction requiring cessation of all work on the development.

---

[11]   See *Jelson Ltd v Derby CC* [2000] JPC 203; see now *RG Kensington Management Co Ltd v Hutchinson IDH* [2003] 2 P. & C.R. 13.

[12]   In accordance with the principle of defining measurable targets (see above), the *"Donee Land"* should be defined with sufficient particularity as to its identifiable spatial characteristics.

If the planning obligation is designed to secure the payment of money to the council, then, again, a positive obligation is not necessarily the most effective approach. For example:

> *"The Applicant shall pay to the Council the [****] Contribution not later than 28 days following Commencement of the Development."*

The theoretical enforcement mechanism for a default is by way of a debt action, but this is of no use if the money has been spent or the owner has gone into liquidation with no visible assets. It is possible to cover the matter by way of a negative clause:

> *"The Development shall not be commenced unless and until the [****] Contribution has been paid to the Council."*

But this approach has limitations in terms of practical enforcement. Consider:

> *"No dwelling forming part of the development shall be Occupied unless and until the Treatment Scheme has been completed."*

It is difficult to believe that a judge would dispossess a family from their home in order to enforce breach of this obligation by a commercial housebuilder.

A better approach in this case might be for the council to require that the costs of carrying out the treatment scheme are secured by a bond or guarantee and then to give the local authority power to enter the relevant land to carry out the agreed works and recover the costs of doing so from the bondsman or the guarantor. Thus, the obligation should contain a well drafted formula providing for the costs of the end project together with an appropriate expert determination or arbitration clause in order to resolve disputes.

If the end project involves defined physical works (e.g. the treatment of derelict land) then Section 106(6) of the 1990 Act provides a statutory right of entry to the relevant local planning authority if there is a breach of a planning obligation which requires those works and gives a right to recover *"reasonable expenses"* in Section 106(6)(b). However, the recovery provision lacks the necessary precision for complex transactions and the exercise of these *"step-rights"* would place the local planning authority in the position of having to carry out the works at its own cost and then to seek to recover those expenses when the developer might (and probably would) argue that they were not *"reasonable expenses"* for the purposes of Section 106(6)(b). All of this might prove unpalatable for the authority which is strapped for cash, hence the need for a bond or guarantee.

The question of practical enforcement becomes more difficult when a risk management scheme not only requires the carrying out of treatment works during the construction process but includes requirements as to long-term monitoring and maintenance. The difficulty lies in the fact that, in many cases, the developer will depart from the site once a development has been completed. Thus, it is necessary that the local planning authority procure some form of long-term security for such monitoring and maintenance. Again, the local planning authority might need to give consideration to the provision of security by way of a bond or guarantee. If, as is often the case nowadays, the developer will be setting up a management company for the purposes of long-term maintenance of on-site infrastructure (such as public open space, sustainable drainage, biodiversity enhancement etc) one solution might be to require the management company to take on the task of future monitoring maintenance of long-term requirements of the risk management scheme. The incorporation of these requirements into the obligations of the management company is not, however, without difficulty. The local planning authority should, if it is prudent, seek to ensure that the chosen management company is financially robust and that it will not expire before these scheme requirements are discharged.

## 15.7    Securing enabling development

It is now clear that applicants for many types of *"enabling development"* may obtain planning permission in certain narrowly defined circumstances.

The fact that an approach is lawful does not, however, mean that it is straightforward in practical terms. In reality there are a number of problems which need to be solved in each case. Clearly, the appropriate legal mechanisms for ensuring that the *"profit"* from the enabling development is paid into the destined project or fund will involve a planning obligation, but it is always extremely difficult to guarantee that the fund will actually reach its proposed destination. For example, if the enabling development is carried out before the fund is paid over (as is usually the case), then how can the local planning authority ensure that the money is forthcoming or is not misdirected? What of the dishonest developer who creates a network of *"shell companies"* to siphon off the profits? What if the landowner goes into liquidation and HMRC or trade creditors claim the proceeds of the enabling development as part of the landowner's assets? There is no single solution.

One solution, or partial solution, might be for the local authority to ensure that the obligation is secured by a third-party bond or guarantee. The shortcoming of this approach is that a bond or guarantee is designed to operate where the planning authority carries out works in default pursuant to Section 106(6), yet it might be that the works which are the subject of the enabling monies will not be specified with any great particularity. In many situations, the landowner will have a list of works of which only some will be selected for funding out of the enabling development. The position is even more problematic if the works are to be specified annually on a rolling programme.

Given that one of the reasons for the enabling development will usually be that the landowner is impecunious, the local planning authority might well be concerned that the landowner could go bankrupt with the result that the proceeds of the enabling development are seized by trade creditors, the tax authorities, etc. Indeed, a trade creditor holding off due to the fact that the landowner has no money might be prompted to pursue recovery of their debt when they find out that a large sum of money is about to be placed in the landowner's bank account out of the enabling development. It might, therefore, be necessary to *"ring-fence"* the proceeds by placing them in a trust fund. Even then, HMRC will probably chase the money in any event.

Another approach is the deposit of the net proceeds arising from the enabling development into a special purpose deposit account and the assignment of all funds in that account to the local planning authority on terms that monies can be drawn down only against proven expenditure on authorised works. Whilst the landowner will protest that the creation of a secured fund is a Draconian interference in their commercial activities, this approach is, in all probability, the only one which guarantees that the enabling proposals will be carried into effect.

If the circumstances of the arrangement permit it, then it might be possible to arrange that the profits from the enabling development are paid to a third-party trustee as they arise and then the trustee will be responsible to ensure that the profits are applied in the agreed way. This could be payments to the developer against proof that the end project is being carried out (e.g. completion certificates) or to the local authority where the authority carries out the works under a default power in the Section 106 obligation.

Another approach may be to structure the development itself in a way which ensures that the money from the enabling development is directed to the desired end project or use. For example, the development could be brought forward in phases and, as each phase is completed, a tranche of the profit is forwarded to the end use.

Ultimately many of these arrangements may turn on the *"covenant strength"* of the developer. A planning obligation with a major multi-national will always be more reliable than one with a *"man of straw"*. Indeed, it may be the case that the local authority will only enter into such arrangements with companies of proven financial worth.

## 15.8     Cash flow and planning obligations

It should be trite, but usually it is not, that those engaged in setting planning obligation should have the matter of cash flow at the forefront of their deliberations. This is because the cash flow models for almost all development schemes will be in deficit up until the developer is in a position to start selling his product. It is a capital-intensive procedure. This means that a developer will, typically, seek to defer expensive commitments under planning obligations until revenue begins to flow. It is important that the local planning authority appreciates this approach because it can affect the quantum of planning benefits which will come with the scheme. Heavy financial commitments at the beginning of the scheme will impact on the financial model and may result in the delivery of fewer benefits than those which are deferred towards the end of the scheme. There is, however, a balance to be struck.

A local planning authority should be astute to what might be loosely described as a *"law of diminishing returns"* or *"marginal utility"*. Whilst it is appropriate to have regard to the cash flow model for a particular development scheme, and to ensure that the frontloading of costs does not render the scheme unviable in its current form, there is a reciprocal danger that loading considerable costs towards the end of the project might, in itself, be counter productive. If one considers the cash flow model in purely commercial terms, then the loading of considerable expenses towards the end of the project might prompt the position where the payment of these expenses at that point in the development programme exceeds the remaining revenues to be gained from the completion of the scheme. The developer might take the view that it is cheaper to suspend the scheme at that point rather than to incur expenses which will not be covered by the marginal sales revenue at that point. To put it bluntly, there is no point in building the remaining houses at a loss.

If benefits are deferred towards the end of a scheme, local planning authorities need to consider whether the marginal cost of delivering those benefits at that time might exceed the marginal revenues which flow from the remaining balance of the scheme. For example, one might have a situation where a developer is proposing to produce a residential scheme comprising 1,100 houses. A sympathetic local planning authority agrees that the costs of providing an extremely expensive highway solution can be put off until the delivery of 1,000 houses, therefore leaving a balance of 100 houses. However, it might be the case that the developer realises that the revenues to be gathered from the remaining 100 houses will not cover the costs of the proposed highway scheme. Accordingly, he might simply cease developing once 999 houses have been completed, the marginal costs of providing the highway scheme exceeding the marginal revenues which might be realised from the completion of the scheme. Accordingly, the payment curve for the costs of discharging a planning obligation needs to be matched to the revenue curve to ensure that this dilemma does not arise.

It should, therefore, follow that the local planning authority needs to strike a balance. In the first instance, it should be ready to accept that frontloading a development scheme with heavy expenditure should be avoided unless there is a good reason for it. Secondly, whilst deferring that expenditure towards the end of the scheme might be acceptable to the developer, it might put the local planning authority in danger of losing that work or income entirely. The balance, therefore, has to be somewhere in the middle. Arguably, matters of timing should not be left to some form of "*Dutch auction*" but should relate to the overall logistics of the scheme and the expenditure should be loaded at points which makes sense in the delivery of the scheme, as opposed to following some form of arbitrary timetable.

### 15.9    Modification of obligations

Section 106A(1) of the Town and Country Planning Act 1990 provides (inter alia) that a planning obligation may not be modified or discharged except by agreement between the appropriate authority and the person or persons against whom the obligation is enforceable.

Section 106A(3) allows a person against whom a planning obligation is enforceable to apply to the local planning authority to modify or discharge a planning obligation within the period of 5 years beginning with the date on which the obligation is entered into.

The administrative process for the management and determination of the application is set out in the Town and Country Planning (Modification and Discharge of Planning Obligations) Regulations 1992.

An authority is entitled to agree to a modification or discharge within the 5-year period on a voluntary basis.

Arguably, the parties to a planning obligation would be wise to ask themselves whether it is overly prescriptive in the first place. If so, then any changes will have to be by way of this cumbersome statutory procedure when, in fact, the prudent drafting of the planning obligation could provide for measured flexibility in any event. For example, if the obligation requires the submission of a scheme to be agreed by the local planning authority, it might be possible to draft a *"tail-piece"* which allows for the subsequent amendment that scheme by agreement in writing. Otherwise, the agreed scheme will become a fixture which cannot be altered save by way of Section 106A.

# Chapter 16

# Planning Conditions And Contaminated Land

## 16.1 Introduction

Somewhat surprisingly, it is difficult to find realistic and useable guidance on the use of planning conditions in connection with land which is, or might be, affected by contamination. These problems are examined in Appendix 1.

## 16.2 The problems with Guidance

Various attempts have been made to provide national guidance on the approach to be taken to the drafting of planning conditions in connection with contaminated land; however, it is fair to say that they have precipitated more confusion than certainty. Unfortunately, it is necessary to go down this particular rabbit hole in order to deal with points which might or might not arise from this national guidance or, indeed, to learn lessons about how things should not be done when drafting planning conditions. It is also worth mentioning, to be fair, that the case law relating to planning conditions is a seemingly never ending changing one, with the result that guidance which might have been written with a certain suite of case law in mind is now out of date.

The National Planning Practice Guidance (NPPG) states that model land contamination conditions can be found in Appendix A of Circular 11/95.[1]

The model planning conditions in Circular 11/95 are, therefore, an appropriate starting point, albeit one then comes to a strange affectation; namely, that, in 2012, the then extant version of the National Planning Policy Framework withdrew the useful explanatory narrative in the Circular but retained the model conditions in the annex to the Circular. Thus, in theory, the model conditions remained intact, but the text which explained them was deleted. Whilst the text was out of date in a number of particulars, deleting it was not helpful in seeking to understand the preserved model conditions and so this chapter will recite both model conditions and the associated explanatory narratives.

The position had been made more complicated by a letter dated 30 May 2008 which was sent by the Deputy Director, Planning – Resources and Environment Policy at the Department of Communities and Local Government to all Chief Planning Officers in England. The letter was said to circulate a new set of model conditions intended for use by local planning authorities during development on land affected by contamination. The explanation for its emergence was:

> *"The publication of PPS23 in 2004 had the effect that there are now two sets of planning conditions published in national planning policy relating to the issue of*

---

[1]    Paragraph: 010 Reference ID: 33-010-20190722 - Revision date: 22 07 2019.

*contamination. In addition to examples of conditions used by local planning authorities provided at Appendix 2B of Annex 2 of PPS23, there are suggested models of acceptable conditions in Appendix A of Circular 11/95 (conditions 56 – 59). These latter model conditions have been overtaken by the policy in PPS23. The intention of circulating these new conditions is to establish a single set of model conditions that is consistent with PPS23 policy. As such I would encourage their use to you. They replace Appendix 2B of Annex 2 of PPS23 and conditions 56 – 59 in Appendix A of Circular 11/95 which are hereby cancelled."*

There was not, in fact, any conflict at all. Appendix 2B of Annex 2 of PPS23 set out *"Some Examples of Conditions Used by Local Planning Authorities"* and added:

*"This Appendix contains some examples of conditions that have been used by local authorities in different circumstances related to development of land affected by contamination. They are not intended as model conditions but they are meant to illustrate the means that some LPAs have adopted to control the potential impacts of contamination on development and land use."* (Emphasis added)

Be that as it may, as noted above, the model conditions in the appendix to Circular 11/95 appear to have been revived by the NPPG, albeit this letter of 2008 does not appear to have been expressly withdrawn. Presumably, it was deemed to be otiose when PPS23 was withdrawn in 2012. This section will proceed on the basis that the letter is no longer extant, albeit the model conditions which were annexed to it will be mentioned below when discussing examples of draftsmanship.

## 16.3    When, and how, conditions may be appropriate
The now withdrawn narrative to Circular 11/95 stated:

*"74. If it is known or strongly suspected that a site is contaminated to an extent which would adversely affect the proposed development or infringe statutory requirements, an investigation of the hazards by the developer and proposals for remedial action will normally be required before the application can be determined by the planning authority. Any subsequent planning permission may need to include planning conditions requiring certain remedial measures to be carried out."* (Emphasis added)

The narrative went on to say:

*"75. In cases where there is only a suspicion that the site might be contaminated, or where the evidence suggests that there may be only slight contamination, planning permission may be granted subject to conditions that development will not be permitted to start until a site investigation and assessment have been carried out and that the development itself will incorporate any remedial measures shown to be necessary."* (Emphasis added)

As mentioned above, when taken together, these paragraphs suggested a dividing line in the use of conditions. If it is *"known or strongly suspected"* that a site is contaminated to an extent which would adversely affect the proposed development or infringe statutory requirements, then permission should not be granted unless site assessments have been provided and proposals for *"remedial action"* have been produced. Conditions are, thus, limited to those which ensure that the *"remediation"* measures are carried out. If there is *"only a suspicion that the site might be contaminated"*, or where the evidence suggests that there may be only *"slight contamination"*, then permission may be granted and conditions can then provide for site assessment and any necessary *"remediation"*.

Somewhat surprisingly, none of the model conditions appear to be drafted to cover the case where there is only a suspicion that the site might be contaminated, or where the evidence suggests that there may be only slight contamination.

Model condition 59 might take up paragraph 74, but it is far from clear. The model condition is for use where soil contamination is *"known or suspected"*[2] and provides:

> *"59. Before the development hereby permitted commences on the site, a soil survey of the site shall be undertaken and the results provided to the local planning authority. The survey shall be taken at such points and to such depth as the local planning authority may stipulate. A scheme for <u>decontamination of the site</u> shall be submitted to and approved by the local planning authority in writing and the scheme as approved <u>shall be fully implemented and completed before any [residential] unit hereby permitted is first occupied</u>."* (Emphasis added)

The matters which are lacking in clarity are threefold. First, as stated above, there is no particular reason why a site should be *"decontaminated"* in order to make it suitable for the proposed use. The focus on decontamination, clearly, fails to capture the aspects of a scheme which include adaptive measures such as ground membrane to prevent the ingress of potentially harmful gases to buildings or passive/active ventilation. This is to say, it would have been preferable to make reference to treatment mitigation or other adaptive measures at this point. It comes up short. Secondly, as is mentioned elsewhere in this book, tying the enforcement mechanism to first occupation is not particularly logical when this could give rise to difficulties where the local planning authority seeks to enforce the breach of this condition against an innocent residential occupier. Thirdly, whilst it might be the case that this condition was drafted in good faith on the basis of being a *"Grampian"* type condition, the form of wording might, now, be problematic as a result of the *Hart* case: see Appendix 1.

The model conditions (in 56, 57 and 58) *"where investigation/remedial proposals carried out/ agreed before planning permission granted"* do not sit well with the above and provide:

---

[2]    There appears to be a drafting error here in that, if the condition is intended to be consistent with paragraph 74 of the narrative, then it should read: *"for use where soil contamination is known or <u>strongly</u> suspected"*.

> *"56. Development shall not begin until a scheme to deal with contamination of the site has been submitted to and approved in writing by the local planning authority.*
>
> *57. The above scheme shall include an investigation and assessment to identify the extent of contamination and the measures to be taken to avoid risk to the [public/buildings/environment] when the site is developed.*
>
> *58. Development shall not commence until the measures approved in the scheme have been implemented."*

No attempt is made to reflect the apparent conceptual distinction drawn by paragraphs 74 and 75 of the narrative.

Unfortunately, the advice in paragraph 74 was at odds with the way in which large sites are packaged and then progressed through the planning system by way of outline planning permissions which are then followed by the determination of reserved matters, often on a phased basis. This means that it is difficult to provide a final treatment scheme for a large phased development before the site layout has been settled by way of reserved matters. For example, an approach which is suitable for the hard-surfaced areas (e.g. car parks, roads etc) will be different to that applicable to sensitive uses (e.g. domestic gardens) and visa versa. A one size fits all approach might be acceptable at an idyllic level, but it might be a blatant misdistribution of financial resources in a *"zero-sum"* financial model.[3]

Finally, the reference to the avoidance of risk is unschooled, because it is not possible to avoid all possible risks for eternity.

## 16.4    Outline planning applications

Neither the NPPF nor the NPPG explain how these principles can be applied to large schemes.

Annex 2 (Development on Land Affected by Contamination) of the now withdrawn Planning Policy Statement 23: Planning and Pollution Control provided one of the more fulsome discussions of the topic:

> *"2.55 Extreme caution should be taken in the granting of outline planning permission unless the LPA is satisfied that it has sufficient information from the applicant about the condition of the land and its remediation and the full range of environmental impacts arising from the proposals to be able to grant permission in full at a later stage. A grant of outline planning permission that cannot be sustained at the detailed approval stage because it becomes apparent that the necessary remediation is not viable or practicable or because the ES (where EIA is required) demonstrates unacceptable adverse impacts*

---

[3]    That is, the budget is a finite one and one may be robbing Peter to pay Paul. Thus, the pursuit of a multi-purpose *"clean up"* might be at the expense of, say, affordable housing.

*could leave the LPA vulnerable to a claim for compensation.*[4] *The LPA should be satis-fied, therefore, that the risks have been properly assessed and, if there is an unacceptable risk, the options appraised sufficiently to identify a viable remediation scheme that will reduce the risks to acceptable level, just as it would with a full application. Outline permissions should not be granted until the LPA is satisfied that it understands the contaminated condition of the site and that the proposed development is appropriate as a means of remediating it. If the LPA is satisfied about this, further investigations and the detailed design of remediation might still be needed. Identifying these issues as reserved matters will enable detailed approval at an appropriate stage and give the developer greater certainty before incurring the costs involved. Where the LPA is minded to grant outline planning permission, the length of time needed for further investigations and detailed design should be considered in determining the timescale for submission of a detailed application on the reserved matters."*

Turning to more modern guidance, under the sub-heading, *"Does an outline application require less information?"* the NPPG states:[5]

*"The information sought should be proportionate to the decision at the outline stage, but before granting outline planning permission a local planning authority will, among other matters, need to be satisfied that:*

- *it understands the contaminated condition of the site;*

- *the proposed development is appropriate as a means of remediating it; and*

- *it has sufficient information to be confident that it will be able to grant permission in full at a later stage bearing in mind the need for the necessary remediation to be viable and practicable."*

This sparse advice[6] does not deal with conditions and does not seem to suggest that the grant of an outline permission subject to a suite of conditions covering assessment, *"remediation"*, mitigation and management is anathema. Unfortunately, the key term *"understands"* is left at large, with no metric for this subjective disposition indicated in the passage. Furthermore, the proposition that the proposed development is *"appropriate"* as a means of *"remediating"* the local planning authority's understanding of the condition of the site has nothing to do

---

[4]   The reference to compensation is unclear and no source is given, so it is difficult to understand the author's concerns.

[5]   Paragraph: 008 Reference ID: 33-008-20190722 - Revision date: 22 07 2019.

[6]   One of the questions which is asked about the NPPG is *"why does it exist?"* A more charitable way of putting it might be that it is unclear as to its target audience. The slim *"advice"* is, often, not only not helpful to the seasoned professional, but also can be a source of confusion because of its over-simplification of complex topics. Arguably, this section is a prime example.

with the suitable for use approach.[7] The reference to *"the need for the necessary remediation to be viable and practicable"* is, however, consistent with an approach which seeks to reflect the "zero-sum" boundaries and the cash flow characteristics of a development scheme.

The NPPG flowchart provides:[8]

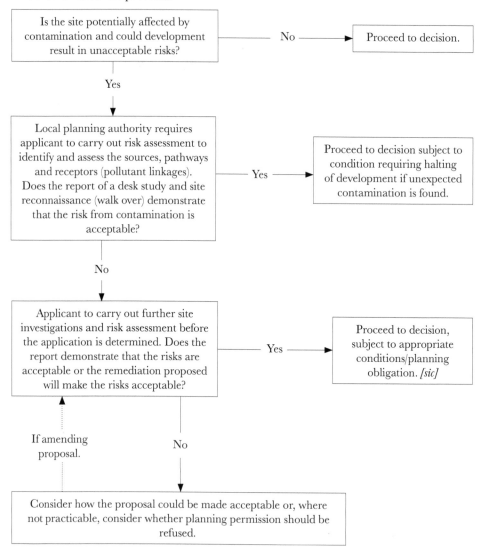

---

[7]   So far as it is worth venturing into this rabbit hole, this seems to conflate town and country planning with Part IIA of the Environmental Protection Act 1990.

[8]   Reformatted from original for purposes of publication.

Again, the flowchart does not suggest that it is wrong to grant an outline planning permission subject to appropriate conditions. And, again, the flowchart does not speak in terms of the complete elimination of all risks but, instead, refers to "*acceptable risks*".

## 16.5 Site characterisation
The NPPG advises[9] that the stages and the factors to consider in framing appropriate planning conditions can include:

- site characterisation;

- submission of the "*remediation*" scheme;

- implementation of the approved "*remediation*" scheme; and

- monitoring and maintenance.

If there is good objective evidence to hypothesise that a site is contaminated to an extent which could make the proposed development unsuitable, then, in all probability, the site characterisation stage will have been completed before the application comes before the planning committee. With, perhaps, a report on the broad options for the remediation scheme, on the other hand, if there is only a suspicion that the site might be contaminated, or where the evidence suggests that there may be only slight contamination, it might be the case that the expense of site characterisation can be left until the principle of the development has been approved and the financial model for the scheme thereby strengthened.

The first sentence of model condition 59 from Circular 11/95 provides a useful starting point for discussion:

> "*59. Before the development hereby permitted commences on the site, a soil survey of the site shall be undertaken and the results provided to the local planning authority. The survey shall be taken at such points and to such depth as the local planning authority may stipulate.*"

It could reasonably be argued that this condition lacks detail and should make reference to an established methodology for the survey.

The model condition annexed to the DCLG letter dated 2008 (see Paragraph 16.2 above) stated:

> "*An investigation and risk assessment, in addition to any assessment provided with the planning application, must be completed in accordance with a scheme to assess the nature and extent of any contamination on the site, <u>whether or not it originates on</u>*

---

9   Paragraph: 010 Reference ID: 33-010-20190722 - Revision date: 22 07 2019.

167

*the site. The contents of the scheme are subject to the approval in writing of the Local Planning Authority. The investigation and risk assessment must be undertaken by competent persons and a written report of the findings must be produced. The written report is subject to the approval in writing of the Local Planning Authority. The report of the findings must include:*

*(i) a survey of the extent, scale and nature of contamination;*

*(ii) an assessment of the potential risks to:*

- *human health,*

- *property (existing or proposed) including buildings, crops, livestock, pets, woodland and service lines and pipes,*

- *adjoining land,*

- *groundwaters and surface waters,*

- *ecological systems,*

- *archaeological sites and ancient monuments;*

*(iii) an appraisal of remedial options, and proposal of the preferred option(s).*

*This must be conducted in accordance with DEFRA and the Environment Agency's "Model Procedures for the Management of Land Contamination, CLR 11".*" (Emphasis added)

Whilst this draft is more fulsome, and refers to (now withdrawn CLR 11) as a quasi-objective standard, it is arguable that the conversational style of the draftsmanship of these "*model*" conditions does not accord with best practice.

For example, the opening condition states:

*"Unless otherwise agreed by the Local Planning Authority, development other than that required to be carried out as part of an approved scheme of remediation[10] must not commence until conditions 1 to 4 have been complied with. If unexpected contamination is found after development has begun, development must be halted on that part of the site affected by the unexpected contamination to the extent specified by the Local Planning Authority in writing until condition 4 has been complied with in relation to that contamination."*

---

[10] The phrase, "*an approved scheme of remediation*" is unclear. This should be a remediation scheme which has been submitted to and approved by the local planning authority pursuant to Condition 3.

The word *"contamination"* should be qualified, otherwise any level of contamination, no matter how small, will trigger this proviso. The phrase *"unexpected contamination"* is ambiguous and, arguably, subjective. It is also important to bear in mind that the discovered problem might not be unexpected contamination per se, but unexpected ground conditions (for example, the discovery of a hidden *"pathway"*). The unexpected event might be the discovery of something which is the potential source of contamination but which is not, at the time, emitting any noxious substances (e.g. an intact underground oil tank). A better phrase would be *"significant risk of contamination which had not been identified in any [****] Assessment submitted with the application documents"*.

The phrase *"Unless otherwise agreed in writing by the local planning authority"* should, nowadays, be omitted because it may be regarded by the courts as being unlawful on account of a conflict with the objectives now covered by Sections 73 and 96A of the Town and Country Planning Act 1990. This unfortunate legal complication poses a considerable problem because, of course, *"remediation"* is an iterative process which must be informed by, and adjusted to, the conditions which are discovered on site as the development progresses. This, by itself, would suggest that a planning obligation should be used with the more complex sites or developments.

Be that as it may, the use of the phrase *"whether or not it originates on the site"* is helpful and could, usefully, be incorporated into similar conditions.

## 16.6 Approval of the *"remediation"* scheme
The second sentence of Circular 11/95 model condition 59 provides:

> *"59. A scheme for decontamination of the site shall be submitted to and approved by the local planning authority in writing and the scheme as approved shall be fully implemented and completed before any [residential] unit hereby permitted is first occupied."*

The problem here, of course, is that the objective of the exercise is not to *"decontaminate"* the site, but to make it suitable for its intended purpose, which means that a scheme will, in all probability, allow for residual contamination which falls below a specified threshold. There is no metricated target and, thus, the objectives and targets of the scheme need to be specified with some particularity.

The phrase *"implemented and completed"* in model Condition 59 is ambiguous and begs the question of whether it refers to two different things or is a drafting redundancy. Note that model Condition 58 (see below) refers to *"implemented"* only, thereby adding another layer of confusion. It is, perhaps, better to use clear and simple expressions such as *"carried out"* or the like.

Model condition 2 annexed to the DCLG letter dated 2008 stated:

> *"2. Submission of Remediation Scheme*

> *A detailed remediation scheme to bring the site to a condition suitable for the intended use by removing unacceptable risks to human health, buildings and other property and the natural and historical environment must be prepared, and is subject to the approval in writing of the Local Planning Authority. The scheme must include all works to be undertaken, proposed remediation objectives and remediation criteria, timetable of works and site management procedures. The scheme must ensure that the site will not qualify as contaminated land under Part 2A of the Environmental Protection Act 1990 in relation to the intended use of the land after remediation.*"[11]

The detailing in this draft condition is to be commended but the conversational style reads more like an extract from aspirational heads of terms rather than a worked-up condition. The main problem is that it does not refer to any published guidance or standards when the objectives and targets of the scheme need to be specified with some particularity. Nor is this rescued by reciting that, "*The scheme must include all works to be undertaken, proposed remediation objectives and remediation criteria*", because the condition itself should provide a clear starting point for the exercise. Subjective words such as "*unacceptable risks*" beg a number of unanswered questions. There is ample technical guidance which could be mentioned.

Again, one has to express concern as to the effect of the condition in light of the *Hart* case: see Appendix 1.

## 16.7    Implementation/verification of the approved "*remediation*" scheme
Model condition 58 (Circular 11/95) provides:

> "*58. Development shall not commence until the measures approved in the scheme have been implemented.*"

The second sentence of model condition 59 concludes:

> "*59. ... and the scheme as approved shall be fully <u>implemented and completed</u> before any [residential] unit hereby permitted is first occupied.*" (As to underlined text, see above).

Model condition 3 annexed to the DCLG letter dated 2008 stated:

> "*3. Implementation of Approved Remediation Scheme*
>
> *The approved remediation scheme must be carried out in accordance with its terms prior to the commencement of development other than that required to carry out remediation,*

---

[11]    The words "*scheme must ensure that the site will not qualify as contaminated land under Part 2A of the Environmental Protection Act 1990 in relation to the intended use of the land after remediation*" do not make sense. The Part IIA criteria are not based on making a site suitable for its intended use. Furthermore, it would be a poor scheme which fails to meet the targets set by Part IIA in any event.

*unless otherwise agreed in writing by the Local Planning Authority.*[12] *The Local Planning Authority must be given two weeks written notification of commencement of the remediation scheme works.*

*Following completion of measures identified in the approved remediation scheme, a verification report (referred to in PPS23 as a validation report) that demonstrates the effectiveness of the remediation carried out must be produced, and is subject to the approval in writing of the Local Planning Authority."*

In all of these model conditions, the requirement that the approved "*remediation*" scheme must be carried out in accordance with its terms prior to the commencement of development will, in all probability, be unrealistic in all but the smaller sites. The condition is predicated on the simple case of a site which will be made suitable for use in its entirety before development commences. This is unnecessary and uneconomic when the site is a large one which will proceed in phases. The expectation that all site adaptation treatment shall take place at the outset will, also, impact on the cash flow model for the site which could, in turn, unnecessarily reduce the budget available for benefits such as affordable housing.

## 16.8    Monitoring and maintenance

Model condition 5 annexed to the DCLG letter dated 2008 stated:

*"5. Long Term Monitoring and Maintenance*

*A monitoring and maintenance scheme to include monitoring the long-term effectiveness of the proposed remediation over a period of [x] years, and the provision of reports on the same must be prepared, both of which are subject to the approval in writing of the Local Planning Authority.*

*Following completion of the measures identified in that scheme and when the remediation objectives have been achieved, reports that demonstrate the effectiveness of the monitoring and maintenance carried out must be produced, and submitted to the Local Planning Authority.*

*This must be conducted in accordance with DEFRA and the Environment Agency's "Model Procedures for the Management of Land Contamination, CLR 11"."*

The draft condition fails to articulate how it will be enforced. This is the most problematic of these draft conditions because it is based on the assumption that the developer will have some control over the site for the period of the scheme, or indeed, that the developer will continue to exist or will remain solvent throughout. Simply providing for periodic surveys and reports makes for an interesting paper-trail, but begs the question of whether it serves any practical purpose. In theory, the local planning authority has a number of options

---

[12]    Again, the phrase "*unless otherwise agreed in writing by the Local Planning Authority*" must be avoided.

available to it when it comes to enforcing planning conditions; however, the reality is that they will be of little avail where the developer has long departed the site or has fallen into liquidation.

Arguably, the better course is to provide for long-term maintenance and monitoring by way of a planning obligation because such an obligation can require financial commitments which are not lawful by way of a planning condition. These obligations can include requirements for bonding or guarantees or, in appropriate cases, the setting up of a management company.

## 16.9 Unexpected contamination
Model condition 4 annexed to the DCLG letter dated 2008 stated:

> *"4. Reporting of Unexpected Contamination*
>
> *In the event that contamination is found at any time when carrying out the approved development that was not previously identified it must be reported in writing imme-diately to the Local Planning Authority. An investigation and risk assessment must be undertaken in accordance with the requirements of condition 1, and where reme-diation is necessary a remediation scheme must be prepared in accordance with the requirements of condition 2, which is subject to the approval in writing of the Local Planning Authority.*
>
> *Following completion of measures identified in the approved remediation scheme a verification report must be prepared, which is subject to the approval in writing of the Local Planning Authority in accordance with condition 3."*

Again, the conversational style of the draft condition leaves much to be desired. The condition does not say when the scheme is to be submitted, which renders the condition ineffectual. A developer could ignore it knowing that any breach of condition notice or enforcement notice would be a nullity, because it could not specify a time period for compliance. This point is of particular importance where a large scheme is evolving in discrete phases.

## 16.10 Drafting problems
The following example is taken from a real-life planning condition in connection with biodiversity. It might, at first blush, appear to be relatively uncontentious; however, it might be the case that it is, in reality, somewhat problematic.

> *The development shall be undertaken in complete accordance with recommendations set out in Section 6 of the Great Crested Newt Survey prepared by [****] dated [****] 2016, Section 4 of the Badger Survey Report prepared by [****] dated [****] 2016, Section 5 of the Reptile Survey prepared by [****] dated [****] 2016, Sections 8.3 and 8.5 of the Ecological Appraisal prepared by [****] dated [****] 2016.*

The first point is that the condition provides that the development should be undertaken in accordance with the number of reports. It is highly unlikely that the authors of those reports would have drafted them with a view to providing prescriptive formulae. Often, they will not have been drafted with legalistic precision. Secondly, it is always possible that there might be conflicts between the various requirements of these diverse reports with no way to reconcile them. For example, the timeline in respect of one topic might interfere with or prejudice activities being carried out for another topic. Or they might, in the absence of an overall critical path analysis, simply be out of sequence with other aspects of the development scheme as a whole. Accordingly, it might be the case that the condition is not enforceable in practical terms. Thirdly, the provision does not say when the scheme must be carried out and by whom.

The following table is extracted from a real-life landscape management plan. Problems could arise if, for example, the local planning authority imposed a planning condition which required that the development be carried out in accordance with a landscape management plan. The document has not been drafted by lawyers and, accordingly, legalistic language has not been used with the result that problems may arise when it comes to the matter of enforcement. The comments below will be taken on an item-by-item basis. The question in each case is whether the local planning authority could, realistically, issue a planning contravention notice or enforcement notice in the event that they consider that a breach of the condition has occurred. It is difficult to see how an inspector or a magistrate would approach the matter.

| Maintenance Schedule | | | |
|---|---|---|---|
| | **Item** | **Frequency** | **Comments** |
| 1 | Weed control | 3 per year | All shrubs, hedges and trees should be monitored for any signs of pests or disease, and appropriate control measures taken. All shrub beds, hedges and tree bases shall be maintained in a weed free condition by removing, by hand, entire weeds, including roots, by forking, digging or hoeing. Only if weed growth is dense shall beds be treated with a glyphosate based herbicide. Herbicide may be applied by spraying, spot treatment or by use of weed wipes. |
| 2 | Watering | To be agreed or as required | Watering may be required during the establishment period of new planting. The appointed management company shall ensure that sufficient water is applied to maintain healthy growth of all soft landscape areas. |

Item 1 (weed control): the first sentence in the comments column refers to *"appropriate control measures"* but this is very judgemental, in the sense that experts might disagree as to what is or is not *"appropriate"* having regard to the nature and extent of the pests or disease. Indeed, it is questionable whether the word *"pests"* has any scientific validity in this particular context. The penultimate sentence uses the phrase *"only if the weed growth is dense shall beds be treated with a glyphosate based herbicide"*. Here again, the question of whether or not weed growth is *"dense"* is judgemental.

Item 2 (watering): The first point here is in the frequency column where the phrase, *"To be agreed, or as required"* is inserted. This is very much like the perilous notion of an *"agreement to agree"* familiar to lawyers and, as such, it is difficult to see how this formula will eventuate to something which is enforceable in law. The first sentence in the frequency column is not a mandatory requirement but is merely hortative. The greatest difficulty here is a reference to an *"appointed management company"*. It is difficult to see how a planning condition can be enforceable against a management company which might have no interest in the land. Be that as it may, there are all the usual problems with whether or not a management company can be held to account in the event that it defaults. Furthermore, the use of the phrases *"sufficient water"* and *"healthy growth"* are, again, judgemental.

The second problem is that no development of any size will proceed in a once and for all fashion. In all probability, there will be some degree of phasing involved. It follows that any condition which seeks to introduce any measures during the course of the development should have regard to matters of timing. That is, of course, particularly so when the initial planning permission is an outline planning permission and the particulars of each phase will emerge during the course of reserved matters approvals.

Accordingly, it is arguable that the better course is not to provide a condition which seeks to promote a simple once and for all requirement but, instead, allows for some degree of sophistication including the provision of a timetable. For example:

> *"No part of the development shall be commenced unless and until a scheme for ecological mitigation (the "Mitigation Scheme") has been submitted to and approved by the local planning authority. The Mitigation Scheme shall be incorporate the recommendations set out in Section 6 of the Great Crested Newt Survey prepared by [****] dated [****] 2016, Section 4 of the Badger Survey Report prepared by [****] dated [****] 2016, Section 5 of the Reptile Survey prepared by [****] dated [****] 2016, Sections 8.3 and 8.5 of the Ecological Appraisal prepared by [****] dated [****] 2016 <u>and shall include a timetable for its implementation. The development shall be carried out in accordance with the timetable and provisions of the Mitigation Scheme."</u>*

There is, however, an unfortunate limitation on the way in which this type of scheme condition can be deployed and this results from uncertainty created by recent case law. It might seem to be sensible, and indeed would be sensible, if the condition provided for variations to the approved scheme from time to time. There might be numerous reasons why the approved scheme does not fit with the way in which the development is emerging onsite. For example, it might be that previously unknown ground conditions have emerged as the works have progressed. It might be the case that the economic viability assessment for the scheme must, then, be revisited and the scheme altered as a result. This is not unusual and may mean that certain *"benefits"* must be trimmed or removed. Accordingly, it might seem appropriate to add the following words to the end of the conditions so as to allow full future variations:

> *"Provided that variations to the approved mitigation scheme may, from time to time, be approved in writing by the local planning authority."*

These additional words are now known as *"tail-pieces"* and have been found to be objectionable. Whether such a *"tail-piece"* will invalidate a condition depends on its substantive effect.[13]

It follows that the local planning authority might be wise to consider whether these complexities are best avoided by dealing with these provisions instead in a planning obligation.

---

[13]   The leading case is *R (Midcounties Co-operative Ltd) v Wyre Forest DC* [2009] EWHC 964 (Admin): see Appendix 1.

# Case study 1

## Nether Farm, Somercotes, Derbyshire

In 2018 outline planning permission was granted for the development of up to 200 houses at Nether Farm, Birchwod Lane, Somercotes. Whilst the application was relatively straightforward, this provides a useful example of how the various components of site assessment and risk assessment operate within the development control process.

The application for planning permission was provided with a Phase 1 Assessment. The assessment noted the proximity of closed former landfill sites and recommended that a Phase 2 Assessment be carried out. The brief for Phase 1 Assessment incorporated:

- A review and assessment of the site history, with reference to potentially contaminated uses.

- Review of regulatory authority and environmental data relating to the site and its environs.

- A site inspection.

- A visit to the mining records office of the coal authority.

- An appraisal of potential environmental risks.

- Development of a Phase 1 conceptual model.

- Preparation of a desk-based coalmining risk assessment.

The Phase 1 Report recommended that:

- A Phase 2 investigation be carried out to include intrusive site investigation to locate mine entries.

- Should signs of potential contamination be evident during construction activities, then a qualified environmental specialist be consulted to assess the risk posed to end-users and the environment.

Armed with these materials, the local planning authority granted outline planning permission in 2018 subject to the pre-commencement condition which required that further work be carried out and that "*remediation*" strategy be provided, viz:

"*No development shall commence until:*

*a) The application site has been subjected to a detailed scheme for investigation and recording of contamination and a report has been submitted to and approved in writing by the Local Planning Authority;*

*b) Detailed proposals in line with current best practice for the removal, containment or otherwise rendering harmless such contamination (the "Contamination Proposals") have been submitted to and approved in writing by the Local Planning Authority;*

*c) For each part of the development, "Contamination Proposals" relevant to that part shall be carried out either before or during such development as appropriate;*

*d) If during development works any contamination should be encountered which was not previously identified and is derived from a different source and/or of a different type to those included in the "Contamination Proposals" then the revised "Contamination Proposals" shall be submitted to and approved in writing by the Local Planning Authority;*

*e) If during development work site contaminants are found in areas previously expected to be clean then their remediation shall be carried out in line with the agreed "Contamination Process;*

*f) Prior to the commencement of any construction works in any area that has been subject to remediation, a verification report shall be submitted to and approve in writing by the Local Planning Authority."*

The Phase 1 Assessment included a review of historical ordnance survey maps between the years 1880 and 2014. Those maps showed that, in 1967, there was opencast mining within 550m of the site. This review showed that the nearby area included a brickworks, sewage works, two collieries and opencast work space, all of which were disused and now grassed made ground. The coal authority report showed that there were a number of shallow coal mine workings within the area. Three mine entries were recorded within the site boundary and a further three mine entries were shown to straddle the boundary. The environmental search data showed that there were two landfill sites located within 500m of the development site which were situated respectively 337m and 367m from the development site and that they had accepted industrial waste. In addition, there were two historical landfill sites located respectively 93m and 141m from the development site, which accepted industrial, inert and special waste and liquid sludge.

As to the Phase 1 conceptual model, it was noted that the mine entries on the site might contain filled clay pits with deep made ground that might be a source of contaminants and ground gas. The remnants of the historical brickworks, collieries and open cast mining might be a potential source of ground gas. It was also noted that there was a coal seam beneath the site and that this coal seam was notoriously gassy and prone to spontaneous combustion. Potential contaminants of concern for the end user including heavy metals, polycyclic aromatic hydrocarbons, herbicides and pesticides. The primary receptors for the site would be construction workers and the residents.

The Phase 2 Assessment was submitted in 2018 and was accompanied with the results of some site sampling which suggested that the risks associated with the development were acceptable for a residential scheme; however, there were two hotspots which needed to be attended to. A further supplementary Phase 2 Assessment was provided in 2019 which corroborated the results of the 2018 Phase 2 Assessment.

The project brief for the Phase 2 Geo-Environmental Assessment required:

• A review of the previous Phase 1 Report.

• A strategy to implement the Phase 2 Geo-Environmental Assessment.

• Recommendations to mitigate against environmental risks.

• A geotechnical design for the proposed development.

The Phase 2 Assessment included intrusive boreholes, trial pits, the analysis of 20 samples for the CLEA screening suite, 4 samples for total petroleum hydrocarbons (TPH)[1] and 3 samples for pesticides. Gas monitoring installations were installed in 9 boreholes.

The CLEA guidance was followed in respect of Generic Assessment Criteria and by reference to published soil guideline values. It was found that the majority of samples analysed for hydrocarbon contamination did not exceed the respective Generic Assessment Criteria for residential end use with private gardens. However marginal exceedances of Dibenz (a,h) anthracene[2] was recorded at two topsoil boreholes, thereby indicating contamination via shallow contamination "*hotspots*". The exceedances were derived from assessment against the appropriate screening value in the Generic Assessment Criteria.[3]

The ground gas monitoring exercise revealed that no methane had been detected. The site was then classified as "*Characteristic Situation 1*" based on a very low flow rates and gas concentrations obtained during gas monitoring visits.

Therefore, it was concluded that gas protection measures for carbon dioxide and methane were not required for the proposed development. However, it was further noted that gas sampling and analysis had not been undertaken at this stage. The risk management and

---

[1]  Total petroleum hydrocarbons (TPH) is any mixture of hydrocarbons that are found in crude oil. Chemicals that occur in TPH include hexane, benzene, toluene, xylenes, naphthalene, fluorene, and other petroleum products.

[2]  Dibenz (a,h) anthracene is a polycyclic aromatic hydrocarbon (PAH) which is a pollutant of smoke, soot, tar and oils. PAHs have been linked to cancers.

[3]  The relevant GAC screening value being 0.30 mg/kg against measurements of, respectively, 0.35 and 0.47.

*"remediation"* section of the report suggested the removal of the shallow soils in the vicinity of the identified hotspots and that this was likely to occur during the topsoil strip of the site. Alternatively, 600mm of clean topsoil could be installed in proximal plots.

The Phase 2 Report ended with the following recommendations for further assessment of the site which should include:

- Should any signs of organic contamination be evident during construction activities, a qualified environmental specialist should be consulted to assess the risk close to end-users and the environment.

- A second phase of ground investigation should be undertaken:

  - to evaluate the risk posed to ground stability from former coal workings through the advancing of rotary boreholes;

  - to identify former mine entries and features on site;

  - to identify additional areas of reworked/made ground;

  - to classify on-site contamination;

  - to identify the depth of the water table and chemical analysis of groundwater; and

  - to undertake gas monitoring and sampling in the deeper rotary boreholes.

The report concluded by saying that the proposed development of the site for residential use was unlikely to pose a significant risk to the end user of the site. It considered that a further ground investigation should be undertaken to further classify the site and its risks. The removal of contamination hotspots was required.

The Phase 2 Assessment was then followed with a *"Phase II Supplementary Ground Investigation"* in 2019. The purposes of the additional report were to:

- Evaluate the risk posed to ground stability from former coal workings through the advancing of rotary boreholes.

- To identify former mine entries *[sic]* on site.

- To identify any additional areas of reworked/made ground.

- To further classify on site contamination.

- To identify the depth to the water table and undertake chemical analysis of the groundwater.

- To undertake gas monitoring and sampling in the window sample and rotary boreholes.

- The assessment of potential risk posed by mine gas.

- Assessment of potential risk posed by volatile organic compounds from the neighbouring landfill.

The Phase 2 supplementary ground investigation incorporated the following:

- The advancing of 10 rotary boreholes to pro forma coal mine workings.

- The excavation of trial pits.

- The excavation of 5 shallow trenches to locate former coal mine shafts.

- The analysis of 20 soil samples.

- The analysis of 8 water samples.

- The analysis of 10 gas samples.

- The monitoring of gas and water levels in boreholes.

A total of 20 soil samples were sent for analysis to an accredited laboratory along with four groundwater samples, 4 surface water samples and 16 gas samples. An assessment of the analysis results for the soil sample taken during this supplementary phase of works did not reveal any contamination in respect of the respective Generic Assessment Criteria for a residential use. Again, the 2 hotspots were noted.

The supplementary gas monitoring and sample phase took place in February and March 2019. 10 rotary boreholes and gas monitoring installations wells were installed.

Gas sampling for volatile organic compounds (VOCs) detected them and was of a type and concentration across the site which tended to be associated with industrial materials i.e. solvents, cleaning agents and fuels.

The VOCs identified were thought to be consistent with the types of waste which were reported to be present within one of the nearby landfill sites. At this stage it was considered that a pathway was present through fractured rock within some or all of the coal seams. This kind of fracturing could occur naturally within coal seams and was not observable via rotary drilling. It was also considered that by means of advancing the boreholes through the coal seams new pathways had been created and that there was not a natural pathway for gas migration to the surface. The risk to surface from volatile organic compounds was considered minimal, but at that stage there was no evidence to substantiate this.

This time the derived gas screening value showed the site as meeting gas "*Characteristic Situation 2*", meaning gas precautions against carbon dioxide and methane were required as per CIRIA (2007).

It was, therefore, recommended that, in conjunction with precautions against carbon dioxide, methane and carbon monoxide, further safety measures be taken to protect against volatile organic compounds in the form of a VOC blocking membrane, which would need to be installed in all properties. A rigorous validation program was also required.

The report therefore recommended, in respect of contamination, that the following should be observed in order to remove the perceived risks to human health[4]:

- Gas protection measures be required across the site to protect the end-user from carbon dioxide and methane risk.

- The gas protection measures should include protection against carbon monoxide.

- A VOC resistant membrane be required across the whole site.

- The installation of the VOC membrane would require robust validation.

- Capping of boreholes was required.

- A detailed "*remediation*" method statement should be prepared, detailing mitigation strategy which effectively removed all risk to human health.

The net result was that it was determined to cover the site in a membrane in order to obviate any problems which might arise in the future from fugitive emissions from the landfill sites.

---

[4]  As noted in Chapter 5 above, it is not possible to obviate all possible risk, nor it necessary to try to do so. The objective of the exercise is to reduce risks to acceptable levels. Furthermore, all measurements are proxies for the condition of the site and not absolutes.

# Case study 2

# Bombardier Site, Crewe

## Introduction

The Bombardier site has been the source of much disquiet at the time of writing. The problem had to do with the fact that 263 houses were built on land which was reputed to be contaminated to a degree which required treatment or other adaptive measures in order to make it suitable for residential use. Planning permission was granted in 2018 and was subject to a suite of contaminated land conditions, of which one was a "*Grampian*" type condition which required that a "*remediation*" strategy be submitted to and approved by the local planning authority before the development was commenced. It appears that this condition was not only not discharged, but also that the dwellings were built nonetheless. The local planning authority then asserted that the whole development was illegal on the basis that a failure to discharge the condition meant that any development purportedly built pursuant to the planning permission did not benefit from that permission. Thus the 263 houses had, it was asserted, been erected without the benefit of planning permission. The developer then made a fresh application for retrospective planning permission in order to regularise the situation.

The question of whether or not the construction of these houses was without the benefit of planning permission turns on the so-called "*Whitley Principle*".[1] At first glance, the local planning to planning authority might appear to have been on solid ground; however, it is necessary to ask what the approval of the "*remediation*" strategy would bring to the scheme in reality (i.e. whether this was a technical breach only). The condition of the site was not unknown in 2018, when the planning permission was granted. It had been the subject of multiple contamination surveys, including a Phase 2 Assessment with intrusive site investigations. These revealed concerns about deposits in made ground and other possible contamination from the previous railway works. The developer had, actually, incorporated a range of adaptive measures in the scheme and this begs the question of whether or not the local planning authority's retrospective approval would have added anything new and whether there was any actual fatal breach of the "*Whitley Principle*".[2]

## The site

This site has to do with the former railway works in Crewe, known as the "*Bombardier Works*" and those who are keen on the history of railways will know that Crewe was one of the great centres of railway engineering, manufacturing and repair during the 19th and

---

[1]    So called after the leading case on the point: F*G Whitley & Sons Co Ltd v Secretary of State for Wales* [1992] 64 P. & C.R. 296.

[2]    See *Agecrest Ltd v Gwynedd CC* (1998) J.P.L. 325; *R v Flintshire County Council and Another Ex Parte Somerfield Stores Limited* [1998] P.L.C.R. 336; *Leisure Great Britain plc v Isle of Wight CC* [2000] P.L.C.R. 88; *R (on the application of Hart Aggregates Ltd) v Hartlepool BC* [2005] EWHC 840 (Admin) and *Greyfort Properties Ltd v Secretary of State for Communities and Local Government and Torbay Council* [2011] EWCA Civ 908.

early 20th century. The Bombardier Works were the historical remains of railway workshops etc from the *"golden age of steam"* which were first used for the building and repair of steam engines and then diesel engines. Unfortunately, the decline of the railways meant that the activities at the Works gradually petered down to the point where the heavy engineering was discontinued. As with many of these workshops, the demand for them fell into decline with the reduction in the railway network and changes in rolling stock and they eventually became empty. The buildings became derelict and eventually the site was cleared and used for housing. That is to say, a classic *"brownfield site"* situation.

There are a number of matters to be taken into account. The first is that the built structures might have contained contaminative materials in themselves, such as asbestos. Secondly, the activities which were carried out in the workshops would have been metal fabrication, welding, paint spraying and activities of that nature, all of which have the potential to contaminate both the buildings and the land upon which those buildings sat. For example, one might find that, perhaps, metal parts were cleaned in some form of solvent and it might also be the case that the solvent was then blown off castings etc (by using airguns) over significant periods of years. There could be a lot of solvent deposited within the fabric of the building and also in the floors and the ground. It might be the case that the buildings were erected on hard pads and floored with hard materials; however, this is not helpful because substances such as oil coolant from the machines tools and volatile organic compounds arising from paint works could be absorbed into the flooring, and would also permeate through the joins.

Next, in all probability, a heavy engineering site may have included oil tanks or tanks which contained some forms of chemicals and, so there is always the danger of historical leak-ages – this is particularly so where those tanks are being dismantled as part of a demolition process. It might, indeed, be the case that there were underground tanks which have been lost to the realms of history, but they still had the potential to leak and cause problems in the future, particularly if disturbed by ground works. Large engineering works would often have electrical substations on site, because they consumed a huge amount of energy and high voltage electricity would have been transferred directly on to the site and then reduced down to workable voltages within on-site electrical substations. The substations and electrical processes that go with them can be contaminative.

Finally, but probably most significantly, one can anticipate that much of an old industrial site will be made ground. This would be where, over time, buildings and equipment have been moved around the site and, in many cases, waste products will simply have been buried on site and then soiled over or hidden under the hard foundations for new build-ings. The potential presence for made ground is always a red flag for the simple reason that one does not know what has been buried in it and one needs to find out what might or might not lie beneath the surface.

Arguably, the first test that needs to be applied is to ask whether there is reasonable objec-tively based suspicion of contamination in relation to a site of this nature, and the answer in connection with the Bombardier site was a clear *"yes"*.

It is possible to postulate a working baseline which is to ask whether there is a reasonable suspicion of a level of contamination which might make the site unsuitable for its proposed use, in order to distinguish objectively sound suspicions from merely fanciful or ephemeral suspicions. If the answer is "*yes*", then the next question is "*where do we go from here?*" The answer has to be to carry out intrusive site investigations. This might be by way of bore-holes, trial trenches etc, but one needs to carry out site investigations to find out whether contamination exists and whether that contamination is a problem. If it is a problem, then it is necessary to come up with a plan to ensure that the site will, once the "*risk management*" plan has been carried out, be suitable for the proposed use or uses.

**Stigma**
The Bombardier Works is a good subject for a case study because it demonstrates the stigmatisation which can be whipped up by uninformed media reports. Here there were headlines such as:

• "Residents in turmoil as every one of the new estate's 263 houses faces demolition".

• "Homeowners at the Coppin Hall Place development in Crewe fear their properties could be worth nothing in a row over planning permission".

• "Toxic residues under the ground means that there is currently no planning permission which could render the properties worthless and result in them being torn down".

• "They were built on the former bombardier train factory site where residues of asbestos, lead, cyanide and arsenic had been found ..."

The mere fact that the houses were built on a site where residues of asbestos, lead, cyanide and arsenic could have been found underneath the land is meaningless unless one has some understanding of the quantum of the materials which were found and also the treatment and adaptive measures which were deployed in the construction of the houses. The reality of the situation was that the developers had carried out extensive site investigations. They had a risk management strategy and they had incorporated appropriate precautions within the buildings themselves. All of this seems to have escaped the reporters. Arguably, the developer had done a relatively good job in sorting out this particular challenge, and what remained to be done to resolve a problem was more technical than fundamental.

**The 2018 Planning Permission (Application No: 18/0079N)**
The permission was for:

> "*The demolition of the existing industrial buildings and structures (including the boundary wall along West Street) and the construction of 263 dwellings comprising 24 apartments and 239 houses, together with other associated works, including the provision of public open space, the laying out of roads and footways (with two new accesses from West Street), and hard and soft landscaping.*"

The conditions relating to land contamination were as follows:

> *"12. a) Any soil or soil forming materials to be brought to site for use in garden areas or soft landscaping shall be tested for contamination and suitability for use prior to importation to site.*
>
> *b) Prior to occupation, evidence and verification information (for example, laboratory certificates) shall be submitted to, and approved in writing by, the LPA."*

**Comment**

This condition is slightly unusual, but it is a prudent one in principle. It makes good sense to ensure that any imported fill materials are free of contaminants. There is, however, an initial problem with the condition; namely, that the verification procedure in sub-condition (b) required that the verification information be supplied and approved prior to occupation. The use of the phrase *"prior to occupation"* is ambiguous and it is not clear whether this is a reference to the first dwelling house on the development or to occupation of the development as a whole. Secondly, it is difficult to see why the requirement in sub-condition (a) is linked to occupation at all. It would seem to be more sensible to ensure that the fill materials are certified as being suitable before they are actually incorporated into the development. Leaving aside any other matters, an incoming residential occupier is not going to be happy to find that his or her garden area is, suddenly, being re-engineered because the verification evidence has proved to be unsuitable. Thus, whilst a welcome condition in principle, the draftsmanship leaves something to be desired.

In the event, it appears that bulk fill containing anthropogenic constituents was recorded as being imported to site in October and December 2019: see extract from Report below.

The contested condition provided as follows:

> *"11. Development shall not commence until:*
>
> *a) A Phase II ground investigation and risk assessment has been completed. A Phase II report shall be submitted to, and approved in writing by, the LPA AND:*
>
> *b) If Phase II ground investigations indicate that remediation is necessary, a Remediation Strategy shall be submitted to, and approved in writing, by the LPA.*
>
> *Prior to the occupation of each phase of the development:*
>
> *c) The remedial scheme in the approved Remediation Strategy shall be carried out.*
>
> *d) A Verification Report prepared in accordance with the approved Remediation Strategy, shall be submitted to, and approved in writing by, the LPA, prior to the occupation of each phase of the development."*

## Comment

Sub-conditions 11(a) and (b) were cast in the *"Grampian"* (aka *"Pre-Commencement"*) form. This meant that, in theory, there was a danger that any development carried out before the discharge of this condition is not authorised by the relevant planning permission: (see Appendix 1).

The local planning authority's officers clearly took the view that the failure of Countryside Properties to discharge this condition prior to the construction of the dwellinghouses in dispute was so severe that the ensuing construction of the dwellinghouses was not authorised by the planning permission. Whether this opinion was right or wrong is debatable. There is an argument that, when one looks to the history of the site, a considerable amount of work had been carried out by the relevant consultants on behalf of Countryside Properties, both in relation to the assessment of the contamination of the site per se and also the adaptation measures which were proposed to be installed so as to isolate the dwellinghouses from any gaseous pollutants.

Sub-conditions 11(c) and (d) embargoed the occupation of each phase of the development until the requirements therein were discharged. However, as with Condition 12, it is not clear whether the reference to *"occupation"* was a reference to occupation of the first dwelling or the entirety of the relevant phase.

### The committee report

The committee report in relation to the application for retrospective planning permission was first submitted to the Council's Strategic Planning Board on 23 March 2023.

The report commenced by saying that the conditions in respect of contaminated land had not been satisfied and this rendered that original consent *"void"* – hence the submission of the application to seek regularisation of the development. One needs to burrow down into this rabbit hole and to seek to understand the very basic legal principles which should have been examined before making this somewhat courageous statement.

It is not clear whether the relevant officers had taken advice from counsel before reaching this conclusion, but it is difficult to see how a failure to discharge the condition rendered the original planning permission *"void"*. The 2018 planning permission was subject to the usual three-year time limit for the commencement of development. Thus, the reality in this case is that the 2018 permission would have expired by effluxion of time because the works which were purported to comprise *"material operations"* for the purposes of Section 55(6) of the Town & Country Planning Act 1990 would have been unauthorised. Even if this were not the case, it is difficult to see how a planning permission which is good on its face can somehow be rendered void ab initio as a result of actions which might, or might not have been, carried out in connection with a condition of that permission. This proposition was completely counter to the current position in UK administrative law.[3] Furthermore, if the

---

[3]   See: Tom Graham – *The Carnwath Report: 30 years on* (almost). Reflections on *"nullity"* and *"invalidity"* - The Journal of Planning and Environmental Law, Autumn 2018.

2018 permission was indeed rendered *"void"*, then the conditions annexed to it would also have been void. Ergo, there could not have been a breach of condition in any event. This being so, the administrative problem would have been whether or not it was expedient to take enforcement action, having regard to the circumstances of the case as a whole. Given the facts of this particular case, one is left to ponder whether or not a requirement for retrospective planning application was, in any event, an overreaction when the proportionate response, in terms of enforcement, would have been to seek to regularise the position by way of the submission and approval of the missing evidence.[4]

Be that as it may, the report went on to say that the main issue for the new scheme was additional information to regularise the issue of contaminated land. Whilst the Environmental Protection Officers were still concerned about certain aspects of the assessments undertaken, they were now satisfied that the main issue, that of human health, had been addressed. The report also noted those officers preferred that their technical findings (which were different from those of the applicant's consultants) should be peer reviewed by another professional.

## Extract from the Report
### Contaminated Land

*This is the main issue with this application, and why it has been necessary to re-submit the application. Environmental Protection comments are therefore presented in some detail below.*

*Following a recent meeting with the applicant and their environmental consultant Environmental Protection (EP) agreed to review the submissions that pertain to the potential risk posed by volatile contamination at the site only. Due to time constraints EP have not reviewed any information pertaining to contact, ingestion and inhalation of dust pathways. EP consider these pathways capable of being resolved, albeit with some potential disruption post any application approval.*

*EP remain unsatisfied with the latest revision of the Remediation Strategy (Rev 8), however the issues pertaining to the vapour risk at the development may be assessed not withstanding our concerns with respect to this document. As such the Remediation Strategy remains unapproved.*

*The following aspects were therefore reviewed on the basis of potential ground gas/ volatile risk:*

- *Importation of bulk fill containing anthropogenic constituents;*

---

[4]   This would have been a classic *"under-enforcement"* approach and Section 173 (11) of the Town & Country Planning Act 1990 would have then had the effect of granting retrospective planning permission for the balance of the development in any event.

- *Polychlorinated Biphenyls (PCBs);*[5]

- *Volatile Organic Compound (VOC) Monitoring Assessment;*

- *Potential volatile contaminants recorded within Made Ground*[6] *left in-situ, including areas where contaminant hotspots were not suitably delineated and excavated;*

- *Tank Removal; and,*

- *Mixture of potentially volatile material with Ordinary Portland Cement before burial.*

## Importation of Bulk Fill

*Further commentary was requested as bulk fill containing anthropogenic constituents was recorded as being imported to site in October and December 2019, which is contrary to the requirements of Section RE-21 of the Remediation Strategy. This section states that material imported to site to achieve proposed ground levels must comprise natural inert soils and aggregate as per the engineering requirements. Concerns were raised as to whether or not importation of soils containing anthropogenic material would require a reassessment of the site's ground gas risk assessment.*[7]

*Further to the above, although no commentary was provided by the consultant pertaining to potential ground gas risk, information pertaining to the donor site has been provided alongside previously unsubmitted import tickets that confirm the provenance of the material. EP are satisfied that the recorded anthropogenic materials are representative of poor segregation at the donor site and that, following an assessment of the site records (exploration hole logs), the materials would not present a significant ground gas risk to the Bombardier site.*

## Polychlorinated Biphenyls (PCBs)

*To date, EP have not received a suitable response from the consultant with respect to this matter. As such, we have undertaken a review of the available information for the site.*

*A previous site assessment undertaken by Aecom (2013) assessed the potential for PCBs to be present at the site. Aecom's study site was significantly larger than the current site and incorporates the works to the east. Aecom noted the presence of two electrical transformers on its site and an internal electrical substation. According to the site's environmental aspects register, the electrical equipment at the site contained no PCBs,*

---

[5]  Polychlorinated Biphenyls (PCBs) are carcinogenic chemical compounds. In 2013, the International Agency for Research on Cancer classified dioxin-like PCBs as human carcinogens.

[6]  See Paragraph 4.2 above.

[7]  This was a valid point. One of the dangers of importing contaminated fill is that the developer might be forced to restart the whole site assessment process.

*although Aecom was not provided with any documentation to confirm this. All buildings historically associated with electrical repair are/were not located on the current subject site, but in the area further east.*

*The applicant's consultant has undertaken PCB testing in the current assessment and were informed of the areas to sample. No PCBs were identified in the testing undertaken (10 No. samples).*

*It is considered by EP that the concrete bases of any substations/electrical infrastructure would provide a measure of protection to the underlying soils with respect to PCBs. Subsequent soil turnover and mixing would dilute any residual impact and decrease the volatile risk to the current development. In light of the above, it is considered that PCBs are unlikely to constitute a vapour risk to the development.*

### Volatile Organic Compound (VOC) Monitoring Assessment

*A series of boreholes were drilled across the final development platform and adsorption tubes installed to obtain VOC samples for laboratory analysis. The results of this analysis were modelled by the environmental consultant to determine whether or not a post-remediation residual risk was present at the site from the volatile contaminants analysed. Some errors have been identified within the submitted models pertaining to compound values, model parameters and equation application, however EP's review and subsequent t reassessment has determined that these errors do not impact the overall conclusion of the submitted assessment. EP are therefore satisfied that the volatile organic compounds modelled do not pose a significant risk to the development.*

### Potential Volatile Contaminants Recorded Within Made Ground Left In-Situ, Including Areas Where Contaminant Hotspots Were Not Suitably Delineated And Excavated.

*Potentially volatile contaminants of concern, which were recorded above the laboratory limits of detection but which do not have remedial targets (within E3P report Ref: 10-880-R3-Rev8), have also been assessed. In addition to the material within the development platform, EP have also considered material left in-situ following hotspot remediation.*

*EP are satisfied with the consultant's assessment for contaminants of concern where authoritative generic assessment criteria have been provided. For the contaminants (2-methylnaphthalene, dibenzofuran, carbazole and anthraquinone) we have reviewed the consultant's risk assessment in detail as no authoritative generic assessment criteria are available for these compounds.[8]*

---

[8] See Paragraph 7.6 on generic assessment criteria.

*Some contradictory information was submitted in the report compared with authoritative UK based guidance. As such, EP have undertaken Detailed Quantitative Risk Assessments (DQRAs) for these substances in order to assess their volatility and, if necessary, whether their concentrations would be capable of causing significant harm to residents. The DQRAs have either concluded that these compounds are not sufficiently volatile within UK ground conditions to pose a significant risk or that on balance the concentrations identified are not sufficient to pose a risk when volatilised into indoor air. EP caveat that these assessments have been undertaken by an officer of the Section and have not been peer reviewed as per standard assessment procedure.*

### Tank Removal

*Queries were raised with regard to a tank recorded by the remedial contractor in plots 259-263. Following further correspondence with the environmental consultant EP are now satisfied that there is no significant residual risk posed to properties in this area.*

*A tank was excavated in the west of the site (Tank Excavation 2). The subsequent delineation of impacted surrounding soils was not sufficiently robust and elevated concentrations of trichloroethene (TCE)[9] were left in-situ. The consultant's report places reliance upon vapour membranes within plots in proximity to this location to protect residents from this residual contamination. The membrane validation information provided for plots in this area is either absent or not in accordance with agreed validation criteria. As reliance could not be placed upon this information, EP undertook a DQRA to determine whether identified concentrations of TCE could potentially pose a significant risk to indoor air at the development.*

*A modelling exercise was undertaken and concentrations of TCE were found to be in excess of site-specific assessment criteria. Further modelling was therefore undertaken to quantify the risk to indoor air utilising site-specific parameters. This concluded that a significant risk to indoor air is unlikely to be present at the recorded contaminant concentrations. EP caveat that this assessment has been undertaken by an officer of this Section and have not been peer reviewed as per standard assessment procedure.*

### Mixture Of Potentially Volatile Material With Ordinary Portland Cement Before Burial

*Material was mixed with Ordinary Portland Cement for geotechnical purposes and buried in the north of the site. The material was chemically tested prior to placement but the material was moved before the receipt of the laboratory results. This material*

---

[9]  It is reported that chronic exposure to trichloroethylene can cause neurological, liver and kidney damage, and have adverse effects on fertility in men who are occupationally exposed. Trichloroethylene is classified as carcinogenic to humans: See Public Health England Trichloroethylene: toxicological overview (Updated 10 June 2021). https://www.gov.uk/government/publications/trichloroethylene-properties-incident-management-and-toxicology/trichloroethylene-toxicological-overview.

*was shown to contain potentially volatile hydrocarbon fractions. As a subsequent exercise to locate this material proved unsuccessful, a modelling exercise was undertaken to ascertain whether or not this material posed an ongoing or future risk to the development via volatilisation and subsequent inhalation. EP still await the final model from the applicant's consultant, however upon their review of the latest submitted model, the errors identified do not adversely impact the presented conclusion that the material does not represent a risk to the development.*

*Two conditions are recommended:*

- *Within 3 months of the approval of this development, a Remediation Strategy shall be submitted to, and approved in writing, by the LPA.*

- *Within 6 months of the approval of the development, a Verification Report for the entirety of the development, prepared in accordance with the approved Remediation Strategy, shall be submitted and approved in writing by the LPA.*

The proposed conditions are problematic. In particular, it is not clear what would happen in the event that the local planning authority fails to approve the *"remediation"* strategy or the verification report within the stipulated time scales. Whilst the developer has control over the timing of the submission of these documents, it does not have control over the approval of them. This begs the question of whether the proposed conditions were, actually, valid.[10] Presumably, a failure to approve by the local planning authority would have to be resolved by way of an appeal which, inevitably, would take a considerable period of time. Accordingly, one wonders whether it might be more appropriate to include these matters in a planning obligation with appropriate clauses for determination by an expert.

---

[10] Or rescued by *Trump v Scottish Ministers* [2015] UKSC 74.

# Appendix 1

# Extended Notes On Conditions

**Legal limits on conditions**

Section 70(1) of the Town and Country Planning Act 1990 provides that a local planning authority may grant a planning permission unconditionally or "*subject to such conditions as they think fit*".

The power to impose conditions is not as wide as the literal words of Section 70(1) might appear to suggest. The courts have, on numerous occasions, held that local planning authorities must observe certain legal principles in imposing conditions.

In *Newbury DC v Secretary of State* [1981] A.C. 578 the House of Lords identified these principles as follows:

*   A condition must be imposed for a planning purpose only and not for any ulterior motive.

*   The condition must fairly and reasonably relate to the development permitted by the planning permission.

*   The condition shall not be so unreasonable that no reasonable planning authority could have imposed it.

In the *Newbury* case, a condition of a temporary permission required the removal of two pre-existing aircraft hangers upon expiry of the permission. The condition was invalid because it did not address anything arising from the change of use. These principles have been developed by the courts in a number of later cases and were endorsed by the Supreme Court in *R (Wright) v Forest of Dean District Council* [2019] UKSC 53.

**The need for precision**

Conditions which relate to land contamination are often burdened with the task of conveying technical requirements in a few words. This is not easy task. The courts have held that a condition may be invalid if it fails to convey its message in terms which should be understood by the reader or fails to provide a formula that can be applied with accuracy in practice; however, the defects must be extreme.

Whilst not a planning case, *R v Fenny Stratford Justices, exp Watney Mann (Midlands) Ltd* (1976) 1 W.L.R 1101 exemplifies the point. There a magistrates' court had made an order, under the Public Health Act 1936, requiring the abatement of nuisance caused by music played in a public house. The order required that the level of noise in the premises should not exceed 70 decibels. The Divisional Court held that the order was void for uncertainty because it did not specify the position where the noise reading was to be taken. The local authority had made the mistake of setting a testable standard in the order but failing to set out the parameters which were essential to the carrying out of the test. One can easily see why this case is important in the context of conditions relating to land contamination where the achievement of measurable standards is central to the exercise.[1]

The position is not made better by the use of subjective language instead. A classic example comes from world of planning enforcement.

In *Metallic Protectives Limited v Secretary of State for the Environment* [1976] J.P.L. 166, an enforcement notice required the occupier of premises to install *"satisfactory soundproofing"* of a compressor and to take all possible action to minimise the effects created by the use of acrylic paint. The Divisional Court held that the notice was a nullity. The mistake was, of course, that the recipient of the notice was not supplied with clear instructions about the nature of the soundproofing. What might or might not be *"satisfactory"* will vary according to the subjective opinions of those one may consult.

One could logically reverse this and say that a condition which shall remove *"unacceptable risk of harm"* is equally subjective. Leaving aside the difficulties of defining what is meant by *"harm"* in this connection, the condition is meaningless without the provision of some objective test which determines when the risk of unacceptable harm is reduced to an acceptable level.

Circular 11/95 called such conditions *"discretionary or vetting"* conditions:

> *"32. Conditions requiring that tidiness, for example, shall be "to the satisfaction of the local planning authority" make the applicant no more certain of just what is required."*

A condition which is defective in this way cannot be rescued by the addition of *"tail-piece"* words such as *"unless otherwise agreed with the local planning authority"* for two reasons. First, because the defect goes to the heart of the condition. It is a fundamental misdirection and so, at law, there is nothing to thus *"vary"*. Secondly, because the *"tail-piece"* might be defective itself: see below.

However, the same paragraph continued:

> *"Conditions which raise these difficulties, however, are not to be confused with conditions which require the submission of a scheme or details for approval which will, when granted, provide the precise guidelines to be followed by the developer."*

**Policy constraints on conditions**
The National Planning Policy Framework (2021) advises:

---

[1]     See also *Kirklees Metropolitan Council v Field* [1997] EWHC 960 (Admin).

*"56. Planning conditions should be kept to a minimum and only imposed where they are necessary, relevant to planning and to the development to be permitted, enforceable, precise and reasonable in all other respects. Agreeing conditions early is beneficial to all parties involved in the process and can speed up decision making. <u>Conditions that are required to be discharged before development commences should be avoided, unless there is a clear justification."</u>* (Emphasis added)

The underlined words allude to *"Grampian type"* conditions, also known as *"pre-commencement conditions"* or *"conditions precedent"*. They indicate the Secretary of State's concerns that such the indiscriminate use of such conditions may slow down the planning process. The footnote refers to Sections 100ZA(4-6) of the Town and Country Planning Act 1990 which require the applicant's written agreement to the terms of a pre-commencement condition, unless prescribed circumstances apply.

The former national advice referred to the so called *"six tests"*; namely, that planning conditions should only be imposed where they are:

• 	 necessary;

• 	 relevant to planning and to the development to be permitted;

• 	 enforceable;

• 	 precise; and

• 	 reasonable in all other respects.

The National Planning Practice Guidance states that any proposed condition that fails to meet any of the 6 tests should not be used. This applies even if the applicant suggests it or agrees on its terms or it is suggested by the members of a planning committee or a third party. Every condition must always be justified by the local planning authority on its own planning merits on a case-by-case basis. Also, conditions which place unjustifiable and disproportionate financial burdens on an applicant will fail the test of reasonableness.

The guidance states that planning permission should not be granted subject to a positively worded condition that requires the applicant to enter into a Section 106 Agreement, or an agreement under other powers, because such a condition is unlikely to pass the test of enforceability. It adds that a negatively worded condition limiting the development that can take place until a planning obligation or other agreement has been entered into is unlikely to be appropriate in the majority of cases.

### Conditions referring to land controlled by the applicant
A condition may impose obligations in respect of any land within the application site, whether that land is owned or controlled by the applicant or not: see *Atkinson v Secretary of State for the Environment* [1983] J.P.L. 599. If a condition refers to land outside the application

site, then this must be land which is within the control of the applicant: see *Peak Park Joint Planning Board v Secretary of State* [1980] 39 P. & C.R. 361.

Section 72(1)(a) provides that a condition may regulate the development or use of any land under the control of the applicant (whether or not it is land within the application site) or require the carrying out of works on any such land so far as it appears to the local planning authority to be expedient for the purposes of or in connection with the permitted development.

In practice, most local planning authorities invite the applicant to show the application site edged in red on the location plan which accompanies the planning application and to show land which is outside the application site but controlled by the applicant edged in blue. This gives the authority the ability to see whether it may impose conditions which include this "*blue land*". Otherwise, the inclusion of land outside the application site might have to be by way of a planning obligation with the relevant landowner.

In *R v Derbyshire County Council, ex. p. North East Derbyshire DC* (1980) it was held that such a condition can have the effect of granting planning permission for the use specified in the condition. Given that the condition in this case related to aftercare on a mining site, it is highly questionable whether the principle would extend to off-site works. Furthermore, one wonders whether this principle still holds good in the very different legal and administrative climate of the 21st century. For example, it would, clearly, be wrongly applied where additional works cause an adverse environmental impact or, indeed, might require an environmental impact assessment.

### Positive conditions and actions outside developer's control

A local planning authority is not entitled to impose a condition which the developer plainly will not be able to discharge. It can only relate to matters over which the developer has control.

A positive condition which requires the developer to carry out works on land outside his control is invalid because he does not have the immediate ability to comply with the condition.

In *Birnie v Banff CC* [1954] S.L.T. (Sh. Ct) 90 planning permission had been granted for the erection of a house, subject to a condition requiring the construction of an access over land not belonging to the applicant. The access was not constructed and the local planning authority took enforcement action. It was held that the authority had no power to impose a condition requiring works on land other than land under an applicant's control and the enforcement notice was quashed.

In *British Airports Authority v Secretary of State for Scotland* [1979] S.C. 200, a condition was imposed concerning the flight path of aircraft taking off and landing at Aberdeen airport. The condition was void because it related to matters over which the applicants had no control. Only the Civil Aviation Authority could control the directions of aircraft.

In *R v Rochdale M.B.C. exp. Tew* [2000] Env. L.R. 1 Sullivan J. held that, even if a condition was theoretically enforceable, it would be invalid if it was not reasonably enforceable. The enforceability of any planning condition had to be considered in the light of the particular facts. A condition which is not reasonably enforceable is not a reasonable condition for the purpose of the *"Newbury"* tests (see above). Enforceability should be considered in a pragmatic and not in a theoretical manner, and should be considered by reference to the terms of the particular conditions, the specific development and the particular site in question. It follows that this guidance is particularly important in connection with the enforcement of conditions relating to verification, monitoring and management.

### *"Pre-commencement"* (aka *"Grampian"*) conditions

Given that it is often important to secure the carrying out of treatment works to allow a development to go ahead, these limitations on the use of positive conditions are not helpful. However, it is possible to circumvent the problem by way of a negative pre-commencement condition.

A negative condition may provide that the permitted development shall not commence unless and until a particular event has occurred. Such conditions are named after *Grampian Regional Council v City of Aberdeen* [1984] S.C. (HL) 58, where the particular event in question was the closure of an off-site highway.

So called *"Grampian conditions"* are now commonly called *"pre-commencement conditions"* or *"conditions precedent"*. Such a condition is said to be *"negative"* in the sense that it prohibits the carrying out of some action on the development site unless and until something else happens (often off-site). For example:

> *"No part of the development shall be begun unless and until the treatment works detailed in the [\*\*\*\*] Report have been completed."*

### Failure to discharge a pre-commencement condition

If the developer fails to discharge a pre-commencement condition and goes ahead with the development, then the breach of planning control can go beyond a mere breach of condition. The development itself may be unauthorised and is deemed to be without the benefit of planning permission. Thus, the failure to comply with such a condition can be fatal. This is because all planning permissions are granted on the basis that each permitted development must be begun within a period stipulated in the conditions to the permission – if the development is not started lawfully within the time limit, then the permission will lapse. In the case of operational development, this act of commencement will be by carrying out a *"material operation"* within the meaning of Section 56 of the 1990 Act and, in the case of material change of use, this will be the initiation of the permitted use. It is now trite law that such acts of commencement count to crystallise a permission if they are lawful and that the carrying out of such an act in breach of some pre-commencement conditions will not normally be lawful for these purposes.

This is sometimes called the *"Whitley Principle"* after the leading case on the point.

In *FG Whitley & Sons Co. Ltd v Secretary of State for Wales* [1992] 64 P. & C.R. 296, planning permission had been granted for mineral extraction, subject to a condition which provided that no working should take place except in accordance with a scheme to be agreed with the local planning authority (or, in the absence of agreement, by the Secretary of State). The developers were unable to reach agreement with the authority and carried out work on the site. An enforcement notice was served in relation to the works and the question for the court was whether those works were lawful and, therefore, prevented the permission from expiring.

In the Court of Appeal, Woolf LJ stated:

> *"As I understand the effect of the authorities to which I am about to refer, it is only necessary to ask the single question; are the operations (in other situations the question would refer to the development) permitted by the planning permission read together with its conditions? The permission is controlled by and subject to the conditions. If the operations contravene the conditions they cannot be properly described as commencing the development authorised by the permission. If they do not comply with the permission they constitute a breach of planning control and for planning purposes will be unauthorised and thus unlawful. This is the principle which has now been clearly established by the authorities."*

The courts have, however, recognised limited exceptions to this general principle. In *Agecrest Ltd v Gwynedd CC* (1998) J.P.L. 325 conditions of a planning permission required a number of infrastructure schemes to be submitted to and approved by the local planning authority before development could commence. Subsequently, however, the local planning authority agreed that the development could commence without full compliance with those conditions. The High Court held that the authority had a discretion in the way in which it dealt with such conditions and that the work did amount to a start of the development.

In *R v Flintshire County Council and Another Ex Parte Somerfield Stores Limited* [1998] P.L.C.R. 336 a permission had been granted for a retail development. A pre-commencement condition in the permission required a study to be made and approved by the council of projected traffic generation and highway effects of the scheme before the development commenced. The study had been carried out with the full knowledge and co-operation of the council and the highway authority. However, the developers had made no actual application to the council for approval of the study, nor was there a record of the council communicating approval to the developer. A rival retail operator tried to persuade the authority to take enforcement action when the development started and then applied to the High Court to force the issue. Carnwath J refused an application for judicial review to quash the council's decision not to consider taking enforcement action against the development, holding that the general *"Whitley Principle"* had to be applied with common sense and with regard to the facts of the particular case. In the instant case it would have been unreasonable for the council to have decided that the planning permission had not been implemented.

It is important to place the *Flintshire* case in its proper jurisprudential setting. A local planning authority cannot vary a condition unless it does so in accordance with statute nor can it waive compliance with a condition or vary it. However, it has a discretion as to whether it takes enforcement action in respect of the breach of a condition. Notwithstanding that the statutory mechanism for the issue of a *"breach of condition notice"* does not require that the authority satisfy itself that such enforcement action is *"expedient"*, the authority is entitled to ask itself this question and, indeed, is required to do so by legislation and treaty obligations outside the 1990 Act. There will be cases where, on any objective assessment, it would be wrong to take enforcement action. Clearly, it would then be irrational if the disputed development is, nonetheless, declared to be of no worth in law. This has been described as the *"irrationality principle"*.

In *Leisure Great Britain plc v Isle of Wight CC* [2000] P.L.C.R. 88 the court considered that any exception to the general *Whitley Principle* should be on a clearly identifiable basis and not simply because the court considered it unfair on the merits to apply the general principle.

In *R (on the application of Hart Aggregates Ltd) v Hartlepool BC* [2005] EWHC 840 (Admin) a permission for mineral extraction was granted subject to a condition (*"Condition 10"*) which provided that: *"The worked out areas shall be progressively back-filled and the areas restored to levels shown on the submitted plan or to a level to be agreed by the Local Planning Authority in accordance with a restoration scheme to be agreed by the Local Planning Authority before extraction is commenced".*

The issue was whether the 1971 permission had lapsed because Condition 10 had not been complied with, in that a restoration scheme had not been agreed by the local planning authority before extraction commenced. This turned on whether the condition was a condition precedent and, if so, whether the breach of it meant that the quarrying which purported to rely on the 1971 permission was, in fact, unauthorised.

Sullivan J held that Condition 10 was not a condition precedent. He referred to the *"Whitley Principle"* and said:

> *"[55] The 1990 Act draws a clear distinction between development without planning permission and development in breach of condition; see s.171(A)(1)(a) and (b). It is important that that distinction is not blurred by an indiscriminate use of the judge-made term "condition precedent"."*

He concluded:

> *"[59] Condition 10 is a "condition precedent" in the sense that it requires something to be done before extraction is commenced, but it is not a "condition precedent" in the sense that it goes to the heart of the planning permission, so that failure to comply with it will mean that the entire development, even if completed and in existence for many years, or in the case of a minerals extraction having continued for 30 years, must be regarded as unlawful.*

> *[60] In my judgment, the principle argued for by the defendant applies only where a condition expressly prohibits any development before a particular requirement, such as the approval of plans, has been met. Condition 10 is not such a condition."*

Hence it was necessary to distinguish between non-compliance with positively worded conditions that require something to be done *"before development takes place"* and conditions which normally contain wording such as *"not to commence development until ..."* or *"no development shall take place until ..."* The former is a breach of condition that can be enforced against. In the latter, development cannot be taken to have lawfully commenced until the condition has been discharged. He added that, even if Condition 10 were a condition precedent, he would have concluded that enforcement action was precluded on the *"irrationality"* principle.

This explanation could be criticised as being somewhat circular as a matter of strict logic, but it seems to be pragmatic. With Condition 10, the parties did not get to the restoration scheme until the extraction was well under way. Hence, it would make no sense to pretend that the development had been commenced unlawfully.

This distinction was continued in *Bedford Borough Council v Secretary of State & Murzyn* [2008] EWHC 2304 (Admin) where an inspector allowed an appeal by a landowner from a decision of the council refusing the grant of a certificate of lawful use or development. The contention of the council in refusing the certificate notwithstanding the beginning of the development in time was that such works were in breach of two conditions of the permission.

Condition 3 stated that:

> *"Before the development is commenced a landscaping scheme to include all hard surfaces and earth mounding shall be submitted for approval by the District Planning Authority, and all planting thereby approved shall be carried out to their satisfaction by a date not later than the end of the full planting season immediately following the completion of that development."*

Condition 4 was that:

> *"Details of all boundary treatments are to be submitted to and approved by the District Planning Authority, prior to the commencement of development."*

The court held that the Inspector had been correct in concluding that two conditions attached to a planning permission for the conversion to a dwelling of a thatched barn did not amount to true *"conditions precedent"* and therefore the principle in *Whitley* had not been engaged and, therefore, breaches of the conditions had not rendered the development as a whole unlawful.

Unfortunately, a later decision of the Court of Appeal has not assisted in the day-to-day application of this increasingly complex doctrine.

In *Greyfort Properties Ltd v Secretary of State for Communities and Local Government and Torbay Council* [2011] EWCA Civ 908, the disputed condition (*"Condition 4"*) stated:

> *"Before any work is commenced on the site the ground floor levels of the building hereby permitted shall be agreed with the Local Planning Authority in writing."*

The loose drafting of this condition left a lot to be desired because, when read in an ordinary way, it seemed to impose a positive obligation on the developer to agree the details with the local planning authority which would be unreasonable because, of course, the developer would not be able to force the authority to agree anything. Instead, a planning inspector had concluded that the condition was a condition precedent and that the failure to settle floor levels was fatal to the validity of access works which had been carried out pursuant to the permission. The Court of Appeal concluded that it was a condition precedent. The Inspector was entitled to find that those ground floor levels were fundamental to the development permitted and that the condition went to the heart of the permission.

As the then case editor for the JPL (Martin Edwards) commented, this is a *"vexed issue"* which *"simply refuses to go away"*: J.P.L. 2012, 1, 39-51.

The lesson which can, however, be derived from this jurisprudence is that, if a local planning authority wishes to put the matter beyond doubt, then it should draft clear and unambiguous conditions. Thus, the current approach is to deduce the effect of a failure to discharge a pre-commencement condition by asking whether it *"goes to the heart of"* the planning permission. Many such conditions govern merely ancillary matters and would not do so. As is so often the situation with town and country planning, this is often a matter of retrospective judgement in each case.

To put it another way, a loose conversational style of drafting is inappropriate when dealing with this highly technical topic.

### *"Scheme"* conditions

The local planning authority is entitled to impose conditions which provide that the detail of matters not particularised in the application may be settled after the planning permission is determined. For example:

> *"No part of the development shall be begun unless and until a risk management scheme for the site has been submitted to and approved by the local planning authority. No dwelling forming part of the scheme shall be occupied unless and until the approved scheme have been completed."*

The above example means that the details mentioned in the condition (i.e. the eponymous *"scheme"*) must be submitted and approved before any works are commenced pursuant to the planning permission. One of the problems with such a condition is that it is very close to Condition 10 in the *Hart* case and Conditions 3 and 4 in the *Murzyn* case (see above) and, accordingly, whilst it might be viewed by some as a form of condition precedent, it is arguable that it does not go to the heart of the planning permission. Therefore, the enforcement of it might be a problem.

It will be seen that the condition in this example not only provides for the approval of details but also stipulates when the works must be completed. The scheme condition holds the actual carrying out of the scheme until a later date – in this case until first residential occupation. The substantive problem with this aspect of the condition is that it is difficult to see why the putative enforcement mechanism is residential occupation when, presumably, any treatment scheme would have been completed long before this occupation takes place. This, again, raises complications in terms of enforcement because it is unclear how a court or planning inspector would react in the event that dwellings are occupied in breach of this part of the condition. It would be surprising if innocent residential occupiers are dispossessed of their properties due to what might turn out to be an administrative error on behalf of the developer.

### Policy limits on *"pre-commencement"* conditions

The utility of pre-commencement conditions was restricted by the advice contained in paragraph 40 of the Annex to Circular 11/95 that there must be *"at least reasonable prospects of the action in question i.e. those stipulated in the condition being performed within the time-limit imposed by the condition"*.

This policy advice was not an expression of the law. A local planning authority is entitled, as a matter of law, to grant planning permission notwithstanding that the developer, on the face of it, appears to have insuperable site-assembly problems.

In *British Railways Board v Secretary of State for the Environment* [1994] J.P.L. 32, the British Railways Board applied for outline planning permission to develop land for housing. On appeal, the Inspector recommended approval subject to the condition that:

> *"13. The works to provide the main access road shall be completed to base course level prior to the commencement of the construction of the residential development hereby approved, and shall be fully completed prior to the occupation of buildings."*

The Secretary of State refused planning permission on the basis that he was precluded in law from granting the permission subject to conditions which appeared to have no reasonable prospect of fulfilment within the five-year life of the permission. The House of Lords held that he had misdirected himself in law in considering that the proposed condition regarding the access road would be invalid.

The Secretary of State responded by saying that the judgment leaves open the possibility for the Secretary of State to maintain, as a matter of policy, that there should be at least reasonable prospects of the action in question being performed within the time-limit imposed by the permission: see Endnote 3 to Circular 11/95.

The issue was raised again in *Merritt v Secretary of State for the Environment, Transport and the Regions* [2000] J.P.L. 371 where Robin Purchas QC (sitting as a Deputy Judge) quashed the decision of an inspector to dismiss an appeal on the ground that the Inspector had erred in law in rejecting a *Grampian* condition relating to the provision of access to the site because, applying Circular 11/95, the Inspector had not been convinced that there was a reasonable prospect that the condition would be fulfilled within the time limit imposed on any permission. The Deputy Judge pointed to the danger in promulgating a policy in an absolute form and that a decision-maker may (wrongly) regard himself as bound to follow that policy. The Inspector had simply applied the policy as a mandatory requirement, without considering whether there was scope for the exercise of discretion.

The Office of the Deputy Prime Minister then sent a letter dated 25 November 2002 to all Chief Planning Officers in England which stated:

> *"As a result of the Judgement in Merritt, paragraph 40 should be amended to read, "It is the policy of the Secretary of State that such a condition may be imposed on a planning permission. However, when there are no prospects at all of the action in question being performed within the time-limit imposed by the permission, negative conditions should not be imposed. In other words, when the interested third party has said that they have no intention of carrying out the action or allowing it to be carried out, conditions prohibiting development until this specified action has been taken by the third party should not be imposed."*

> *The foot note [sic] at the bottom of page 16 [of the then NPPF] should be replaced with:*

> *"A policy of refusing permission where there was no reasonable prospect of planning conditions being met could be lawful, but sound planning reasons for the refusal should be given and it should be made clear that this was only a starting point for consideration of cases."*

This appears the final word – at least for now.

### Legal limits on "*pre-commencement*" conditions

Section 14 of the Neighbourhood Planning Act 2017 created a very important limitation on the unfettered use of pre-commencement conditions. From 1 October 2018, a local planning authority must obtain the written agreement of the applicant before imposing such conditions on a planning permission.

The 2017 Act inserted new Section 100ZA into the Town and Country Planning Act 1990. This provides that an outline planning permission for the development of land may not be granted subject to a "*pre-commencement condition*" without the written agreement of the applicant to the terms of the condition: Section 100ZA(5). Section 100ZA(6) then adds that the requirement under Section 100ZA(5) does not apply in such circumstances as may be prescribed. The detailed provisions are now set out in the Town and Country Planning (Pre-commencement Conditions) Regulations 2018 (S.I. 2018, No. 566).

A *"pre-commencement condition"* is defined in Section 100ZA(8) as a condition imposed on a grant of planning permission (other than a grant of outline planning permission within the meaning of Section 92 of the 1990 Act) which must be complied with:

(a)    before any building or operation comprised in the development is begun; or

(b)    where the development consists of a material change of use of any buildings or other land, before the change of use is begun.

References to a condition includes a limitation: Section 100ZA(13).

The formula in Section 100ZA(8)(a) above is odd because, of course, a *Grampian* condition is not a condition *"which must be complied with ... before any building or operation comprised in the development is begun"*. It is a condition which prohibits that commencement unless and until certain specified events have taken place. To take an example:

> *"The [****] scheme shall be agreed prior to the start of the development."*

Whilst this can be read as a pre-commencement condition, its more natural meaning is that it is a condition which goes to the matter of timing. If, for example, this formula were used in a contract, then it would be a requirement as to the date of delivery and not some form of embargo on the start of the development. Furthermore, unlike a contractual obligation, this condition cannot bite until the development has commenced, that is to say, after the stipulated date for delivery. Accordingly, the better course is to avoid these contortions and, if a pre-commencement condition is intended, then it should be expressed in clear terms e.g.:

> *"No part of the development shall be commenced unless and until the [****] scheme has been submitted to and approved by the local planning authority."*

Even then, Martin Goodall has noted that some conditions in this form are, in practice, unenforceable. He gives this example:

> *"A scheme shall be submitted to and approved by the Local Planning Authority before any site clearance or development works commence on site to ensure the retention and protection of all existing trees on the site and to ensure that such trees are not damaged in the course of the development. All works subsequently carried out shall be in strict accordance with the approved scheme."*

He points out that the conditions attached to a planning permission only take effect when the permission is implemented by starting a *"material operation"* under Section 56 of the 1990 Act. If the development is not started, then the conditions do not bite. The problem is that the removal of trees or other vegetation is not an activity which falls within the definition of a *"material operation"* because it does not normally amount to *"development"* within the definition in Section 55 of the 1990 Act. Thus, this clearance work does not implement the planning permission and would not amount to starting the development.

So, at that point in time, the conditions in the planning permission will not have come into effect and they cannot be enforced.

Be that as it may, rather than trying to distinguish which conditions fall within Section 100ZA(8) and which do not, the better course is for the local planning authority to provide the full suite of proposed conditions to the applicant. Indeed, this is good practice in any event, not least because it might save practical difficulties at a later date and, perhaps, appeals which could have been avoided.

Sections 100ZA(5) and 100ZA(8) apply to permissions which arise from relevant grants of planning permission. References to a *"relevant grant of planning permission"* are to any grant of permission to develop land which is granted on an application made under Part III of the 1990 Act and include the modification of any such grant: Section 100ZA(13).

Article 2(1) of the 2018 Regulations (see above) provides (in effect) that the agreement of the applicant under Section 100ZA(5) of the 1990 Act is not needed in relation to a relevant grant of planning permission where:

(a)    the local planning authority or, as the case may be, the Secretary of State gives notice in writing to the applicant that, if planning permission is granted, the authority or the Secretary of State intends to grant that permission subject to the pre-commencement condition specified in the notice; and

(b)    the applicant does not provide a substantive response to the notice no later than the last day of the period of 10 working days beginning with the day after the date on which the notice is given.

Where notice has been given under paragraph 2(1)(a), the application for planning permission must not be determined until the period given in the notice for a substantive response to be received has expired unless, before that expiry, the local planning authority or, as the case may be, the Secretary of State receives a substantive response, or written agreement to the terms of the proposed pre-commencement condition: paragraphs 2(2) and 2(3).

### "Wheatcroft" conditions
A planning condition may modify the development proposed by the application.

In *Kent County Council v Secretary of State for the Environment and Another* (1976) 33 P. & C.R. 70 Sir Douglas Frank QC (sitting as a deputy judge in the Queen's Bench Division) upheld a condition which had the effect of removing a proposed access road from a scheme for an oil refinery. The substance of the permission was the construction of the refinery, to which all else was ancillary. The operator's acceptance of the condition imposed was evidence that it was not such as to make the refinery unworkable and that, accordingly, the condition was not invalid.

Such conditions are often called "*Wheatcroft*" conditions after *Bernard Wheatcroft Ltd v Secretary of State for the Environment* (1982) 43 P. & C.R. 233 where proposals for a housing development were reduced in size by condition. The test for the validity of such a condition being whether or not the proposed modification is so fundamental that to apply it by condition would frustrate the normal public participation processes. Forbes J stated:

> "*I should add a rider. The true test is, I feel sure, that accepted by both counsel: is the effect of the conditional planning permission to allow development that is in substance not that which was applied for?. Of course, in deciding whether or not there is a substantial difference the local planning authority or the Secretary of State will be exercising a judgment, and a judgment with which the courts will not ordinarily interfere unless it is manifestly unreasonably exercised. The main, but not the only, criterion on which that judgment should be exercised is whether the development is so changed that to grant it would be to deprive those who should have been consulted on the changed development of the opportunity of such consultation, and I use these words to cover all the matters of this kind with which Part III of the Act of 1971 deals.*
>
> *There may, of course, be, in addition, purely planning reasons for concluding that a change makes a substantial difference.*"

In *Breckland District Council v Secretary of State for the Environment and Hill* (1993) 65 P. & C.R. 34 an application for a 16-pitch gypsies' caravan site was accompanied by a plan which identified the site as being 0.47ha. The application was refused by the council. On appeal, the Inspector accepted an amended plan increasing the site to 0.6ha. and thus bringing it nearer to three dwellings in the vicinity. Mr David Widdicombe, QC (sitting as a Deputy High Court Judge in the Queen's Bench Division) quashed the Inspector's decision on the basis that the result must not be substantially different from the development applied for, the amendment to the plan was substantial and the decision that it was not substantial was perverse.

The approach of Forbes J in *Wheatcroft* was heavily criticised by John Howell QC (sitting as a Deputy High Court Judge in the Queen's Bench Division) in *Holborn Studios Limited, R (on the application of) v The Council of the London Borough of Hackney* [2017] EWHC 2823 (Admin):

> "*[73] In my judgment this conflation of the substantive and procedural constraints on the powers of the local planning authority is flawed. It is quite possible for a person to be deprived of an opportunity of consultation on a change which would not result in a permission for a development that is in substance not that which was applied for. Thus, for example, a proposed change to the external appearance of a new building or to the proposed access to it might be said not to result in a development that is in substance different from that applied for, or not to involve a "substantial difference" or a "fundamental change" to the application, but it may still be a change about which persons other than the applicant may want to make representations and would be deprived of the opportunity to do so if not consulted about it. On the other hand to say that any change about which others may want to make representations is to be*

*classified as one that involves a "fundamental change" or a "substantial difference" to the application, or one which makes the development something that was not in substance what was applied for (as would be the result of using the loss of an opportunity to be consulted as the "main criterion" of whether or not there is such a change), deprives such terms of meaning."*

With respect, this seems to take Forbes J out of context. In *Wheatcroft*, the condition reduced the size of the scheme. It is difficult to see how this could be objectionable to the public. Nor did Forbes J's *"rider"* turn on the matter of substance, in the sense of quantum or scale. The question of procedure turns, instead, on that which is important to members of the public. Hence why Forbes J said:

*"The main, but not the only, criterion on which that judgment should be exercised is whether the development is so changed that to grant it would be to deprive those who should have been consulted on the changed development of the opportunity of such consultation."*

Counter to John Howell QC, it could be equally said that a proposed change to the external appearance of a new building, or to the proposed access to it, might be said to result in a development that is in substance different from that applied for because it may be a change about which persons other than the applicant may want to make representations.

Subject to these limitations and this note of caution, it would, for example, be possible to modify proposals by condition to change their effects. Thus:

*"The development shall be carried out in accordance with the approved drawings save that Drawing XXX (titled "****") shall be replaced by Drawing YYY (titled "Revised ****")."*

### The "*Proberun*" case
*Medina Borough Council v Proberun Ltd* (1991) 61 P. & C.R. 77 is important because it shows that a local planning authority cannot go back against a grant of an outline planning permission on the retrospective ground that technical arrangements are not satisfactory.

There the developer's land was joined to a highway by a narrow lane which was in its ownership. The developer did not own any other land surrounding the site. On the refusal of an application to renew an earlier lapsed full planning permission for an extensive housing development on the site, under which access to the highway via the lane had been accepted, the developer appealed to the Secretary of State. The Secretary of State granted an outline planning permission only and attached a condition to the permission providing that details of the design of the buildings, the means of access and landscaping must be submitted to the local authority for approval. Subsequently, the local planning authority refused to approve an access which used the lane only. The authority made it quite clear that the only access which would satisfy them would be over land not in the developer's ownership and an inspector then dismissed the developer's appeal on the grounds that the proposed access contained serious flaws and did not meet required standards.

The Court of Appeal decided that where permission is granted subject to the details of access being approved and the applicant owns or controls no other land than that set out in the application, then details cannot be turned down simply because the local planning authority deems them to be unsatisfactory. It is enough that they are the best that can be achieved on the application site. To expect the developer to provide access on land outside their control was an abuse of power and unlawful.

In *R v Newbury DC Ex p. Chieveley Parish Council* [1999] P. & C.R. 51 Carnwath J drew a distinction between, on the one hand, the effective nullification of an outline permission, and on the other hand, the refinement of the scheme at the reserved matters stage (@ p.1156):

> "In my view, while the general approach as explained in Medina is not in doubt, its application must depend on the circumstances. Much will depend on the scope of the matters left open by the outline permission. In Medina the issue was as narrow as the strip within which room for access had to be found. By contrast, if one takes the example, given earlier, of an outline permission for residential development of a defined area, with all matters reserved, including numbers and form of housing, I cannot see how questions of traffic generation can be irrelevant in fixing the acceptable density and the form of access. Medina merely shows that any limitations imposed at that stage cannot be such as to nullify the principle of residential development."

**Effect of invalid conditions**

In *Kent CC v Kingsway Investments (Kent) Ltd* [1971] A.C. 72, the House of Lords held that certain conditions were valid. However, the Lords went on to say that if the invalid conditions are unimportant, incidental or merely superimposed on the permission, then the permission might endure. If the conditions are part of the structure of the permission, then the permission falls with it.

In *Fisher v Wychavon District Council* [2001] J.P.L. 694, the Court of Appeal was faced with a decision notice which purported to be the grant of permission for the permanent stationing of a caravan on the one hand, but then included conditions which suggested it was a temporary permission only. Unfortunately, the situation was compounded by a typographical error which masked what the temporary period was intended to be. The court struck down the permission. They did not seek to correct the permission by the use of a "*blue pencil*" and (para. 27) adopted Wade: Administrative Law, 8th ed. (2000) at p.295:

> "The court may be particularly disinclined to perform feats of surgery where an invalid condition is one of the terms on which a discretionary power is exercised. If an invalid condition is attached to a licence or to planning permission, the permission without the condition may be such as the licensing authority would not have been willing to grant on grounds of public interest. The right course for the court is then to quash the whole permission, so that a fresh application may be made."

In *R v St Edmundsbury BC exp. Investors in Industry Commercial Properties Ltd* [1985] 1 W.L.R. 1168 the court stated that a condition requiring a development to provide for small retail outlets as well as a supermarket had neither been unreasonable nor been imposed for considerations other than those of planning. Alternatively, it was not so fundamental as to render the whole permission void and was, accordingly, severable and the grant of permission was not void on account of the imposition of the condition. The condition related to retail sales, though not necessarily to food retail sales, and envisaged retail entities not forming part of the supermarket activities as such. It was within the general ambit of the permission sought, and the purpose of the condition was to improve the facilities that the development would afford, particularly to the local area.

### *"Tail-piece"* conditions

Many permissions have, over the years, been granted subject to conditions which allow for minor variations to the matters prescribed by them by agreement with the local planning authority. For example:

> *"The development shall be carried out in accordance with the approved layout plan* <u>*unless otherwise agreed in writing by the local planning authority.*</u>*"*

The underlined words are now known as *"tail-pieces"* and have been found to be objectionable.

The leading case is *R (Midcounties Co-operative Ltd) v Wyre Forest DC* [2009] EWHC 964 (Admin). Whether such a *"tail-piece"* will invalidate a condition depends on its substantive effect. There, two such conditions were challenged; one was held to be defective and the other was not.

One imposed limits on the retail floorspace of a new superstore and continued *"unless otherwise agreed in writing with the Local Planning Authority."* Ouseley J held that the effect of the tail-piece was to enable development to take place *"which could be very different in scale or impact from that applied for, assessed or permitted, and it enables it to be created by means wholly outside any statutory process."*

The second condition identified the drawings in accordance with which the development was to be carried out. It added *"unless other minor variations are agreed in writing after the date of this permission and before implementation with the Local Planning Authority"*. Ouseley J stated:

> *"[79] I do not regard this tail-piece as unlawful. Its clear scope is to enable "minor variations" to an obligation otherwise to develop "in strict accordance" with plans and drawings. Both those parts of the condition operate to limit the flexibility which the tail-piece provides."*

In the event, Ouseley J held that he could excise the offending tail-piece from the first condition so as to leave the balance (and the permission) intact.

In *R (Warley) v Wealden DC* [2011] EWHC 2083 (Admin) permission was granted for lighting at a tennis court subject to a condition which provided that the court should not be operated outside prescribed times "*without the prior consent in writing of the Local Planning Authority*". Mr Rabinder Singh QC (as he then was) sitting as a deputy High Court Judge concluded that these words were inappropriate and severed them from the permission.

Regardless of whether such conditions can be saved by severance, the lesson to be learned is not to use such "*tail-pieces*". Section 96A of the 1990 Act now provides a statutory mechanism for minor variations to planning permissions and this should be used. More significant variations to a scheme should be made via Section 73 of the 1990 Act or a new application.

## Discharge of conditions

Article 27 of the Town and Country Planning (Development Management Procedure) (England) Order 2015 (S.I. 2015/595) provides that, on an application for any consent, agreement or approval required by a condition or limitation attached to a grant of planning permission, the authority must give notice to the applicant of their decision within a period of 8 weeks or such longer period as may be agreed by the applicant and the authority.

Article 28 provides a mechanism for deemed discharge of certain planning conditions where the applicant has given notice in accordance with Article 29 (called a "*deemed discharge notice*"). A condition to which Section 74A(2) of the 1990 Act applies is deemed to be discharged where the applicant has given such notice, in relation to that condition, and the period for the authority to give notice to the applicant of their decision on the application has elapsed without the authority giving notice to the applicant of their decision. Deemed discharge takes effect on the date specified in the deemed discharge notice or on such later date as may be agreed by the applicant and the authority, unless the authority has given notice to the applicant of their decision on the application before that date.

A deemed discharge notice may not be given unless at least 6 weeks have elapsed beginning with the day immediately following that on which the application under Article 27 is received by the local planning authority or such shorter period as may be agreed in writing between the applicant and the authority for serving a deemed discharge notice has elapsed: Article 29(2).

Deemed discharge does not apply where the condition falls within the exemptions listed in Schedule 6 of the 2015 Order or, in relation to that condition, the applicant and the local planning authority have agreed that the provisions of Section 74A of the 1990 Act (deemed discharge of planning conditions) do not apply.

## Challenging conditions

If the applicant is unhappy with a planning condition then they have a number of options available to them:

- a High Court challenge if they believe that the condition is ultra vires;

- an appeal against the condition to the Secretary of State;

- an application for renewal of the permission under the streamlined procedure in regulation 3(3) of the Town and Country Planning (Applications) Regulations 1988;

- an application to for planning permission which is not subject to the condition under Section 73 of the 1990 Act;

- seeking a *"non material amendment"* under Section 96A of the 1990 Act; or

- an application for a new planning permission.

Each of these actions is subject to its own limitations:

- A High Court challenge must be started within six weeks of the date of grant of the planning permission.

- An appeal against a condition must be started within three months of the date of grant of the planning permission.

- An application for renewal is not available if the permission has lapsed, the development has begun or if the time-limit for the submission of reserved matters has expired.

- An application to vary is not available if the permission has lapsed.

A High Court challenge can be precarious because, if the court feels that the condition is fundamental to the permission, it may quash both the condition and the planning permission. There is established authority for the proposition that, if an authority has imposed a wrongful condition, then it is guilty of taking into account an improper consideration thereby vitiating its subsequent decision as a whole.

Similarly, an appeal to the Secretary of State reopens the question of whether or not the planning permission should have been granted whether with or without the disputed condition.

By contrast, an application to vary under Section 73 is a much safer course because the local planning authority (or the Secretary of State on appeal) must review the condition only and cannot upset the original permission.

# Appendix 2

# Generic Site Assessment And Detailed Assessment

It might be the case that the reader requires some further explanation of the somewhat technical language associated with site assessments or about the interaction between the many and varied sources of guidance.

### Generic site assessments
One difficulty is understanding the role of generic site assessments.

*"Model Procedures for the Management of Land Contamination"* - Contaminated Land Report 11 (see below) provided two useful definitions:

- *"Generic quantitative assessment"*: Risk assessment carried out using generic assumptions to estimate risk or to develop Generic Assessment Criteria.

- *"Generic assessment criteria"*: Criteria derived using generic assumptions about the characteristics and behaviour of sources, pathways and receptors. These assumptions will be protective in a range of defined conditions.

Generic assessment criteria are *"generic"* because they are settled by reference to broad assumptions which will not, normally, be replicated on a site-by-site basis. For example, the CLEA guidance (see below) is based on a hypothetical generic site for which assumptions are made as follows:

- Soil type.

- Below ground level of contamination.

- Width of source zone parallel to the wind direction.

- Wind speed.

- For organic substances, that there is no free product.

It is important to note at the outset that Generic Assessment Criteria are intended to provide a screening or sifting mechanism at an early stage in the process and are intended to field the need for a site-specific assessment for each potential contaminant until the scheme proposals are more advanced, both in terms of site knowledge and financial confidence. It follows that the criteria must be very conservative, otherwise undesirable contaminants may slip though the net because the thresholds are set too high. It also follows that later refinement of the site assessment should be to reduce the extent of the treatment or adaptive actions which would be required if the rude Generic Assessment Criteria were applied in an unrefined model.

If these ground rules are not understood then the particular threshold set out in model procedures can be taken to represent *"magic numbers"*. This is the quantitative thresholds are taken to be definitive when that is exactly the reverse of the reasons for providing them.

### ICRCL Guidance Note 59/83

Guidance on the assessment of potentially contaminated land has a long history. As is often the case, it is helpful to look at the back-story in order to understand the current position.

The substantive starting point is the document called *"Guidance on the Assessment and Redevelopment of Contaminated Land"*, otherwise known as *"ICRCL Guidance Note 59/83"* (second edition, July 1987), which was published by the Inter Departmental Committee on the Redevelopment of Contaminated Land.

Guidance Note 59/83 sought to draw together a number of earlier and separate guidance notes with the intention of providing a generic and overarching approach which would as act as an initial screening. The production of this guidance should, to a large extent, have provided for consistency of decision-making by those bodies which adopted or accepted it.

The Guidance Note turned, to a large extent, on the concept of *"trigger concentrations"* which depend upon the intended use of the site. Examples of these concentrations were given for the principal contaminants. The Guidance Note provided that if, after thorough investigation, the samples from the site show values below the prescribed *"lower trigger concentrations"*, then it was reasonable to regard the site as uncontaminated and to proceed with the development accordingly. If, however, the result exceeded the *"upper trigger concentrations"*, then it followed that some adaptive action would be required if the chosen form of development was to proceed. This was set out in a diagrammatic form as follows:[1]

---

[1] Reformatted from original for the purposes of reproduction.

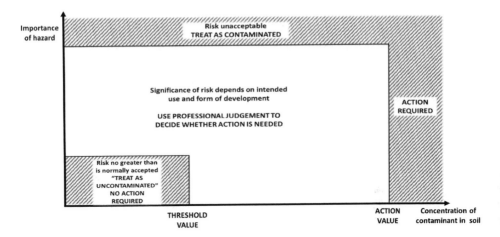

*Interpretation of "Trigger Concentrations"*

The *"tentative trigger concentrations"* were set out in two tables. One table, Table 3, set out the concentrations for selected inorganic contaminants. The second table, Table 4, set out concentrations for contaminants associated with former coal carbonisation sites. Table 3 was set out as follows:

| Contaminants | Planned uses | Trigger Concentration (mg/kg air dried soil) | |
|---|---|---|---|
| | | Threshold | Action |
| Group A: Contaminants which may pose hazards to health | | | |
| Arsenic | Domestic gardens, allotments | 10 | * |
| | Parks, playing fields, open space | 40 | * |
| Cadmium | Domestic gardens, allotments | 3 | * |
| | Parks, playing fields, open space | 15 | * |
| Chromium (hexavalent) | Domestic gardens, allotments | 25 | * |
| | Parks, playing fields, open space | | * |

| Chromium (total) | Domestic gardens, allotments | 600 | * |
|---|---|---|---|
| | Parks, playing fields, open space | 1,000 | * |
| Lead | Domestic gardens, allotments | 500 | * |
| | Parks, playing fields, open space | 2,000 | * |
| Mercury | Domestic gardens, allotments | 1 | * |
| | Parks, playing fields, open space | 20 | * |
| Selenium | Domestic gardens, allotments | 3 | * |
| | Parks, playing fields, open space | 6 | * |
| **Group B: Contaminants which are phytotoxic but not normally hazards to health** | | | |
| Boron (water-soluble) | Any uses where plants are to be grown | 3 | * |
| Copper | Any uses where plants are to be grown | 130 | * |
| Nickel | Any uses where plants are to be grown | 70 | * |
| Zinc | Any uses where plants are to be grown | 300 | * |

The first point to make, in connection with Table 3, is, of course, that the lists of contaminants and *"planned uses"* are noticeably short. Furthermore, the final *"action"* column is populated by asterisks and, when one goes to the accompanying notes, they state that action concentrations will be specified in the next edition of ICRCL 59/83. The third edition never appeared. The *"threshold"* values would, nowadays, be described as *"soil guideline values"* or *"soil concentrations"* (see below).

Table 4 was set out as follows:

| Contaminants | Planned uses | Trigger Concentration (mg/kg air dried soil) | |
|---|---|---|---|
| | | Threshold | Action |
| Polyaromatic hydrocarbons | Domestic gardens, allotments, play areas | 50 | 500 |
| | Landscaped areas, buildings, hard cover | 1,000 | 1,000 |
| Phenols | Domestic gardens, allotments | 5 | 200 |
| | Landscaped areas, buildings, hard cover | 5 | 1,000 |
| Free cyanide | Domestic gardens, allotments, landscaped areas | 25 | 500 |
| | Buildings, hard cover | 100 | 500 |
| Complex cyanides | Domestic gardens, allotments | 250 | 1,000 |
| | Landscaped areas | 250 | 5,000 |
| | Buildings, hard cover | 250 | No limit |
| Thiocyanate | All proposed uses | 50 | No limit |
| Sulphate | Domestic gardens, allotments, landscaped areas | 2,000 | 10,000 |
| | Buildings | 2,000 | 50,000 |
| | Hard cover | 2,000 | No limit |
| Sulphide | All proposed uses | 250 | 1,000 |
| Sulphur | All proposed uses | 5,000 | 20,000 |
| Acidity (pH less than) | Domestic gardens, allotments, landscaped areas | pH5 | pH3 |
| | Buildings, hard cover | No limit | No limit |

Again, the point to note is that the list of contaminants was relatively short, albeit, in this case, the "*action*" column is fully populated.

It will also be noted that the trigger concentrations have, in many cases, an uneasy match with the proposed uses. For example, the thresholds for complex cyanides are the same for domestic gardens and hard cover, when one would expect that the latter would carry a much higher threshold value. This is against the obvious differentiation when one comes to the action levels in the final column and suggests a degree of over-conservatism in the threshold values.

The narrative to the Guidance Note stated that for the purposes of setting trigger concentrations, contaminants could be divided into three categories:

*   Those which may present a hazard even in very low concentrations, examples being methane and asbestos. For these, any measurable concentration required action to be considered or taken. Their threshold concentration was, therefore, effectively zero.

*   Those for which a given concentration in the soil produce a measurable effect on a "*target*", examples being sulphate, sulphur, organic compounds, cytotoxic metals and cyanide.

*   Those for which no "*dose-effect*" relationship between the concentrations in the soil and the effects have been determined experimentally. There was, at the time, insufficient evidence to specify precise trigger values of these contaminants.

The Guidance Note went on to say that the tentative trigger values were based on professional judgement after taking into account the available information. It emphasised that:

> "*These assessments are seldom simple. As may be seen from Tables 3 and 4, trigger concentrations are only available for a limited range of contaminants, though these are generally the most important. For most contaminants, it is very difficult at present to set upper values at which the concentration would automatically be considered undesirable or unacceptable. Given the paucity of information about some contaminants and the difficulty of obtaining it for others, it is unlikely that some of these values could ever be derived experimentally. The assessment of risks and of the need for remedial action must, therefore, depend on subjective or qualitative criteria.*" (p.12 @ para.37)

The notion of "*subjective or qualitative criteria*" is in need of exploration, because a qualitative approach is not subjective and, almost by definition, is not criterion-based. It is, essentially, a site-specific analysis based upon data derived from that particular site as assessed by reference to the nature of the proposed development.

ICRCL Guidance Note 59/83 was in existence, and applied in practice, for 20 years, up until 2003. The robust question to be asked is whether, notwithstanding the laudable motives behind the publication, it was of any great value on a day-to-day basis? Perhaps, there are lessons to be learned nonetheless.

Clearly, the threshold approach was very limited in terms of its content and the Guidance Note made it clear that it was secondary to subjective or qualitative evaluations. The fact that action levels were never published for Table 3 had the unfortunate side effect that regulators were often tempted to take exceedances of the lower threshold as meaning that adaptive action was required. Perhaps the best way to put it is that the Guidance Note provided a useful starting point for screening or sifting sites which might or might not be contaminated. However, ultimately, it did not carry one any great distance into the assessment process.

The Guidance Note was withdrawn in 2003 on the reasoning that the guideline values were out of date and not in line with Part IIA of the Environmental Protection Act 1990 and associated policy.

### The CLEA model

The CLEA package consists of Contaminated Land Reports (CLRs) 7 to 10, the CLEA 2002 software, toxicological reports (TOX) and Soil Guideline Values (SGVs).

The modelling basis for the CLEA guideline values is set out in:

• CLR 9: *"Contaminants in soils: collation of toxicological data and intake values for humans"*.

• CLR 10: *"The CLEA model technical basis and algorithms"*.

*"Model Procedures for the Management of Land Contamination"* (Contaminated Land Report 11 (CLR 11)) was published in 2003 and sought to draw the threads created by CLR 9 and CLR 10 and other documents together in an overarching document. It stated that the technical approach presented in the Model Procedures was designed to be applicable to a range of non-regulatory and regulatory contexts. These included development or redevelopment of land under the planning regime.

CLR 11 was withdrawn in October 2020, in favour of the LCRM, but still remains a useful source of information for those interested in this topic.

The application of generic assessments within the overall risk management process is well illustrated by Figure 1 of CLR 11 on page 78.

CLR 11 (Page 8) addressed the matter of costs and benefits:

> *"At several stages of the risk management process, judgements have to be made about the relative costs and benefits of particular courses of action or decisions. This "cost–benefit analysis" is an inherent part of the management of environmental risks in a sustainable way, and is a formal component of particular stages of regulatory regimes. It allows for the structured and transparent balance of the costs (usually, but not always, in financial terms) against benefits, which can be wide-ranging depending on the context – for example, enhanced health and environmental protection, increased commercial confidence in the condition of the land or simply greater certainty in ultimate decision making. The scope and particular criteria for any cost–benefit analysis will depend on the context."*

## Generic quantitative risk assessment

The purpose of generic quantitative risk assessment is to establish whether Generic Assessment Criteria and assumptions are appropriate for assessing the possible risks and, if so, to apply them to establish whether these are actual or potentially unacceptable risks. It also determines whether a further detailed assessment is required.

At the beginning of this generic quantitate risk assessment stage the assessor has an outline conceptual model for the site and the context of the risk assessment, and has identified some possible pollutant linkages of concern that justify further assessment.

During this stage the assessor considers the availability and appropriateness of Generic Assessment Criteria to simplify the assessment of the site. If Generic Assessment Criteria can be used, or developed, for some or all of the possible pollutant linkages, the assessor determines what information (e.g. about contaminants, pathways and receptors and other properties of the site and its setting) is needed to apply the criteria in an appropriate way.

Further information is then collected about the site and its surroundings through intrusive site investigation. This includes information on the actual presence, and extent of, contaminants, pathways and receptors that may form pollutant linkages and give rise to unacceptable risks, and information on other characteristics of the site that are relevant to the risk assessment and decision-making process.

The assessor refines the conceptual site model as a result of the investigations, and potential pollutant linkages are confirmed for evaluation. If appropriate, the assessor uses Generic Assessment Criteria to assess one or more potential pollutant linkages.

The final part of this stage is consideration of the next steps: this can include further work to complete the generic quantitative risk assessment or detailed quantitative risk assessment; for example, when Generic Assessment Criteria are not appropriate or sufficient to assess the risk. Assessment using Generic Assessment Criteria may also lead straight to the stage of options appraisal or, where no potential health and environmental risks have been identified, to an exit from the process.

At the end of this stage, the assessor should have established:

*   What pollutant linkages can be evaluated using Generic Assessment Criteria and assumptions.

*   Whether unacceptable risks associated with these linkages can be identified.

*   What further action is appropriate.

Key outputs from this stage are:

- A decision record – the pollutant linkages identified based on the development of the conceptual site model; the Generic Assessment Criteria used to assess risks; the unacceptable risks identified; and the proposed next steps in relation to the site.

- An explanation of the development of the conceptual site model (in particular the results of site investigation); the selection of criteria and assumptions; the evaluation of the potential risks; and the basis for the decision on what happens next.

**Further Reading**

CLR 7 Overview of DETR reports on the assessment of contaminated land.

CLR 8 Potential contaminants for the assessment of land.

CLR 9 TOX Contaminants in soils: Consolidated main report.

CLR 9 TOX 1 Contaminants in soils: Arsenic.

CLR 9 TOX 2 Contaminants in soils: Cadmium.

CLR 9 TOX 3 Contaminants in soils: Chromium.

CLR 9 TOX 4 Contaminants in soils: Cyanide.

CLR 9 TOX 5 Contaminants in soils: inorganic Lead.

CLR 9 TOX 6 Contaminants in soils: inorganic Mercury.

CLR 9 TOX 7 Contaminants in soils: Nickel.

CLR 9 TOX 8 Contaminants in soils: Phenol.

CLR 9 TOX 9 Contaminants in soils: Polycyclic Aromatic Hydrocarbons.

CLR 9 TOX 10 Contaminants in soils: Selenium.

CLR 10 The CLEA model: Technical basis and algorithms.

CLR 10 GV 1 Guideline values for Arsenic contamination in soil.

CLR 10 GV 2 Guideline values for Cadmium contamination in soil.

CLR 10 GV 3 Guideline values for Chromium contamination in soil.

CLR 10 GV 4 Guideline values for Cyanide contamination in soil.

CLR 10 GV 5 Guideline values for inorganic Lead contamination in soil.

CLR 10 GV 6 Guideline values for inorganic Mercury contamination in soil.

CLR 10 GV 7 Guideline values for Nickel contamination in soil.

CLR 10 GV 8 Guideline values for Phenol contamination in soil.

CLR 10 GV 9 Guideline values for Polycyclic Aromatic Hydrocarbons contamination in soil expressed as benzo(a)pyrene toxic equivalent concentrations.

CLR 10 GV 10 Guideline values for Selenium contamination in soil.

CLR 11 Model procedures for the management of contaminated land: introduction and overview.

CLR 11 MP 1 Model procedures: risk assessment.

CLR 11 MP 2 Model procedures: evaluation and selection of remedial measures.

CLR 11 MP 3 Model procedures: implementation of risk management actions.

# Appendix 3

# Site Adaptation Treatment Techniques In More Detail

This Appendix is not intended to be a duplicate guide to treatment techniques but focuses on those which may be of interest during the planning process. In accordance with the convention, they are divided into "*in-situ*" and "*ex-situ*" treatments.

As the classifications imply, "*in-situ*" is treatment which does not move the contaminant to the surface. And "*ex-situ*" treatment includes the movement of the pollutive materials. As one may expect, in-situ treatment is, as a generality, more attractive to those involved in the planning process.

### In-situ treatment
SP1001 provides commentary on twelve treatment profiles for in-situ treatment techniques and they are summarised below, albeit with some additions and with some extra narrative. They are:

(1)   Chemical oxidation and reduction.

(2)   Electro-remediation.

(3)   Enhanced bioremediation using redox amendments.

(4)   Flushing.

(5)   Monitored natural attenuation.

(6)   Permeable reactive barriers.

(7)   Phytoremediation.

(8)   Sparging.

(9)   Stabilisation/solidification.

(10)  Thermal Treatment.

(11)  Venting.

(12)  Vitrification.

## Bioremediation[1]

> *"Bioremediation is an engineered technology that modifies environmental conditions (physical, chemical, biochemical, or microbiological) to encourage microorganisms to destroy or detoxify organic and inorganic contaminants in the environment".*[2]

Bioremediation is a biological process that stimulates microbes to use harmful contaminants as their source of food and energy. Certain microorganisms eat toxic chemicals and pathogens, digesting and eliminating them through changing their compositions into gases, like ethane and carbon dioxide[3]. Some contaminated soil and water conditions already have the right counter-microbes. Here, human intervention can speed up the natural amelioration by boosting microbial action. Microbial actors like fungi and aerobic bacteria are mixed into the soil or water[4]. In cases where the right microorganisms are low in numbers or entirely absent, *"amendments"*[5] by way of *"bioaugmentation"*[6] or *"biostimulation"*[7] may be used.[8]

### Advantages of In-Situ Bioremediation (ISB)

- Transformation of organic contaminants to innocuous substances.

- Accelerated ISB can provide volumetric treatment, treating both dissolved and absorbed contaminant.

- In-situ bioremediation can often be faster than pump-and-treat processes.

- Lower costs than many other treatment options.

- The zone of treatment using bioremediation can be larger than with other treatment technologies.

---

[1]   SP1001, p.14.

[2]   Introduction to in-situ bioremediation of groundwater (December 2013 prepared by the US Office of Superfund Remediation and Technology Innovation - prepared for (inter alia) the US Environmental Protection Agency).

[3]   Greenhouse gases?

[4]   Adapted from https://www.waste2water.com/bioremediation-benefits-and-uses/.

[5]   The addition of reagents which release oxygen, creating aerobic conditions or which stimulate the removal of oxygen and the generation of hydrogen, creating anaerobic conditions: per SP1001, p.14.

[6]   The addition of highly concentrated and specialised populations of specific microbes into a contaminated site to enhance the rate of contaminant biodegradation. The addition of degrading microorganisms to supplement the indigenous populations: See Adams GO, et al: *Bioremediation, biostimulation and bioaugmentation: a review*. This paper also provides useful commentary on large, and very large, oil spills (including Deepwater Horizon and the Amoco Cadiz). Int J Environ Bioremed Biot 2015 - and Abdulsalam et al. *Comparison of biostimulation and bioaugmentation for remediation of soil contaminated with spent motor oil*. Int J Environ Sci Te 2011; 8:187–94. (2011).

[7]   The modification of the environment to stimulate existing bacteria capable of bioremediation (Adams ibid).

[8]   Bioaugmentation and biostimulation were used to treat the Deepwater Horizon oil spill of 2010, where 3.19 million barrels of vented near the Gulf of Mexico - https://www.aftermath.com/content/3-examples-of-bioremediation/.

- It can be used to treat soil and groundwater with minimal site disturbance and is a relatively simple technique.

- As an in-situ (versus ex-situ) technology, there is:

  - typically, little secondary waste generated;

  - reduced potential for cross-media transfer of contaminants;

  - reduced risk of human exposure to contaminated media.

### *Limitations of In-Situ Bioremediation*

- It may be difficult to apply to a heterogeneous subsurface.

- There might be uncertainty over the appropriate quantity of supply of "*amendments*" for treatment and toxic intermediate breakdown products may be formed.

- Some contaminants may not be completely transformed to innocuous products.

- The intermediate produce may be more toxic and/or mobile than the parent compound.

- Some contaminants cannot be biodegraded (i.e., they are "*recalcitrant*").

- Coagulation.

- Difficult to implement completely in low-permeability or heterogeneous aquifers.

- Heavy metals and toxic concentrations of organic compounds may inhibit activity of indigenous microorganisms.

- Microbe not developed for recent spills or for recalcitrant compounds.

The typical timescale for bioremediation is circa 6 months to 3 years.[9]

### *Vitrification*[10]

In-situ vitrification uses extremely high temperatures (typically 1,400 to 2,000°C) to melt soil in the ground. The high temperatures cause the thermal or chemical destruction of contaminants or they are incorporated within the vitrification product.

---

[9]  SP1001, Contaminated Land Remediation Contaminated Land Remediation CL:AIRE (2010); Table 1.3: Lines of evidence to verify remediation and typical timescales for in-situ remediation processes.

[10]  SP1001, p.23.

The potential advantages of vitrification are that it is applicable to a wide range of contaminants and can be used to tackle otherwise difficult to treat contaminants. However, it is expensive and energy intensive. Furthermore, off-gas needs to be carefully controlled (due to volatilisation of organics and some metals) and the volume reduction in sub-soil raises the risk of subsidence because the soil function is damaged or destroyed, thus sub-soil with high water content can be problematic. There may also be concerns over the reuse of treated material and stability of the vitrified glass.

The typical timescale for vitrification is circa 1 year.[11]

### *Solidification and stabilisation*[12]
Solidification and stabilisation use binders and additives to reduce the mobility of metal contaminants. In solidification, contaminated soils are mixed with a physical binding agent such as cement, bitumen, asphalt and thermoplastic binders to form a crystalline, glassy, or polymeric mass which have low leaching rates. In stabilisation, chemical reactions are induced between the stabilising agent and metal contaminants.

It can be used to treat recalcitrant contaminants (e.g. metals, PCBs and dioxins). The processing equipment occupies a relatively small footprint and the physical properties of the soil are often improved by the treatment. The limitations to the treatment are that it does not destroy or remove the contaminants; it may be difficult to predict long-term behaviour; it may result in an overall increase in the volume of material and reagent delivery; and effective mixing can be difficult to achieve. It may require long-term maintenance of protection systems and/or long-term monitoring.

The typical timescale for solidification and stabilization is up to 1 year.[13]

### *Soil flushing*[14]
Soil flushing involves the use of water or appropriate washing solution. Acids, bases and surfactants are added to water and used as extraction or flushing solutions to recover metals, organic and oil contaminants like phenol. After flushing, the solution is recovered using wells or trenches and is treated at the surface to remove contaminants. A good understanding of site geology and hydrogeology is required to prevent loss of contaminant and soil flushing solution beyond the capture zone and to allay regulatory concerns.

The potential advantages of the treatment include that the process can be designed to treat specific contaminants (including both organic and inorganic compounds) and it can be used in both pathway management and source control. The limitations include that low permeability or heterogeneous soils are difficult to treat; the risk of worsening the situation

---

[11]  SP1001, Table 1.3.

[12]  SP1001, p.20.

[13]  Ibid SP1001, Table 1.3.

[14]  SP1001, p.15.

by producing more toxic or mobile compounds; its effectiveness can be hindered by a shallow water table; and the above ground separation and treatment can be expensive.

The typical timescale for soil flushing is circa 1 to 3 years.[15]

### Electro-remediation[16]

Electro-remediation (aka *"electrokinetics/electro-reclamation"*) is applicable to metal contaminants and involves passing a low intensity electric current between electrodes. An electrical gradient initiates the movement of contaminant metals by electro-migration and metals arriving at the electrodes can be removed. It works best with fine grained materials such as clays. It is an emerging technique with few UK case studies. The limitations include that it needs a soil water content of soil greater than 10% to be effective; buried services or metallic objects or ore deposits can cause problems; it is possible for the soil to heat up to temperatures that may cause damage to soil, flora and fauna; and carbonate-rich materials limit its application.

The typical timescale for electro-remediation is circa 1 to 3 years.[17]

### Soil venting[18]

In-situ venting involves the movement of air through the unsaturated zone via extraction and/or injection wells which induces contaminant removal by either of two mechanisms:

- Volatile contaminants partition into the air as it moves upwards through the soil. The resulting vapour is collected and treated at surface if necessary.

- Aerobic bacteria, stimulated by the supply of oxygen, consume contaminants as a food source (biodegradation).

It is not applicable to inorganic compounds due to their low volatility.

The potential advantages of the treatment include that it can be cost-effective; it can treat many organic compounds; it can induce physical and biological processes; and minimal site disturbance. The limitations include that it may be limited by the structure of the soil; its effectiveness can be hindered by a shallow water table unless water is pumped out; it is limited by the depth of contamination; and the verification of treatment can be difficult.

The typical timescale for soil venting is circa 1 to 3 years.[19]

---

[15]  SP1001, Table 1.3.

[16]  SP1001, p.13.

[17]  SP1001, Table 1.3.

[18]  SP1001, p.22.

[19]  SP1001, Table 1.3.

### *Chemical oxidation and reduction*[20]

In-situ chemical methods involve the addition of chemicals to soil or groundwater to oxidise or reduce the contaminants thereby degrading them, reducing their toxicity, changing their solubility, or increasing their susceptibility to other forms of treatment.

The advantages are that reactions are fast and can result in complete degradation; it is applicable to a wide range of organic contaminants; and costs are low. The limitations include that it may require large volumes of reagent; it gives rise to environmental considerations from using aggressive reagents; and toxic intermediate breakdown products may be formed. Also, groundwater may be coloured by reagents; precipitation reactions may be reversible with changes in redox conditions over time; and it may be difficult to facilitate contact between contaminants and reagents in the treatment zone.

The typical timescale for chemical oxidation and reduction is up to 1 year.[21]

### *Thermal treatment*

Thermal treatment involves increasing the temperature in the ground and can lead to enhanced contaminant removal by one or more of several methods: increased volatilisation; reduced viscosity; increased solubility in water; decreased adsorption; drying of the soil can increase air permeability which may improve extraction; and direct application of heat may accelerate chemical reactions which may result in contaminant destruction. In addition, after the application of the heating process, subsurface conditions can be suitable for accelerating biodegradation of residual contaminants. It is limited to enhancement of VOC/SVOC recovery.

There are four main methods for in-situ heating: injection (steam or hot air); electrical resistance heating; electromagnetic heating (radiofrequency or microwave); and thermal conductive heating. The heating methods have differing ranges of applicability for contaminants and soil and groundwater conditions, treatment efficiencies, and cost.

Potential advantages include that it is applicable to a wide range of soil types, applicable to difficult dense non-aqueous phase (DNAPL) contaminants and causes minimal site disturbance. The limitations include that buried objects or utilities may cause operating problems; potential for damage to soil structure, fauna and flora and impacts on groundwater quality; and the enhanced mobility of contaminants might lead to migration outside the treatment zone.

The typical timescale for thermal treatment is up to 1 year.[22]

---

[20]  SP1001, p.12.

[21]  SP1001, Table 1.3 @ p.12.

[22]  SP1001, Table 1.3.

### Monitored natural attenuation[23]

Natural attenuation relies upon natural physical, chemical and biological processes reducing the load, concentration, flux or toxicity of contaminants within a specified timescale. It *"is often used as a polishing step at the end of a remediation scheme to manage any residual contamination".*[24]

The potential advantages include that there is less generation or transfer of treatment wastes; it is less intrusive (as few surface structures are required); and it can be used in conjunction with, or after, other treatment methods. The overall cost is likely to be lower than many active treatment technologies. Furthermore, this approach can be married to phytoremediation (see below) and the provision of *"net biodiversity gain"* for the purposes of the Environment Act 2021, thereby combining the costs (see below).[25]

The typical timescales for monitored natural attenuation are highly dependent on the specific contaminant treatment design and could be between 1 and 30 years. Hence, it requires a long-term commitment to monitoring and a contingency plan if the contaminants or groundwater do not behave as predicted. This might mean the need to consider the provision of financial security for these long-term management arrangements by way of Section 106 Agreements and management companies or bonding.

The limitations of the technique also include that it requires extensive site investigation; it requires significant depth of understanding of local geology and hydrogeology; subsurface conditions may change over time; and it may result in renewed mobility of previously stabilised contaminants.

### Permeable reactive barriers[26]

A permeable reactive barrier (PRB) is an engineered treatment zone placed in the saturated zone to treat contaminated groundwater as it flows through. PRBs can be designed in a variety of configurations, depending on the contaminants to be treated, the layout of the area requiring treatment and the requirements of the land user(s). There are two basic types of PRB:

- Funnel-and-gate™: contaminated groundwater is directed to a permeable reactive zone (the *"gate"*) by impermeable barriers, such as a cut-off wall (the *"funnel"*).

- Continuous wall: a reactive treatment zone is placed in the subsurface across the complete flow path of the contaminated groundwater.

---

[23]  SP1001, p.16.

[24]  Table 4.3 @ p.94.

[25]  See also Table 2.8 @ p.54.

[26]  SP1001, p.17.

Its advantages are that it is a solution for inaccessible or dispersed source; it is relatively easy to maintain and monitor; and causes minimal above-ground disturbance. The limitations of the technique include that there may be a loss of reactive capacity over time (requiring replacement of reactive media); loss of permeability due to precipitation of metal salts or biofilm production; it requires a significant depth of understanding of the local geology and hydrogeology; and it may be limited by the depth of the contamination below ground. Also, it may be necessary to dispose of reactive media as a hazardous waste.

The typical timescale for permeable reactive barriers is up to ten years.[27]

### Phytoremediation[28]

Phytoremediation uses living plants to contain, disperse, stabilise, extract and/or destroy contaminants. It is probably best described as an *"emerging technique"* (per Nathaniel (2007)). It uses the natural ability of vegetation to extract, accumulate, store, and/or degrade organic and inorganic substances. In some cases, the selected flora can extract and store specified contaminants. The flora is then harvested and the stored contaminants removed with the harvested flora.

The advantages are low cost and the provision of vegetative cover. The possible and considerable potential benefit is that it may enhance biodiversity and, given the statutory duty to promote biodiversity net gain in the Environment Act 2021, its use might help discharge this duty.

Unfortunately, whilst potentially attractive in connection with structural landscaping (such as public open space or biodiversity gain land), the problem is that the applied research on this topic is somewhat limited. It is, in part, hampered by the fact that specific species of flora have to be matched to specific contaminants and this is thus a very wide ranging, time consuming and expensive area of research.[29]

The other limitations of the technique include that it moves the contaminants to biomass which may create a hazardous waste; the depth of treatment is limited; high concentrations of contaminants can be toxic to plants; and it may require a further waste reduction process to concentrate contaminants in harvested biomass (e.g. incineration). Furthermore, contaminants can be moved from depth to the surface which may expose surface receptors to them; transfer of contamination across media (e.g. from soil to air); and products may be mobilised into groundwater or bioaccumulated in animals.

The typical timescale for phytoremediation is up to 10 years.[30]

---

[27]  SP1001, Table 1.3.

[28]  SP1001, p.18.

[29]  See Table 2.11 @ p.56. Also p.83. Also: *"Phytoremediation advances in the lab but lags in the field"* – Carolyn Beans (PNAS – 2017).

[30]  SP1001, Table 1.3.

**Sparging**[31]
Sparging involves the injection of air (or other gases) below the water table to promote volatilisation and/or biodegradation of contaminants from soil, water and the vapour phase, but it is not suitable for the treatment of inorganic contaminants. It offers enhanced clean-up rates relative to groundwater pump and treat techniques; it can be highly cost-effective; and involves minimal site disturbance.[32]

The limitations of the technique are that it should only be applied to unconfined aquifers where injected air can freely reach the unsaturated zone and be subsequently collected; it should not be applied where significant free phase hydrocarbons are present (due to the risk of contaminant mobilisation); and the need to ensure a uniform air flow to avoid spreading the contaminant plume.

The typical timescale for sparging between 6 months and 3 years.[33]

**Soil vapor extraction**[34]
In "*soil vapor extraction*" a low-pressure air stream is applied to a well in unsaturated soil to induce the controlled flow and capture of sub-surface air and gases, including volatile and some semi-volatile contaminants.

**Ex-situ treatments**
Ex-situ techniques are those that are applied to excavated soil, or treatments of contaminated water or gaseous emissions that take place at the surface.

The treatment profiles mentioned in SP1001 are:

•     Biological treatment.

•     Chemical oxidation and reduction.

•     Soil washing and separation processes.

•     Stabilisation/solidification.

•     Thermal treatment.

•     Venting.

•     Vitrification.

---

[31]   SP1001, p.19.

[32]   SP1001, p.19.

[33]   SP1001, Table 1.3.

[34]   Not mentioned in SP1001.

- Water and gas/vapour treatment.

They are summarised below.

### Biological treatment
Biological treatment is an ex-situ biological method which exploits existing microbial processes to degrade, or reduce the toxicity of, contaminants in soil. Several different biological treatment configurations are available; namely, biopile, windrow turning, landfarming, composting and slurry-phase bioreactor.

The potential advantages are that it can result in complete contaminant degradation; soils can often be reused on site; and preservation or enhancement of soil structure (except for slurry-phase bioreactor). The limitations include that heavier organic contaminants are difficult to degrade; there is potential for formation of toxic intermediate breakdown products; and conditions must be carefully controlled to ensure complete and consistent treatment.[35]

### Chemical oxidation and reduction
Chemical oxidation and reduction involves the addition of chemicals to excavated soil to oxidise or reduce the contaminants thereby degrading them, reducing their toxicity, changing their solubility, or increasing their susceptibility to other forms of treatment.[36]

The potential advantages are that it facilitates contact between contaminants and reagents in excavated soil and can treat a wide range of contaminants. Limitations are that it may require large volumes of reagent; may affect soil structure; and generate toxic intermediate breakdown products. Also, control is needed to prevent leaching into water courses, as some reagents are aggressive.

### Soil washing and separation[37]
Soil washing and separation is an ex-situ physical/chemical method using an aqueous solution (typically water) to separate contaminants and/or contaminated soil particles from uncontaminated material.

The potential advantages are that it is applicable to a wide range of contaminants and reduces the volume of contaminated material (which may reduce the cost of disposal or treatment by another technology). Limitations include that it may be uneconomic to treat small volumes; it is uneconomic to treat material with a high fine content; and a water processing unit is likely to be required, which will add cost. Also, contaminant depleted fractions may not meet the required decontamination standards and therefore it will require disposal or further treatment.

---

[35]   SP1001, p.26.
[36]   SP1001, p.27.
[37]   SP1001, p.28.

### Stabilisation and solidification[38]

Stabilisation and solidification is an ex-situ physical/chemical method involving a reaction between a binder and soil to reduce the mobility of contaminants by physical encapsulation or chemical immobilisation. The potential advantages include that it can be used to treat recalcitrant contaminants (e.g. heavy metals, PCBs and dioxins); the process equipment occupies a relatively small footprint; the physical properties of the soil are often improved by treatment; and treated material can be reused on site or be re-classified for less expensive disposal. Limitations include that it does not destroy or remove the contaminants; it may be difficult to predict long-term behaviour; it may result in an overall increase in volume of material; and reagent delivery and effective mixing can be difficult to achieve. Also, it may require long-term maintenance of protection systems and/or long-term monitoring.

### Thermal treatment[39]

The ex-situ thermal method involves the use of heat to destroy organic contaminants or enhance their mobility and facilitate their recovery and treatment. It is applicable to a wide range of organic and some inorganic contaminants and there is potential for high contaminant removals. Limitations include that incineration can be expensive with high energy costs; material may need screening and pre-treatment; and it may result in loss of organic matter in the soil, which restricts its use post-treatment. Also, emissions must be carefully controlled in case incomplete combustion products are formed.

### Venting[40]

Ex-situ venting is a development of in-situ venting, the difference being that the soil is excavated for treatment. Venting is a means of removing organic compounds and some semi-volatile organic compounds from unsaturated soils. Soil can be engineered to suit contaminant properties and decontamination requirements and (unlike in-situ venting) it is not limited by the heterogeneity of the subsurface. The limitations include the potential for loss of volatile contaminants over permitted emission levels during excavation, unless properly managed and health and safety concerns at all stages.

### Vitrification[41]

Ex-situ vitrification uses electricity to produce high temperatures to destroy organic contaminants or immobilise inorganic contaminants within a glass-like material. It is applicable to a wide range of contaminants and contaminated materials and is able to treat otherwise difficult to treat contaminants. Limitations include that off-gas needs to be carefully controlled (due to volatilisation of organics and some metals), it is expensive and energy intensive, the entire soil function is destroyed and material with high water content can be problematic. Also, there may be concerns over the reuse of treated material and stability of the vitrified glass (especially where the product might be classified as a radioactive waste).

---

[38]  SP1001, p.29.

[39]  SP1001, p.30.

[40]  SP1001, p.31.

[41]  SP1001, p.32.

### Water and gas/vapour treatment[42]

Both in-situ (e.g. venting and sparging) and ex-situ decontamination techniques produce contaminated water and gaseous streams which requires treatment at the surface. Water and gas/vapour treatment is the generic term for such treatments.

---

[42] SP1001, p.33.

# Appendix 4

# Critique Of The Planning Inspectorate's Suggested Conditions

(as updated to May 2023)

*Contaminated land – for use only in smaller developments (84)*

*No development shall commence until an assessment of the risks posed by any contamination, carried out in accordance with British Standard BS 10175: Investigation of potentially contaminated sites - Code of Practice and the Environment Agency's Model Procedures for the Management of Land Contamination (CLR 11) (or equivalent British Standard and Model Procedures if replaced), shall have been submitted to and approved in writing by the local planning authority.* (a)

*If any contamination is found, a report specifying the measures to be taken, including the timescale, to remediate the site to render it suitable for the approved development shall be submitted to and approved in writing by the local planning authority.* (b) *The site shall be remediated in accordance with the approved measures and timescale and a verification report shall be submitted to and approved in writing by the local planning authority.* (c) *If, during the course of development, any contamination is found which has not been previously identified, work shall be suspended and additional measures for its remediation shall be submitted to and approved in writing by the local planning authority.* (d) *The remediation of the site shall incorporate the approved additional measures.* (e) *and a verification report for all the remediation works shall be submitted to the local planning authority within [****] days of the report being completed and approved in writing by the local planning authority.* (f)

[Lettering (a-f) added]

Notes:

(a)   The reference to a British Standard is to be commended.

(b)   No timetable is provided for the authority's consideration and approval of the assessment. This is typical of this type of pre-commencement condition; however, it needs to be borne in mind that this might delay delivery of a scheme if the authority is dilatory. Also query whether *"remediation"* is used as, or should be construed as, a term of art: see Chapter 3 of this book.

(c)   This sentence is predicated on the assumption that the existence of any *"contamination"*, however small, will require treatment. There is no mention of a risk assessment. It might be the case that the level of risk is so small that no such action is needed. Also, the condition makes no mention of mitigation schemes. For example, a site may be subject to low levels of landfill gas emissions which can be counteracted by mitigation measures such as those currently set out in CIRIA C665 or the imposition of an "*Article 4 Direction*" by the Local Planning Authority.

(d)     This provision is ambiguous. At worst, it might be argued that it is ultra vires because it seems to provide that the authority will automatically approve the report. At best, the approval or not of the verification report seems to be devoid of any consequences. This text does not say what the result of approval or not approval is supposed to be.

(e)     Again, there is the presumption that the unexpected contamination poses unacceptable risks and must, inevitably, be treated.

(f)     Again, the role of the verification report is unclear.

### Contaminated land – risk assessment (80)

*No development shall commence until an assessment of the risks posed by any contamination shall have been submitted to and approved in writing by the local planning authority. This assessment must be undertaken by a suitably qualified contaminated land practitioner, in accordance with British Standard BS 10175: Investigation of potentially contaminated sites - Code of Practice and the Environment Agency's Model Procedures for the Management of Land Contamination (CLR 11) (or equivalent British Standard and Model Procedures if replaced), and shall assess any contamination on the site, whether or not it originates on the site.*

*The assessment shall include:*

* *a survey of the extent, scale and nature of contamination;*

* *the potential risks to:*

    * *human health;*

    * *property (existing or proposed) including buildings, crops, livestock, pets, woodland and service lines and pipes;*

    * *adjoining land;*

    * *ground waters and surface waters;*

    * *ecological systems; and*

    * *archaeological sites and ancient monuments.*

*Use with conditions (81) to (83).*

The obvious rejoinder is that this condition appears to have no regard to the way in which a large and phased scheme will evolve. It places an embargo on the commencement of all development notwithstanding that the permission may be in outline and the developer might not be coming to the final phases of the scheme for a number of years. Furthermore, if there have been reasonable concerns that the site might be subject to significant contamination, then it is difficult to see why the application has come to the planning committee without prior site investigations and assessments.

### Contaminated land – remediation scheme (81)

*No development shall take place where (following the risk assessment) land affected by contamination is found which poses risks identified as unacceptable in the risk assessment* (a), *until a detailed remediation scheme shall have been submitted to and approved in writing by the local planning authority. The scheme shall include an appraisal of remediation options, identification of the preferred option(s), the proposed remediation objectives and remediation criteria, and a description and programme of the works to be undertaken including the verification plan.* (b) *The remediation scheme shall be sufficiently detailed and thorough to ensure that upon completion the site will not qualify as contaminated land under Part IIA of the Environmental Protection Act 1990 in relation to its intended use.* (c) *The approved remediation scheme shall be carried out* (d) *[and upon completion a verification report by a suitably qualified contaminated land practitioner shall be submitted to and approved in writing by the local planning authority] before the development [or relevant phase of development] is occupied.* (e)

[Lettering (a-e) added]

*Use with conditions (80), (82) & (83).*

Notes:

(a)   The determination as to acceptability or otherwise is a matter for the local authority only, albeit having regard to expert advice.

(b)   Again, it is not clear whether "*remediation*" includes mitigation etc.

(c)   This cross-reference to Part IIA of the Environmental Protection Act 1990 posits, of course, a wholly incorrect test. The proper standard is "*suitable for use*". This usage could distort the thrust of the condition as a whole.

(d)   This points up the difficulty with "*scheme conditions*", which is that their force relies on those drafting the scheme with lawyers' precision, otherwise it will not be possible to show whether there has been an enforceable breach of the condition or not. The reality is that such approved schemes are often worded in a way which is enough for the purposes of an engineer, but which lack the precision which is needed by a lawyer in seeking to enforce them.

(e)     It is only at this point that the matter of phasing is mentioned. Again, it is not clear whether *"remediation"* includes mitigation.

### Contaminated land – reporting of unexpected contamination (82)

*Any contamination that is found during the course of construction of the approved development that was not previously identified shall be reported immediately to the local planning authority. (a) Development on the part of the site affected shall be suspended and a risk assessment carried out and submitted to and approved in writing by the local planning authority. (b) Where unacceptable risks are found remediation and verification schemes shall be submitted to and approved in writing by the local planning authority. These approved schemes shall be carried out before the development [or relevant phase of development] is resumed or continued. (c)*

[Lettering (a-c) added]

*Use with conditions (80), (81) & (83).*

Notes:

(a)     It might be the case that a developer will comply with this reporting requirement, but it would be the naïve draftsman who relies on it. The better course is to impose a requirement for ongoing surveys and assessments as the development progresses rather than relying on a *"one-hit"* approach which turns, in the main, on an assessment of the whole site at the beginning of the process. This particular condition is useful as *"belt and braces"* but it is not a proper substitute for conditions which provide for ongoing measures as the development progresses. It might be argued that such an approach is overly complicated for a condition and this may, indeed, be a valid complaint, in which case, it might be argued that the better approach is to deal with larger schemes by way of planning obligations rather than conditions.

(b)     This would need more than a risk assessment only. The developer should carry out appropriate surveys and tests before moving to the risk assessment.

(c)     The drafting of the last two sentences appears to be rushed. The greater detail in Condition 82 should be replicated mutatis mutandis.

### Contaminated land – long term monitoring and maintenance (83)

*No development shall take place (a) until a monitoring and maintenance scheme to demonstrate the effectiveness of the proposed remediation shall have been submitted to and approved in writing by the local planning authority. (b) The approved scheme* *shall be implemented, and the reports produced as a result, shall be submitted to the local planning authority within (\*\*) days of the report being completed and approved in writing within (\*\*) days of receipt. If any of these reports identifies any discrepancy with the verification report then a protocol, including timescale, for the necessary remediation shall be submitted to the local planning authority within a further (\*\*) days and approved in writing within (\*\*) days of receipt. Thereafter, any necessary remediation and verification shall be carried out in accordance with the approved protocol.* (c)

**[Lettering (a-c) added]**

*Use with conditions (80) to (82).*

Notes:

(a)    Again, the above-mentioned concerns about a large phased scheme need to be repeated. In practice, it will be years before the developer comes to the later phases, if ever.

(b)    This detailed wording of this condition is at odds with its title and the title given to the eponymous scheme. It is apparent that, in reality, the scheme is not about long-term ongoing decontamination or mitigation measures after the necessary works have been carried out. It is to *"demonstrate the effectiveness of the proposed remediation"* notwithstanding that this is the function of the verification report in Condition 80. The initial mis-direction is shown by the words, *"The approved scheme shall be implemented"*. If, notwithstanding, the condition is construed on the basis that the scheme is, indeed, for long term maintenance and monitoring, then the obvious flaw is that no duration is specified.

(c)    If the condition is for long-term maintenance and monitoring, then this gives rise to the perennial problem that the developer might not continue in existence, or remain solvent, for the chosen duration of the scheme. This might not be a problem where any flaws in the relevant works will show up quickly, but it might be a major problem where the authority is seeking some form of security for decades. Not for the first time, one is left to wonder whether the better approach to complex schemes is by way of planning obligations because the authority can bring into play mechanisms such as bonding arrangements, management companies and escrow accounts to provide for long-term financial security.

# Appendix 5

# Illustrative Examples Of Conditions/Planning Obligation Clauses[1]

## Site Assessment
The Development shall not Commence unless and until:

- The site has been surveyed to determine whether it is affected any Contamination or has the potential to be Contaminated and the survey report shall have been submitted to and approved in writing by the local planning authority.

- If the survey indicates that the site is Contaminated or has the potential to be contaminated, then no development shall Commence until a risk assessment of any Contamination of the site has been completed and the survey report and Risk Management Plan shall have been submitted to and approved in writing by the local planning authority.

- The survey, risk assessment and Risk Management Plan must be undertaken by a suitably qualified contaminated land practitioner, [in accordance with British Standard [****] and Model Procedures [****] or equivalent British Standard or Model Procedures if replaced], and shall address any Contamination, or potential for Contamination. The survey report and risk assessment shall include a survey of the sources, extent, scale and nature of any Contamination or potential Contamination.

- For the purposes of [this Clause] [these conditions] the expression "*Contamination*" shall mean such contamination or pollution (whether or not it originates on the development site) as may cause the site to be unsuitable for its proposed use or which may (whether in consequence of the development or otherwise) adversely affect the environment or any land in the locality of the site and shall include actual or potential risks to:

  - human health;

  - property (existing or proposed) including buildings, crops, livestock, pets, woodland and service lines and pipes;

  - adjoining and nearby land;

  - ground waters and surface waters;

---

[1]    These examples are illustrations and are not intended to be templates or precedents.

- ecological systems (both fauna and flora) and habitats; and

- archaeological sites and ancient monuments.

And "*contaminant*" and "*contamination*" shall be construed accordingly.

Where the development is to be delivered in phases, then the above provisions shall apply mutatis mutandis on a phase-by-phase basis.

## Treatment scheme
Where a survey report and risk assessment have been carried out and approved by the local planning authority and Contamination or potential Contamination is found which would, in the opinion of the local planning authority, make the development unsuitable for its proposed use or otherwise pose risks identified as unacceptable in the risk assessment then no development shall take place until a treatment scheme for the site shall have been submitted to and approved in writing by the local planning authority.

The treatment scheme shall include an appraisal of treatment options, identification of the preferred option(s) (with measurable outcomes), the proposed risk management objectives and criteria, and a description and programme of the works to be undertaken including a Verification Plan and a monitoring and maintenance scheme to demonstrate the effectiveness of the proposed treatment scheme.

Where the development is to be delivered in phases, then the above provisions shall apply mutatis mutandis on a phase-by-phase basis.

## Verification
The development shall not Commence unless and until a Verification Plan has been submitted to and approved by the local planning authority (whether as part of a treatment scheme or otherwise).

For the purposes of this [condition/clause] "*Verification Plan*" means a document that sets out the requirements for gathering data/evidence to demonstrate that decontaminative treatments meet all the treatment and/or mitigation objectives and criteria stipulated in [the approved Risk Management Plan Ref: ****] and will include monitoring, sampling and testing criteria, and identify all those records that should be retained to demonstrate compliance these requirements (e.g. field monitoring data, laboratory data, level surveys above and below capping layers).

No part of the development shall be occupied unless and until a Verification Report has been submitted to and approved by the local planning authority.

The Verification Report will have regard to ["*Guidance for the Safe Development of Housing on Land Affected by Contamination*" – *R&D66: 2008 Volume 1* or equivalent guidance if replaced)] and will include:

(1)   A description of the site background.

(2)   A summary of all relevant site investigation reports.

(3)   A statement of the treatment objectives.

(4)   A description of the treatment works.

(5)   The verification data (sample locations/analytical results).

(6)   Project photographs.

(7)   As built drawings.

(8)   Records of consultations with Regulators.

(9)   Duty of Care paperwork.

(10)  Environmental monitoring data.

(11)  A description of any residual contamination.

(12)  Any arrangements for post treatment management.

For the purposes of this [condition/clause], *"treatment"* shall include decontamination works and mitigation.

Where the development is to be delivered in phases, then the above provisions shall apply mutatis mutandis on a phase-by-phase basis.

**Reporting of unexpected contamination**
Any contamination which is found during the course of construction of the approved development that was not previously identified shall be reported immediately to the local planning authority.

If the local planning authority so notifies the developer in writing then development on the part of the site affected shall be suspended until a risk assessment in relation to possible contamination has been submitted to and approved in writing by the local planning authority and (where unacceptable risks are found) Treatment and Verification schemes have been submitted to and approved in writing by the local planning authority. These approved schemes shall be carried out before the development [or relevant phase of development] is resumed.

The local planning authority shall be entitled to enter and inspect the site of the development at all reasonable times so as to ascertain whether unexpected contamination is occurring or potentially about to occur.

Where the development is to be delivered in phases, then the above provisions shall apply mutatis mutandis on a phase-by-phase basis.

### Contaminated land – for use only in smaller developments

No development shall commence until an assessment of the risks posed by any contamination, carried out in accordance with [in accordance with British Standard [****] and Model Procedures [****] or equivalent British Standard or Model Procedures if replaced] shall have been submitted to and approved in writing by the local planning authority.

If any contamination is found which is unacceptable to the local planning authority, then no development shall take place until a scheme specifying the measures to be taken to treat the site to render it suitable for the approved development, including the timescales, and the timing of a verification report shall have been submitted to and approved in writing by the local planning authority. The site shall be treated in accordance with the measures and timescale in the approved scheme.

The verification report shall be submitted to the local planning authority in accordance with the said scheme and approved in writing by the local planning authority.

If, during the course of development, any contamination which is unacceptable to the local planning authority is found which has not been previously identified, then work shall be suspended and shall not recommence until additional measures for its treatment shall have been submitted to and approved in writing by the local planning authority. The treatment of the site shall then incorporate the approved additional measures and a verification report for all the treatment works shall be submitted to the local planning authority within [****] days of the report being completed and approved in writing by the local planning authority.

# Index